PRAISE FOR *CYBER SECURITY FOUNDATIONS*

'The authors of this book have a lot of experience of teaching people about cyber security, and it shows. If you want to understand the main dimensions of cyber security, this is the book for you. It covers the long-term principles with up-to-date examples, so it's easy to follow but gives you a great foundation in the topics that matter.'
Professor Andrew Martin, Professor of Systems Security, University of Oxford

'An accessible and engaging introduction to cyber security, aimed at those new to the topic as well as for readers looking to broaden their knowledge. It provides excellent coverage of this broad discipline, building on the authors' many years of combined experience of teaching and researching in this field. An excellent first introduction to cyber security.'
Professor Steve Schneider, Director of Computer Science Research Centre, University of Surrey

'An essential resource for any master's student studying cyber security. Aligned with the CyBOK, it covers the core concepts that are essential for those looking to advance in this field. I particularly liked the structure used for each chapter, starting with clear learning objectives, followed by an in-depth exploration of fundamental topics, then highlighting key points, suggested exercises and further reading. The exercises are well-suited for incorporating into taught modules, providing practical and challenging tasks that reinforce the material covered in each chapter. Overall, a valuable addition to any cyber security curriculum.'
Dr Natalie Coull, Head of Division of Cyber Security, School of Design and Informatics, Abertay University

'This comprehensive guide on cybersecurity expertly bridges specialized knowledge across a wide range of areas, making it an invaluable resource for college and university programmes. In an era where interconnected knowledge is crucial, it fulfils the vital need for cohesive and accessible cyber-security education.'
Professor Rei Safavi-Naini, NSERC/Telus Industrial Research Chair and Alberta Innovates Strategic Chair in Information Security, University of Calgary, Canada

'*Fundamentals, technology and society*: this book does exactly what it says on the tin! It provides a broad but precise coverage of the fundamental principles and technology of cyber security while not shying away from discussing societal aspects of cyber security, from cybercrime to usable security. The book's breadth-over-depth approach, but without compromising rigour, hits the right note and should appeal to students, professionals and the curious reader alike.'

Professor Carlos Cid, Director, Simula UiB Cyber Security Research Centre, Bergen, Norway

'Fresh and clear, crafted to help cyber security newcomers confidently navigate the complexities of the field.'

Professor Panagiotis Papadimitratos, Professor of Software and Computer Systems, KTH Royal Institute of Technology, Stockholm, Sweden

'Presents readers with an accessible and engaging tour through the landscape of key topics in cyber security. The book offers a means to build knowledge and understanding of both technical and non-technical aspects, with each chapter containing clear learning objectives and relevant supporting examples and exercises. The resulting book delivers a means to understand cyber security in its wider context, forming a valuable reference for those already interested in the issues, as well as a route into it for those without prior background in the area.'

Professor Steven Furnell, Professor of Cyber Security, University of Nottingham

'Provides a clear and comprehensive roadmap to understanding the essential principles of cyber security.'

Professor Debi Ashenden, Director of the Institute for Cyber Security, University of New South Wales, Australia

'A great guide to navigate the complex maze of cyber security. It helps aspiring experts to orient themselves and demystifies the topic for a broader audience. The exercises complete the picture and make the book a valuable teaching resource. Overall, the authors have pulled off a tour-de-force by writing a highly accessible introduction to this ever more important topic.'

Professor Bart Preneel, Full Professor at University of Leuven, Belgium

Cyber Security Foundations

Fundamentals, technology and society

Keith M Martin
Jassim Happa
Konstantinos Mersinas
Guido Schmitz

KoganPage

Publisher's note

Every possible effort has been made to ensure that the information contained in this book is accurate at the time of going to press, and the publishers and authors cannot accept responsibility for any errors or omissions, however caused. No responsibility for loss or damage occasioned to any person acting, or refraining from action, as a result of the material in this publication can be accepted by the editor, the publisher or the authors.

First published in Great Britain and the United States in 2025 by Kogan Page Limited

Kogan Page
Kogan Page Ltd, 2nd Floor, 45 Gee Street, London EC1V 3RS, United Kingdom
Kogan Page Inc, 8 W 38th Street, Suite 90, New York, NY 10018, USA
www.koganpage.com

EU Representative (GPSR)
Authorised Rep Compliance Ltd, Ground Floor, 71 Lower Baggot Street, Dublin D02 P593, Ireland
www.arccompliance.com

Kogan Page books are printed on paper from sustainable forests.

ISBNs
Hardback 978 1 3986 1474 1
Paperback 978 1 3986 1472 7
Ebook 978 1 3986 1473 4

British Library Cataloguing-in-Publication Data
A CIP record for this book is available from the British Library.

Library of Congress Control Number
2024057399

Typeset by Integra Software Services, Pondicherry
Print production managed by Jellyfish
Printed and bound by CPI Group (UK) Ltd, Croydon CR0 4YY

CONTENTS

PREFACE

We are delighted you have reached the opening page of *Cyber Security Foundations: Fundamentals, technology and society*! Every word in this title is important, so in this preface we explain why, set out our vision for the book, explain what it covers and suggest how the book might be used.

Context

In 1992, Royal Holloway, University of London launched a pioneering postgraduate programme in Information Security. This was a visionary initiative because, at that time, no university anywhere in the world offered a similar programme. The 1992 MSc in Information Security syllabus was rooted in the relatively primitive computing technology of the day, but primarily targeted a future, anticipated world where digital technology would ultimately become ubiquitous and need securing.

That world has well and truly arrived. Over three decades later, over 4,000 students have graduated from this master's programme, which has maintained its core focus while evolving to address the many exciting developments that have subsequently occurred. In 1992, for example, few people imagined powerful computers in everybody's pockets and an ability for anyone to have a global audience for their personal images and observations.

In 2002, Royal Holloway launched a new online MSc in Cyber Security through the University of London Worldwide. This aligns closely with the established campus programme, but has a contemporary structure inspired by the Cyber Security Body of Knowledge (CyBOK), an initiative driven by the UK National Cyber Security Centre (NCSC) to develop an established body of knowledge relating to cyber security.

The idea for this book arose from the development of this new MSc, in which all four authors were involved. In preparing the new programme, we were reminded how cyber security has become such an enormous field, touching on many different issues across technology and society. While extensive resources are available on each specialist topic, we felt that many students struggle with bringing seemingly disparate aspects of cyber security knowledge together in order to develop a coherent understanding of the wider field. This is precisely what this book attempts to do.

Vision and philosophy

Essentially, this book presents an overview of the foundations of cyber security, outlining the core challenges, technologies and societal aspects, and how these interrelate. We have designed it to be a starting point for learning about cyber security.

As much of society has embraced digital technology and moved an ever-increasing number of services and related data into online environments, the importance of securing the supporting digital environments has magnified. It is increasingly recognized that cyber security (the security of these digital environments) is not simply a technical matter. While cyber security does involve core technology to protect computers, networks and related infrastructure, it also requires prudent governance and an understanding of how society (individuals and organizations) engages with digital environments – both in terms of presenting threats to such environments and being a crucial part of the defence against such threats.

The vision and philosophy of the book is based around five concepts:

1. Painting the big picture. A comprehensive book about cyber security in its entirety would be vast and unwieldy. This book is not such a text. Rather, the central aim of this book is to introduce readers to the many different interrelated facets of cyber security, aiming for breadth while limiting depth. This book thus paints the big picture. Nothing more, but certainly nothing less.
2. Focused on principles and core theory. Cyber security is a contemporary subject where specific technologies and concepts can emerge rapidly, sometimes significantly over-hyped. This creates the impression of a fast-moving subject that any book would struggle to capture other than for a brief moment in time. However, over 30 years of evolution of cyber security educational programmes at Royal Holloway has demonstrated that, while technologies come and go, the fundamental principles of cyber security change much less than some people imagine. This book focuses on foundations and principles rather than fashion. Much of what we cover will be just as valuable 30 years from now.
3. CyBOK-informed. The NCSC's CyBOK initiative consists of a series of white papers on specific cyber security topics, each written by leading global experts and clarifying what they believe to be the core knowledge concerning those topics.[1] The CyBOK initiative was initially designed to guide designers of new cyber security education programmes, but has subsequently gained a broader reputation as a general source of cyber security wisdom. Although CyBOK is much too broad to cover in any single programme (or book), and is arguably incomplete, it nonetheless provides an excellent resource. We have designed this book so that CyBOK is sprinkled throughout our coverage, with most CyBOK knowledge areas featuring in at least one chapter. Indeed, this book might serve as a useful aid for anyone trying to interconnect the various CyBOK documents.

4 Aimed at (budding) cyber security professionals. Royal Holloway's postgraduate programmes, CyBOK, and thus this book, are all aimed generally at a cyber security professional audience. We thus assume that readers are either students seeking to enter the cyber security profession, or are already working there. Since there are many roles that such a reader could fulfil, the material we cover focuses on developing the broad foundational knowledge that a (budding) cyber security professional should know, independent of the roles they eventually fulfil.
5 Accessibility. While some readers might already be experts in certain topics covered in this book, we imagine that other knowledge areas are relatively unfamiliar. This book thus assumes that each subject is new to the reader, making no assumptions about prior knowledge.

This book is intended to be a launch pad, a support for foundational knowledge-building and a source of inspiration. We will equip you with what we hope is a valuable frame of reference by means of which you can further develop your cyber security knowledge and interpret future developments. You can, and should, read more deeply and fill in some of the cyber security knowledge gaps that we will leave you. Securing our digital future is going to need people who understand the fundamental, technological and societal aspects cyber security. That means it's going to need you!

Organization and contents

The organization of this book is based around a conceptualization of cyber security as being a subject concerning fundamentals, technologies and societal aspects. We now briefly introduce the nine chapters, which begin with foundational issues and then proceed to examine technological and then societal cyber security.

1 **Cyber security fundamentals: Core security concepts, guidance and ecosystem** This chapter will clarify our vision of what it means to provide cyber security. It considers core ideas and terminology, importantly setting out the main security services that cyber security delivers. It will also discuss fundamental cyber security principles, as well as outlining the main players in the cyber security ecosystem.
2 **Cryptography: The toolkit of fundamental digital security mechanisms** This chapter explores the role of cryptography in supporting cyber security. It explains the functionality and purpose of the main cryptographic tools we use today, as well as exploring the wider infrastructure surrounding cryptography and how this impacts the overall security of digital systems.
3 **Computer system security: Securing core digital technology** Computer systems are core technological components in today's digital environments. This chapter

discusses the main security approaches that computer systems use to protect their digital resources. This includes protection provisions provided by the operating system, as well as mechanisms for authentication and authorization.

4 **Network security: Securing the technology backbone** Most computer systems are connected to one another by large, distributed networks, most notably the internet. This chapter reviews core network security threats and technologies. This includes issues to do with addressing, routing and different networking layers, as well as technologies such as firewalls and intrusion detection systems.

5 **Software and application security: Securing computer programs** This chapter introduces the principles concerning security of software and applications, including issues relating to malicious software. It outlines the most common software vulnerabilities that can be introduced during software development, as well as exploring techniques for secure programming and software development.

6 **Cyber security management: Enabling and supporting organizational cyber security** A major factor in securing digital systems is putting in place appropriate management and governance to ensure that the underlying security technologies are integrated into wider organizational processes. This chapter will address the main approaches to practical cyber security management, including risk management, incident management, compliance and the key role that people play in supporting organizational cyber security.

7 **Cybercrime: Threats presented by malicious actors** A major threat to digital environments arises from activities associated with cybercrime. This chapter takes a broad look at cybercrime, considering the different types of cybercrime and the varied motivations of cybercriminals. It also discusses why social engineering is such an important component of cybercrime.

8 **Privacy: Addressing the risks presented by data collection** This chapter considers the role of privacy in digital environments. It considers what privacy means in different contexts. This includes organizational contexts, where legal privacy requirements present risk management challenges, through to individual privacy preferences. It looks at the role of technology in threatening privacy, as well as supporting privacy through use of privacy-enhancing technologies.

9 **Human aspects: The role of personality, behaviour and culture in cyber security** This chapter will explore the role that humans and their actions play in cyber security. It will look at both individual personality and behaviour, as well as group behaviour in the form of security culture. This chapter explains why an appreciation of human aspects is important in the design of cyber security. It also considers how to approach the changing of human security behaviour.

Key features

This book was designed for anyone wishing to inform themselves about cyber security, whether a student, a cyber security professional seeking to broaden their knowledge or a curious general reader desiring an introduction to this fascinating field.

As a companion for educational programmes relating to cyber security, by taking a breadth-over-depth approach to cyber security we imagine that the book will best support a general educational module on cyber security, such as might be found on a computer science or management programme at either undergraduate or postgraduate level.

For students specializing in cyber security who might be studying educational modules focusing on individual chapter topics, the content of this book will be informative but is unlikely to be sufficient. We suggest that the primary role of this book for such students is to highlight key issues and integrate knowledge obtained within different areas of specialism. The latter is particularly important because most programmes must deliver specialist modules in some sort of sequence, thus students inevitably learn the details of some topics before others. Since an important role of this book is to help the reader understand how the many varied aspects of cyber security fit together, this book thus presents a tour of cyber security that such a student could engage with at the start, during and perhaps even as a closing summary of their cyber security studies.

To aid educational readers, we have included several additional features within each chapter. These are:

- Learning objectives. These specify the main topics that a chapter will cover.
- Key points. This identifies the main lessons to be taken away from a chapter.
- Exercises. These are directed tasks that can be optionally undertaken in order to gain a deeper understanding of the material covered in a chapter.
- Further reading. This lists some core resources that can be used to explore the chapter material in greater depth.

Note

1 *The Cyber Security Body of Knowledge,* www.cybok.org/ (archived at https://perma.cc/JC7A-QNNH)

ACKNOWLEDGEMENTS

Much of the material covered in this book is loosely based on the learning materials developed by both ourselves and other colleagues on Royal Holloway's MSc in Cyber Security, which is operated through the University of London Worldwide. We would thus like to extend our extreme thanks to those other colleagues, some of whom also assisted with reviewing the material in this book. In particular, we would like to thank Peter Komisarczuk (Cyber security fundamentals), Ahmad Salman (Software and application security), Andrew Dwyer and Chris Mitchell (Cyber security management), Martin Warren (Cybercrime), Erin Hales and Elizabeth Quaglia (Privacy), Lizzie Coles-Kemp and Anete Poriete (Human aspects) and Fauzia Idrees. We would also like to thank the many Royal Holloway cyber security students with whom we have interacted and who have informed our approaches to discussing and reasoning about cyber security.

Keith expresses his deepest gratitude to Anita, Kyla and Finlay, who had to put up with numerous angsts over word counts, deadlines and extended edits. Yes, the 'cyber book' is finished, and would not have been without your unconditional love and presence.

Jassim thanks his family Mani, Kyran, Kai, Mum, Dad, Karim, Gerd, Anne, Sushma and Geir. Thank you for all your support and love throughout the years. It really means the world to me.

Konstantinos dedicates this book to his late father, mentor, role model and 'skipper in the seas of life', Charilaos Mersinas. Your keen intuition, instant perceptiveness and steady hand continue to navigate me through life's open seas. As I stare at the glittering horizon, I thank you, Dad.

Guido would like to thank his partner, Astrid, and parents, Ingrid and Roman, for their ongoing support of his academic endeavours.

WALKTHROUGH OF TEXTBOOK FEATURES AND ONLINE RESOURCES

Learning objectives

A bulleted list at the beginning of each chapter summarizes what you can expect to learn, to help you to track your progress.

LEARNING OBJECTIVES

- What cyber security means and what it protects
- Identification of fundamental security services provided by cyber security
- Definitions of core concepts relating to cyber security attacks and defences
- Obtaining guidance on cyber security from different sources
- An introduction to different cyber security players and their various roles

Real-world examples

A range of case studies illustrates how key ideas and theories are operating in practice to help you to place the concepts discussed in real-life context.

REAL-WORLD EXAMPLE TLS

To illustrate these security services in context, consider the security technology Transport Layer Security (TLS), which is a widely deployed network protocol used to establish a secure communication channel between two devices.

Exercises

Questions and exercises throughout the text encourage you to reflect on what you have learnt and to apply your knowledge and skills in practice.

EXERCISE

1 Take a moment to reflect on all the different digital environments (at home, at work and when out and about) that you engage with on a typical day. For each one, from your own personal perspective, write down the worst security incidents that could occur (for example, data that it would be embarrassing to expose, digital functionality that it would be disastrous not to have available, etc.).

Further reading/resources

Provides guided access to some key readings in the area to help you further develop your skills and understanding.

FURTHER READING

- Anderson, R (2021) Security Engineering: A guide to building dependable distributed systems, 2nd edn, Wiley
- National Initiative for Cybersecurity Careers and Studies (2023) Explore terms: A glossary of common cyber security words and phrases, https://niccs.cisa.gov/cybersecurity-career-resources/vocabulary (archived at https://perma.cc/D8XQ-DUNH)

Key points

Key learning points at the end of each chapter summarise the main themes of the chapter and act as a useful revision tool.

KEY POINTS

- Cyber security involves protecting all aspects of our digital environments, including data, technology and human and societal aspects.
- The goals of cyber security include realization of fundamental security services, such as confidentiality and data integrity.

Glossary

A detailed glossary is included at the end of the book for quick reference to key terms and definitions in the book.

References

Detailed references provide quick and easy access to the research and underpinning sources behind the chapter

Online resources:

This book includes online resources for lecturers and students comprising:

- lecture slides
- self-test questions
- further resource links
- mapping the book to CyBOK knowledge areas

These resources can be accessed through the Kogan Page website:
www.koganpage.com/cyber-security-foundations

01 Cyber security fundamentals

Core security concepts, guidance and ecosystem

This chapter introduces the topic of cyber security by considering a number of fundamental issues. Firstly, we explore what cyber security might mean, including a clarification of what it is that cyber security aims to protect. We then consider the elemental security services that cyber security provides, as well as how they relate to one another. We introduce fundamental terminology relating to cyber security attacks and defences, as well as considering who attackers might be and how their capabilities vary. Next, we discuss good practice in cyber security, introducing policies, standards and good cyber security principles. Finally, we provide a model of the cyber security organizational ecosystem, identifying some of the major players.

LEARNING OBJECTIVES

- What cyber security means and what it protects
- Identification of fundamental security services provided by cyber security
- Definitions of core concepts relating to cyber security attacks and defences
- Obtaining guidance on cyber security from different sources
- An introduction to different cyber security players and their various roles

What is cyber security?

In this section, we consider what cyber security means. Cyber security is a surprisingly hard concept to precisely pin down and define, so we first consider an instinctive approach, based on personal experiences. We then consider what cyber security aims to protect. Finally, we discuss definitions and related concepts, using these to motivate the remaining chapters of this book.

Defining cyber security through personal experience

In considering the full scope of what cyber security is, a productive starting point is your own instinctive feelings as to what you imagine it to be. These arise from your own digital experiences in your personal life and at work. Take a moment to contemplate this.

You will be aware of the increasing prevalence of digital technologies and services. You will also be aware of the rising value of the data that these technologies and services process and generate. You will thus, undoubtedly, recognize the importance of making sure that our digital world operates as intended, since we all have a great deal at stake.

You will be aware of some of the threats we face from use of digital technologies. The fact that digital technologies connect to one another, in many cases via the internet, means that a wide range of actors with malicious intent could cause us harm, for example by stealing our data or disrupting our digital activities. These dangers could arise from almost anywhere, since the internet has global reach. It is likely that you have even experienced such events, perhaps through having a password compromised, having inadvertently connected to a phishing invitation (you will certainly have received many of them!) or having had a computer virus on one of your digital devices.

You will also be aware of some of the techniques we deploy to help secure digital technologies and services. Almost everyone is familiar with passwords and anti-virus software. In choosing to read this book, it is likely that you have an awareness of many other techniques such as encryption and firewalls. At work, you may have come across further aspects of digital defence such as organizational security policies. You have probably also formed some personal views on the benefits, drawbacks and frustrations of engaging with some of these security controls.

It is likely, therefore, that you regard cyber security as a blanket term, covering all matters relating to digital threats and defences. Your intuition is arguably as good as any formal definition. The UK's National Cyber Security Centre, for example, defines cyber security as 'how individuals and organizations reduce the risk of cyber attack',[1] the latter concept being defined by the US National Institute of Standards and Technology as 'any kind of malicious activity that attempts to collect, disrupt, deny, degrade, or destroy information system resources or the information itself'.[2] In other words, however fuzzy your intuitive cyber security definition might be, you are, essentially, correct![3]

Digital environments

In this book, we will avoid formally defining cyber security and, instead, demonstrate the scope of what we regard as cyber security through consideration of a

Figure 1.1 Layers of a digital environment

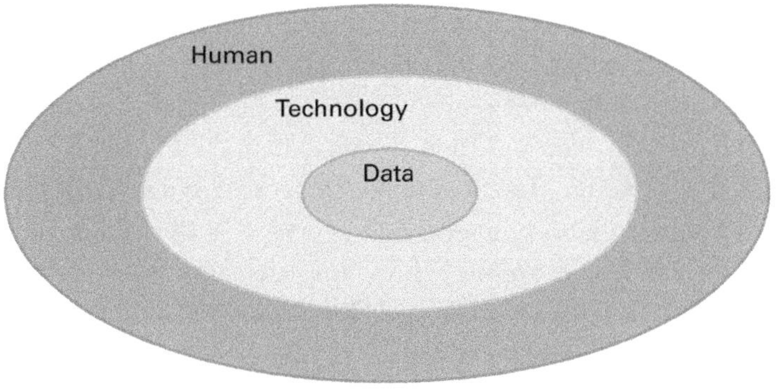

wide range of topics relating to the defence of, and attacks on, digital environments. This will include knowledge from a rich diversity of fields of expertise, including computer science, criminology, economics, law, management, mathematics and psychology. We first need to clarify the nature of what cyber security seeks to protect.

Loosely speaking, we will consider digital environments to consist of three fundamental layers, as depicted in Figure 1.1.

1. *Data layer*. This is the most elemental of the layers, since data is the digital representation of the information that we generate, exchange and use. We need to pay close attention to the security of data wherever it exists in our digital systems, whether at rest on devices, in transit over networks or during processing. Arguably the most fundamental controls we can apply to protect data are provided by cryptography, which is the subject of Chapter 2.
2. *Technology layer*. Digital data only exists because of the digital technologies that we have developed to assist our daily lives. Most digital devices are computers, whether their primary use is traditional computing (such as a laptop) or whether they are embedded computers within technologies such as cars. We consider the security of computers in Chapter 3. The ability to communicate with other devices over networks enhances greatly the utility of our digital devices, hence we discuss network security in Chapter 4. Software and applications are the main mechanisms we use to perform tasks using computers, so we focus on their security in Chapter 5.
3. *Human layer*. Ultimately, digital technology exists to serve human needs, which is something that we must not overlook when considering security aspects. The interface between humans and digital systems is arguably the most difficult layer

of our digital environments to secure. In Chapter 6, we consider how organizations can best approach this interface through effective cyber security management and governance. Of course, the human layer is also the origin of most of the threats our digital systems face, so we look specifically at cybercrime in Chapter 7. One particularly complex aspect of digital systems concerns the relationship between humans and data that relates to them, as well as the wider impacts of processing human-related data within digital systems. We consider matters relating to this in Chapter 8, where we discuss information privacy. Finally, in Chapter 9 we focus on humans themselves, examining how humans and their actions can either strengthen or diminish cyber security, and how to use these insights to support the creation of secure digital environments.

While this layering is merely conceptual, it helps us not just to comprehend the structure of this book, but also to remind ourselves that any notion of cyber security must consider all three digital environment layers, and how they interrelate, in order to be effective. For example, we will see in Chapter 2 that encryption (which operates on the data layer) requires secret keys that need to be stored on devices (which needs consideration of the technology layer) whose security often depends on safekeeping by human users (the human layer). An important role of this book is thus to demonstrate the interrelationship between the various topics we discuss in order to cultivate a holistic approach to cyber security.

Security, privacy and safety

We have already indicated the fuzziness of cyber security as a concept and stated that we will not formally define it. We now briefly mention some related concepts that you may well come across.

Firstly, *cyber* security has not always been the primary terminology for the subject matter of this book. When computers first emerged as a commercial technology in the 1970s, the term *computer* security was common. Computers were not so widely networked and the threats presented by cybercrime were barely imaginable, hence the focus of what we now call cyber security was simply on the security of computing devices. As computers became more widely deployed by organizations, and the internet developed in the late 1980s, the term *information* security entered common usage. This was because the value and vulnerability of data, and thus of the information it represents, became more appreciated. As we moved into the new century, the terminology *cyber* security became more popular. This partially captured the more embedded nature of computing, especially the ubiquity of mobile phones, but also probably rose to prominence because *cyber* was a more evocative word that more readily drew attention to an emerging societal threat. Today, some people refer to *digital* security, perhaps due to greater acceptance of the normality of digital technologies in our everyday lives. For our purposes, information, cyber and digital security are essentially the same, although information security is arguably a more general concept since it includes information not in digital form.

The term *privacy* is just as complex to define, since it means different things in different contexts. Privacy relates to security, but captures a range of ideas concerning access to, and control of, data. We defer a discussion on defining privacy to Chapter 8.

Security is also associated with the notion of *safety*. There is no universal view as to how these terms relate. Some argue that safety is a more emotional concept, others that safety only applies with respect to unintended harms. We make no distinction between security and safety, arguing in Chapters 8 and 9 that aspects of security can also be emotional. We frame cyber security primarily through consideration of malicious threats, and observe that most cyber security controls de facto provide protection against unintended harms, such as accidents.

Finally, security is always a relative term, not an absolute one. We will see throughout this book that no digital environment can be completely secure. Further, what security might mean is always contextual and relative to nuanced notions of risk that are not universal. What one person regards as secure, another might not. Our objective in this book is to present a framework for reasoning about cyber security, mindful of the impossibility of eliminating every threat we face when using digital systems.

Cyber security services

Another way of thinking about cyber security is to consider the core security functionality that we might want to realize when using a digital technology or service. In this section, we introduce some important *security services* that will feature throughout the later chapters of this book. We then introduce a particular security technology, TLS, which will serve to illustrate these security services, as well as to provide a case study that we will return to in later chapters.

Entities

Before specifying our security services, it is worth noting an important aspect of digital interaction that is of relevance throughout this book. While we often imagine a digital interaction as occurring between human beings, such as when you send an email to a friend, this is only partially true. Rather, it is your computer (more precisely the browser or email client software) that is exchanging data with your friend's computer. Similarly, when you digitally interact with your mobile bank online, your phone is communicating with the computer system of your bank. While this observation might seem pedantic, we will see throughout this book that from a cyber security perspective there are many situations where this difference matters enormously. For the purposes of introducing these security services, we will thus use the term *entity* to capture an abstraction that could represent, for example, a human being, an organization, a digital device or an application running on a digital device. Whenever we consider cyber security in context, in later chapters, it is always worth returning to this observation and making sure that you are clear which entities are in play, and any resulting security implications.

Confidentiality

The first aspect of security that most people think of relates to secrecy. This is particularly poignant in digital environments, where data can be so easily communicated, stored and replicated. Data *confidentiality* is the ability to restrict access to data to only authorized entities. When data is in transit across networks then the primary mechanism for providing data confidentiality is encryption, which we discuss in Chapter 2. When data is at rest then the main techniques are either encryption or enforcing access control, which we discuss in Chapter 3. Other techniques for supporting confidentiality include use of secure multiparty computation, which we discuss in Chapter 8.

Integrity

Digital data is prone to modification, either accidentally, due to data degradation (such as by the addition of noise on a channel) or by deliberate manipulation. *Data integrity* is the ability to detect modification of data since creation by an authorized entity.

Unlike confidentiality, there are different levels of data integrity that we might consider. For example, some data integrity techniques can detect unintended, but not deliberate, data manipulation. *Data origin authentication* is a strong data integrity service that enables a verifying entity to not only detect deliberate manipulation of data, but also gain assurance of which entity was the authorized data creator. *Non-repudiation* is a yet stronger data integrity service that enables a verifying entity to prove to a third party which entity was the authorized data creator. We will see examples of a range of cryptographic data integrity mechanisms in Chapter 2.

Note that data integrity benchmarks against a point of authorized data creation. One common approach to designing a data integrity mechanism is for a single authorized data creator to compute and send a data integrity check value that a verifying entity can later recompute. Alternatively, sometimes the authorized creator consists of multiple entities and the integrity of data is benchmarked against a belief that data is correct due to its widespread consistent propagation throughout a digital system. An example of this is the creation of blockchains, which will be discussed in Chapters 2 and 8.

Entity authentication

The reach and invisibility of our digital networks means that one of the biggest challenges we face in digital environments is ensuring that communications are taking place between intended entities. The ability to digitally masquerade so easily is one of the main facilitators of cybercrime, as discussed further in Chapter 7. *Entity authentication* is the ability to confirm that a specific entity is engaged in a digital communication session. Note that unlike confidentiality and data integrity, entity authentication is a security service that applies in real time, such as during a login or when setting up a secure network channel. We discuss examples of entity authentication techniques in Chapters 2 and 3.

When considering entity authentication it is particularly important to consider precisely what 'entity' we are authenticating. This may be a human user, often tested for by means of passwords, PINs or biometrics, or a device, often represented by a cryptographic key stored on that device. In many situations, it is desirable to authenticate a combination of entities through a *multifactor authentication* process. For example, when logging on to a corporate network many users are required to present a password as well as some information sent to their mobile phone. The entities being authenticated in this situation are a combination of the human user (who has hopefully memorized the password and may have used something like face recognition to activate the phone) and the phone itself (with a de facto belief that this is a device normally only under the control of the intended human user).

Entity authentication is often confused with user identification, but it is important to recognize that entity authentication does not always identify a human user, even when a human might be using a digital device. For example, mobile network operators always undertake entity authentication of a service requestor before connecting a mobile phone call. In this case, the authenticated entity is really the SIM card inserted into the calling mobile phone, which contains a cryptographic key. The network operator conducts entity authentication in order to ensure payment of the call. In some cases, this process will result in identification of a human user, such as when confirming the SIM enables the network operator to identify a user with a contract and later charge them for the service. However, some SIMs are prepaid and purchased without the network operator knowing which human user they belong to. In such cases, entity authentication enables the operator to confirm there is credit on the account, but does not result in human user identification.

Authorization

Entity authentication is a real-time service confirming which entity is making a digital connection. If the purpose of entity authentication is access to a computing environment of some sort, then we next need to determine what an authenticated entity is allowed to do. *Authorization* is the ability to determine which digital resources an entity is permitted to access and what they can do with them. Note this separation between entity authentication and authorization – while closely related, they perform subtly different roles.

There are many different ways to manage authorization. Specific resources such as digital files can be directly associated with permissions that define what a given entity can do with the resource. Alternatively, resources can be stored in a location, such as a folder, which has its own permissions that govern what an entity can do with all resources contained there. Authorization can apply to individual entities, or apply to groups of entities, such as when using classification systems or authorization roles. We discuss authorization in more detail in Chapter 3.

Anonymity

Anonymity is a more problematic security service to define because, while you may have an instinctive feeling for what this *might* mean, there are many subtleties. For example, it might sound like anonymity should mean the opposite of entity authentication, except that we discussed previously the case of prepaid SIMs on mobile phones that enable entity authentication of the SIM while the human owner of the SIM is, essentially, anonymous. Anonymity is often associated with confidentiality, since one way of supporting anonymity is to provide confidentiality of the identities of underlying entities.

While anonymity normally relates to preventing identification of an entity involved in a digital interaction, merely hiding identity often provides only a weak notion of anonymity. For example, suppose a user is issued with an anonymous website access token that does not reveal their identity. Each time the user uses the token to access the website, the user's identity remains hidden; however, because they use the same access token each time, the website is able to determine a clear browsing pattern for this (anonymous) user which might reveal information about them – such as their likely time zone, work patterns, etc.

Anonymity is a security service that is often associated with problematic digital activities. We will see in Chapter 7 how anonymity plays a significant role in cybercrime. However, there are many legitimate reasons why anonymity might be desirable, particularly to support information privacy. We explore this issue in more detail in Chapter 8.

Availability

Availability is the ability to access a digital resource (data, device or service) whenever needed. We have come to rely on digital resources so much that it can be extremely frustrating when they are not available, even for a short while. While availability of some resources is merely desirable, availability of an increasing number of digital resources is crucial. Today, the likes of hospitals, banks and power networks rely on digital resources whose unavailability could have catastrophic consequences. As we will discuss in Chapters 4 and 7, many cyber attacks explicitly target availability, such as denial of service attacks that aim to disrupt service provision and ransomware attacks that make data unavailable.

Although there are some general system design approaches that aid availability, such as using replication (including backups) to avoid single points of failure, few security technologies explicitly address availability. Rather, everything discussed in this book indirectly supports availability. Taking a holistic approach to cyber security is the best way to defend against the types of cyber attack that can make systems unavailable. We consider this issue particularly in Chapter 6, where we explain how cyber security management and governance supports availability of an organization's digital environment. This includes the need to anticipate, and recover speedily from, the consequences of unavailability. We include in Chapter 6 a case study of an organization suffering from, and responding to, unavailability of its systems during a major cyber attack.

REAL-WORLD EXAMPLE TLS

To illustrate these security services in context, consider the security technology *Transport Layer Security* (TLS),[4] which is a widely deployed network protocol used to establish a secure communication channel between two devices (see Figure 1.2). You have probably come across TLS most commonly when you enable a secure connection between your client web browser and a remote web server, with use of TLS often indicated by a small padlock in the browser address bar and the prefix https used before the web address. We will stick with this specific use of TLS when we review the various

Figure 1.2 Transport layer security

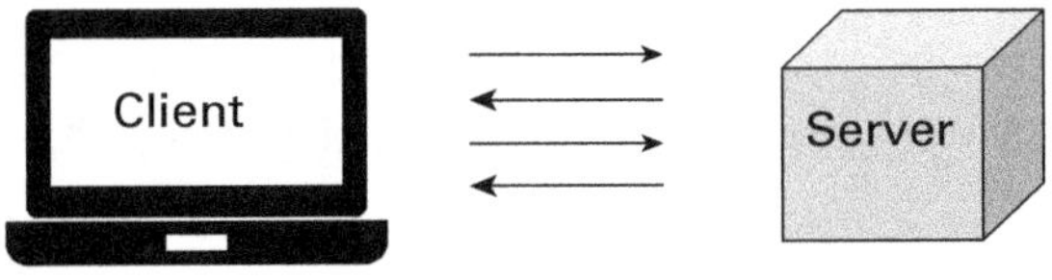

security services just discussed. Specifically, we will consider whether TLS provides these services and, if not, how these services might relate to use of TLS.

- *Confidentiality*. Since anyone can potentially view any data sent over the internet, in this case between a browser and a remote web server, it is imperative that TLS provides confidentiality of the data exchanged over the connection.
- *Integrity*. Because data sent over the internet can be intercepted and modified, TLS needs to provide strong data integrity. It is important that both entities are confident that data sent over the resulting secure channel came from one another, so data origin authentication is a necessary service. On the other hand, for most data there is no need for either a browser or web server to prove to a third party that they were the true originator of exchanged data, so non-repudiation is an unnecessarily strong service. Should we want non-repudiation, it can be provided within the data itself, for example a webmail application could compute a digital signature on data that is then sent to the server over TLS.
- *Entity authentication*. It is important that a web browser can determine whether it is communicating with a genuine web server, otherwise, for example, fraudulent websites could readily fool customers into making payments for fake products. On the other hand, a web server has less need to know exactly which client browsers are connecting to it. Even in the case of making payments, what a service provider operating a website needs are valid payment details and a delivery address – they do not need to know exactly who is making the request for purchase. TLS thus always provides entity authentication of the server, and only optionally provides entity authentication of the client.
- *Authorization*. The purpose of TLS is only to establish a secure communication channel between two entities – it does not govern what those entities have access to once the channel is established. For example, we might use TLS to protect the connection between a student's web browser and a university's educational web portal. The authorization policies of the university govern which services and materials the student can access, but these are applied beyond the TLS connection itself.
- *Anonymity*. TLS can be used to establish a secure connection between any two entities, whether their identities are known to one another or not. Thus, while anonymity is not a security service explicitly provided, TLS supports anonymity should this be required. For example, the anonymity software Tor works by establishing a network of intermediary routers between a web browser and the destination web server, with each connection protected using TLS.
- *Availability*. While availability is not a service directly provided by TLS, use of TLS supports availability indirectly. For example, by helping to ensure a web browser is

communicating with a genuine server, use of TLS reduces the risk of a browser connecting to a malicious server that could attack the client's computer. On the other side of the connection, by protecting user credentials passed from the browser to the server, the risks of a criminal stealing credentials and using them to later attack the server are also reduced.

Defining cyber security through services

The security services we have described in this section provide one helpful way of thinking about some of the objectives of cyber security, but they do not paint the full picture. For one thing, there are additional security services that might be needed in specific settings, such as *accountability* (the ability to establish responsibility for an action, such as deletion of a file). In addition, the security services we described focus on the data and technology layers of our digital environment and do not reflect all of the more human aspects of cyber security that we explore in Chapter 9.

There is a popular tendency to frame cyber security in terms of just three of these services: confidentiality, integrity and availability (often referred to as the *CIA triad*). While there are situations where focusing on these three important services is constructive, particularly when contemplating security of data itself, it is also arguably an overly simplistic means of capturing what cyber security is about. We will leave you to decide, whenever you come across the CIA triad, whether its use in a specific context has captured all of the important issues requiring consideration.

Cyber attack and defence

Another way of contemplating cyber security is to consider it from the perspective of cyber attacks and defences. In this section, we introduce some important terminology relating to this way of thinking. We then consider the range of adversaries we might encounter and their differing capabilities. Finally, we consider the potential flow of a cyber attack.

Core terminology

We now introduce some core terminology that will be useful throughout this book.

An *asset* is a resource within a digital environment that we wish to protect. An asset may be data itself, whether it resides in a file, database, email repository or with a cloud storage service provider. An asset may also be a device on which data resides, such as a mobile phone, desktop computer, network server or a data centre. An asset may even be a service, such as a managed service for supporting human resources or user authentication. When seeking to secure any digital environment, it is crucial to first identify the relevant assets that require protection.

A *vulnerability* is a weakness in a digital environment that could threaten the security of an asset. A vulnerability can exist at any layer of the digital environment. For example, a vulnerability could be unprotected critical data, inappropriate device access permissions or staff ignorance concerning organizational security policies. While it is impossible to identify all vulnerabilities in a system, it is important to identify as many as possible and respond to them. In some cases, it may be possible to eliminate a vulnerability. For example, a password written down on a piece of paper attached to a computer screen represents a vulnerability that destruction of the paper will eliminate. On the other hand, a weak password represents a vulnerability we can reduce, not eliminate, by replacement with a stronger password.

A *threat* is anything that could exploit a vulnerability to harm or disrupt an asset. Threats can arise from many different sources, including environmental incidents, accidents and malicious activities. A *cyber attack* is a threat arising from a malicious source. As we discuss in Chapter 6, a major part of cyber security management is to anticipate threats and determine to what extent they require defensive actions.

A *risk* is a complex concept that emerges from a combined analysis of the likelihood of a particular threat arising and the impact the threat might have should it manifest. A highly impactful threat such as complete destruction of a data centre by an earthquake might not present much risk if the data centre is located in a region of seismic stability. On the other hand, a relatively low-impact threat, such as an employee being locked out of their account because they have failed three times to supply a valid password, might become a significant risk to business operations if employees are asked to change their passwords every week and, as a result, an epidemic of lockouts unfolds. Risk management is discussed in Chapter 6.

A *control* is a measure put in place to address a risk. Controls can be applied to any layer of a digital environment. Indeed, in most situations, different controls are likely to be applied at all three layers. For example, considering a simple password-based employee login process to a corporate computer system, cryptography will be applied at the data layer to protect stored passwords, system security controls will be applied at the technology layer to protect the password database, and users should be given password selection guidance at the human layer to help them select appropriate passwords. Note that while many security controls aim to prevent threats from materializing, others are used to detect security issues or to react to them. A major objective of this book is to provide an overview of the many different types of control that could be deployed.

Adversarial capabilities

In a perfect world (which we do not live in!) the only need for cyber security would arise from accidents, carelessness or natural events. Unfortunately, our digital environments are also vulnerable to attack by people who intend to cause harm. The motivations behind cyber attacks are broadly similar to any other acts of malice by human beings (financial gain, politics, power, revenge, etc.) but the digital environment has several features that encourage certain behaviour and influence the types of malicious event that occur. These include:

- *Distance*. The greatest benefit of our digital environments also presents the most significant danger – a malicious actor can launch a cyber attack against a digital asset from anywhere in the world.
- *Anonymity*. Cyber attacks can be launched under a degree of anonymity, which makes them attractive to certain types of attacker and presents attribution challenges for anyone seeking to confirm the source of an attack, such as criminal investigators.
- *Costs*. Just as digital environments have brought down the costs (financial, effort and time) of many legitimate activities, they have also reduced the costs of conducting many malicious activities.
- *Scale*. Cyber attacks can be deployed at scales unimaginable for non-digital attacks, with some types of cyber attack lending themselves to automation.
- *Complexity*. Our digital environments are complex and arguably less understood by most human users, which creates opportunities for attackers to exploit confusion and ignorance.

A wide range of potential adversaries may seek to attack our digital environments in different ways. We explore this issue in more detail in Chapter 7 but, for now, give a high-level four-part characterization[5] of common sources of cyber attack:

1. *Interpersonal offenders*. A range of undesirable online behaviours originate from individual offenders seeking to cause harm to a specific human target, often one known to them personally. In most cases, attacks from interpersonal offenders take the form of bullying or harassment, including release of sensitive private information. Attacks from interpersonal offenders can be extremely sinister, including online stalking, grooming and extortion. Targeted cyber attacks of this type often require limited resources to conduct.
2. *Career criminals*. These are the source of a significant percentage of cyber attacks, whether operating in small syndicates or as part of large criminal organizations. The motivation for almost all cyber attacks by career criminals is financial gain through fraud. This may involve theft or deception to obtain access to digital

credentials, which are then used to access funds unlawfully, or holding entire data sets to ransom by breaking into computer systems and denying the data owners access to their own digital assets. Career criminals tend to be well resourced, conducting cyber attacks at scale. Criminals also often sell their attack capabilities as a professional service.

3 *Hacktivists*. A different threat arises from hacktivists, who are attackers motivated primarily by political objections to an organization's activities. Hacktivists tend either to seek to deny an organization access to its own digital assets, or to obtain and then expose information about the organization that might be politically damaging. While not every organization may regard itself as a likely target of hacktivism, it is often hard to anticipate how future events might change this risk. Hacktivists tend to be determined and well resourced.
4 *Nation states*. The most powerful potential attackers of a digital environment are those sponsored by nation states. There are many reasons why a nation state might launch a cyber attack, including espionage, hostile action and international political manoeuvring. Cyber attacks by nation states can take any form, but commonly include data theft, denial of access to critical services and, increasingly, disinformation campaigns. Nation state attackers often seek to avoid direct attribution by, for example, conducting attacks through intermediaries. It is extremely hard to defend a digital environment against a committed nation state attacker.

Note that some attackers are hard to classify into just one of these categories (for example, an unfairly dismissed disgruntled employee who attacks their employer could be regarded as both a criminal and a hacktivist) and others cross multiple categories (for example, a criminal gang hired by a nation state to undertake a cyber attack). It is also worth emphasizing that we are not taking any moral stance on the motivations behind any cyber attack (there may, on occasion, be good reasons for conducting any of these attacks). What is always important, from a purely defensive point of view, is that when determining how best to provide cyber security, it is important to consider who likely adversaries are and what their different capabilities might be.

Flow of a cyber attack

Some (not all) cyber attacks are multistage processes, each of which may need separate defensive controls to counter. There have been several attempts to propose models that capture the flow of certain types of cyber attack.[6] While there is no such thing as a generic cyber attack, considering different phases that are common to many types of attack can be constructive.

Many cyber attacks undergo elements of the following four phases, a simple example of which is depicted in Figure 1.3.

Figure 1.3 Phases of an example cyber attack

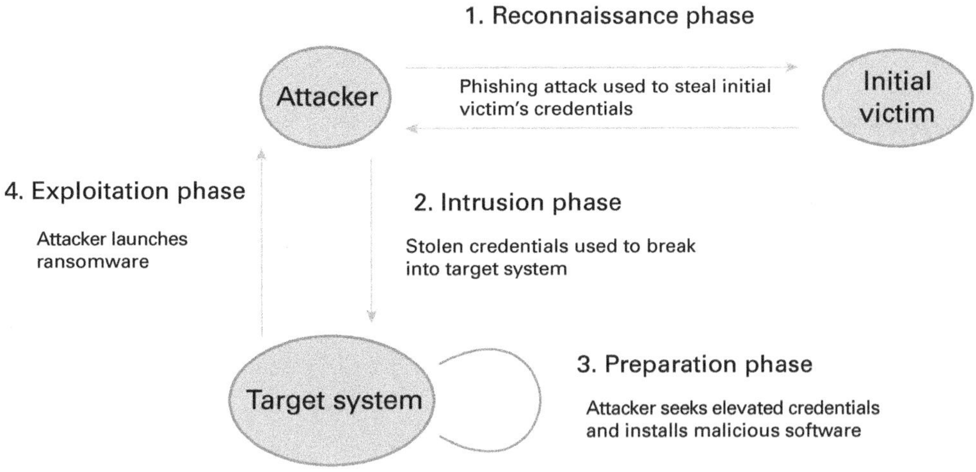

1. *Reconnaissance.* This scoping phase is where potential weaknesses in a system are assessed from the outside. This may involve network scans or probing for access opportunities (perhaps by means of a phishing campaign).
2. *Intrusion.* This involves a breach of the system's defences. This could be via an unprotected network, using stolen credentials or by persuading a genuine user to install malicious software inadvertently.
3. *Preparation.* Having gained access to a system, this phase involves whatever preparatory activities are required before implementing the main cyber attack. This could involve seeking further internal credentials, elevating known credentials to those of a higher privilege or installing additional software.
4. *Exploitation.* This is the activation of the main attack, which could be anything from stealing data, disrupting services or conducting a ransomware attack by encrypting critical data.

There may be significant time gaps between these different attack phases. In particular, following intrusion into a system, sometimes a long time elapses before exploitation. Note also that sometimes different attackers conduct different phases. For example, some attackers conduct reconnaissance activities and then sell the results to others.

The cyber security controls discussed throughout this book help to defend against these different attack phases. For example, access control techniques discussed in Chapter 3 and software development practices discussed in Chapter 5 help to defend against intrusion, internal network monitoring techniques such as intrusion detection systems discussed in Chapter 4 can help to detect anomalous activity associated with preparation, and cyber security management and governance controls discussed in Chapter 6 reduce the risks of serious damage during all four phases.

Cyber security guidance

In this section, we discuss sources of guidance on cyber security. We start by introducing security policies then discuss the important role played by cyber security standards. Next, we outline some general cyber security principles. Finally, we discuss an attempt to define the scope of cyber security in more detail.

Security policies

It should be clear from our discussions that cyber security means different things in different contexts. The nature of the digital environment, specific security services required, range of threats faced, tolerable levels of risk and cyber security principles to apply all vary in different situations. Within a particular context, it is thus important to establish specific cyber security objectives and priorities.

A *security policy* is a set of rules or principles governing cyber security within a context. This context could be organizational, where an organizational security policy defines the overall cyber security objectives of the entire organization (see Chapter 6). The context could also be quite specific, such as an access control policy defining the rules that govern which entities have what types of access to digital assets (see Chapter 3). Whatever the nature of a security policy, within the context to which it applies it provides the benchmark guidance against which to make relevant design, implementation and management decisions.

Since security policies provide the 'local' guidance reference for practising cyber security within a specific context, it is important they are written clearly and communicated to all relevant parties. Indeed, cyber security policies are themselves a type of cyber security control since, without them, there is a risk of inappropriate or inconsistent deployment of other controls.

Cyber security standards

A cyber security *standard* is a document, or set of documents, that specify how a cyber security system, process or technology should work. Cyber security standards are either advisory, such is the case for many standards governing practices (which often need to be tailored to specific environments), or prescriptive, such is the case for many standards specifying technologies. There are many advantages of basing cyber security on standards, including:

- *Best practice.* Standards provide sources of best practice. Many aspects of cyber security (for example, the cryptographic algorithms discussed in Chapter 2) are very difficult to design and implement without significant expertise.
- *Compatibility.* Conforming to standards enables cyber security techniques deployed within one digital environment to be compatible with those deployed in another. This is particularly so, for example, with network security protocols (see Chapters 2 and 4) whose primary purpose is to connect different digital environments securely.
- *Confidence building.* Deploying widely respected cyber security standards enables others to build confidence in the cyber security of a digital environment. In some cases, conformance with specific cyber security standards is mandatory for compliance reasons.

A wide range of standards bodies produce cyber security standards. These vary in their topic coverage, means of production and accessibility. They include:

- *ISO.* The International Organization for Standardization (ISO)[7] produces standards on a wide range of topics. ISO standards on cyber security management are particularly influential, as we will discuss further in Chapter 6. ISO has a network of national expert groups who feed into the international standards decision-making process. While widely respected, one issue concerning ISO standards is that they require a subscription to access.
- *NIST.* The US National Institute of Standards and Technology (NIST)[8] produces a wide range of cyber security standards for the US Federal Government. Although it is a national body, NIST standards are widely adopted internationally and are freely available. For example, we will see in Chapter 2 that NIST standardized many of the most commonly deployed cryptographic algorithms.
- *IETF.* The Internet Engineering Task Force (IETF)[9] is a self-governing body producing cyber security standards relating to core internet technologies. Expert volunteers from a range of organizations cooperate to develop IETF standards in an open manner.
- *ETSI.* The European Telecommunications Standards Institute (ETSI)[10] is a regional standards body that focuses on producing standards relevant to telecommunications. Despite its regionality, ETSI is globally influential and is a major player in the development of cyber security standards for telecommunications.
- *OASIS.* OASIS Open[11] is a non-profit organization that produces cyber security standards supporting open source software. While anyone, as an individual, can

participate in an OASIS standardization process, OASIS funds its activities through an organizational membership model.

- *HomomorphicEncryption.org.*[12] Formed as a collaboration between researchers in industry, government and academia, this group focus on the development of an open standard for a very specific type of cyber security technology called homomorphic encryption (see Chapter 8).

Note that some cyber security standards define cyber security controls or practices whose development was driven by the associated standards body (such as NIST's Advanced Encryption Standard, discussed in Chapter 2). Other cyber security standards incorporate existing cyber security controls or practices, some of which may have been developed independently and grown into de facto standards (such as ISO 27001, discussed in detail in Chapter 6, which is based on a standard BS 7799 developed by the UK Government that later gained considerable global traction).

Cyber security principles

It is impossible to provide general principles that apply to cyber security in every setting since different digital environments have different facets and exceptions to every rule tend to exist. We now outline 10 principles, synthesized from a range of sources,[13] most of which apply to many settings. Later chapters will discuss any principles that apply to specific topics.

1. *Clarity over uncertainty.* It is important in cyber security to be clear what your security objectives are. This starts with a clear understanding of which assets require protection. In most cases, it is advisable to adopt a sound risk-based approach that clarifies likely threats, which controls merit adoption and what residual risk remains (see Chapter 6). Response and recovery from any cyber attack that occurs is normally much smoother if such an incident was anticipated and prepared for. Good cyber security practice involves trying to minimize surprises!
2. *Simplicity over complexity.* A system that has a simpler design is much easier to analyse, enabling, for example, risk management of the system to be more reliable. Cyber attackers often exploit complexity, seeking weaknesses in a complex system that designers have missed. Attackers, after all, hold a distinct advantage since they only need to find one point of vulnerability.
3. *Transparency over obscurity.* While it may seem tempting to hide certain details about the working of a cyber security system as a layer of defence, this is often unwise. There is always a risk that the system has not had sufficient scrutiny and that it may contain weaknesses as a result. It is also often difficult to keep design details secret since reverse-engineering techniques (deconstruction of a system

through careful analysis) might later expose them. While there exist specific environments where openness is not always appropriate (for example, military systems), 'security by obscurity' is generally frowned upon.

4 *Continuity over staticity.* Digital environments and the cyber threats they face are constantly in flux. So, too, must defensive responses to these threats be under continuous review. As we will discuss further in Chapter 6, policies and processes relating to cyber security should be regularly reassessed. Cyber security is a continuous process, not a static achievement.

5 *Comprehensiveness over isolation.* When seeking to protect a digital environment, we should take a holistic view and not treat any of the component parts in isolation. It is particularly important to recall the three different layers we proposed in Figure 1.1, and make sure we consider how cyber security controls deployed in one layer might affect those in another. When working on the details of any aspect of cyber security, it is important to keep this bigger picture firmly in mind. This book aims to provide you with a comprehensive high-level overview of cyber security.

6 *Positivity over negativity.* In general, cyber security design should focus on enabling what is permitted, rather than excluding what is not. The main risk with the latter approach is that it requires a complete assessment of what is not permitted, which is particularly challenging to undertake in a dynamic attack environment where attacker capabilities may evolve in anticipated ways. Focusing on enabling positive operations creates a system that can fail in a safe manner. When considering organizations, we will also discuss in Chapters 6 and 9 the importance of developing a positive security culture rather than a negative one. Cyber security is most effective when seen as enabling capabilities, not preventing them.

7 *Prudence over generosity.* It is generally wise to restrict any entities (users, devices, systems) within a digital environment to having the minimum capabilities and access to resources they require to operate fully, but not more than that. This includes allocating least privileges and making sure that resources such as memory and disk space are shared only with entities that need them (see Chapter 3). By being prudent, rather than generous, a system designer can reduce the attack surface available to a potential adversary.

8 *Robustness over fragility.* It is important that cyber security systems are designed to withstand cyber attacks as best they can. While nobody sets out to design a fragile system, various design aspects can help to reduce the risk of inadvertent fragility. The avoidance of single points of failure reduces the risk that an attack disabling a core digital functionality leads to wider disruption. The adoption of a 'defence in depth' approach to cyber security means that an attacker

overcoming one cyber security control may still be prevented from obtaining their objectives by means of other controls. Strong systems are normally more secure systems.

9 *Forethought over afterthought.* Cyber security should be considered from the outset when developing any new digital technology or service. Retrofitting security controls to something already in deployment is often problematic and leads to suboptimal design decisions.

10 *Reputation over innovation.* Cyber security tends to be an area where it is generally better to adopt tried-and-tested approaches rather than adopt innovative approaches that have not yet gained wide acceptance. This is one reason why cyber security standards play such an important role. Providing strong cyber security is hard, so it is wise to follow established good practices. For example, in cryptography, the subject of Chapter 2, a well-known maxim is 'don't roll your own crypto', which refers explicitly to the fallacy of designers without sufficient expertise attempting to invent their own cryptographic algorithms. This is not to say there is no place for innovation in cyber security, but the precautionary principle advises against pursuing innovation until implications, including those impacting security and privacy, are well understood.

Defining the scope of cyber security

There is a plethora of information available about cyber security, making it hard to know who to turn to for reliable knowledge – apart from this book, of course! In the next section, we will discuss different players in the wider cyber security ecosystem, many of whom are good sources of cyber security knowledge and advice. Later chapters contain links to sources more specific to each of the topics under consideration. Here, we briefly introduce an initiative by the UK Government to provide an informal specification of core knowledge relating to cyber security.

The Cyber Security Body of Knowledge (CyBOK) project[14] aims to establish a set of open resources that define foundational bodies of knowledge (overview documents written by subject experts) in areas relating to cyber security. Initially conceived as a resource for developing education and professional training, the CyBOK document bank has become a source of cyber security knowledge across a broader audience within academia, industry and government.

Figure 1.4 shows the way CyBOK v1.1 presents the relationships between its 21 knowledge areas. Subject matter associated with the data and technology layers is central, with areas relating more closely to the human layer surrounding them. While CyBOK remains a work in progress and there are some omissions (CyBOK v1.1

Figure 1.4 CyBOK knowledge areas

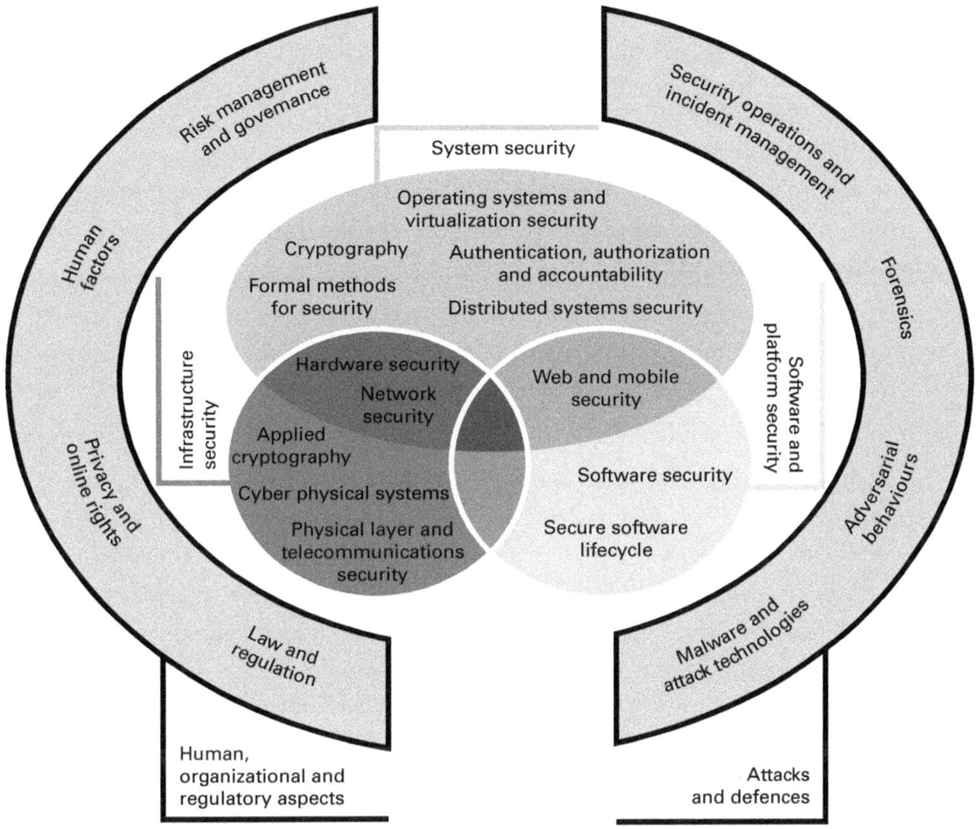

does not cover much of what we discuss in Chapter 9), this attempt to structure and detail core knowledge in cyber security is interesting and relevant. Indeed, CyBOK indirectly influenced the scope of this book, with this and subsequent chapters covering material that touches upon most CyBOK knowledge areas.

The cyber security ecosystem

We close this chapter by presenting a brief outline of the various organizations that engage with cyber security, and discussing how they interact. First, we present a simple model identifying three classes of engagement with cyber security. We then explore each class in a bit more detail.

Cyber security ecosystem model

Figure 1.5 depicts a simple model identifying three different ways in which organizations engage with cyber security. The model features three classes of engagement.

1. *Cyber security consumers.* A consumer of cyber security is an organization maintaining a digital environment that seeks to make it secure.
2. *Cyber security producers.* A producer of cyber security is any organization creating cyber security products or services made available, commercially or otherwise, to consumers.
3. *Cyber security enforcers.* An enforcer of cyber security is any organization providing cyber security enforcement services to both producers and consumers, where such services might relate to statutory or regulatory expectations, monitoring or audit, or provision of standards, certification, education and advice.

We must emphasize that this is a *simple* model. *All* organizations are cyber security consumers (indeed, we are all, as individuals, consumers). Some organizations fall into all three classes, often structured in such a way that some units within the organization serve a role as producers (or co-producers, since they might purchase a cyber security solution and then modify it to meet local requirements) and others as enforcers (for example, internal audit departments). Nonetheless, this class distinction is a useful means of introducing some of the different players and roles in cyber security.

Figure 1.5 Cyber security ecosystem model

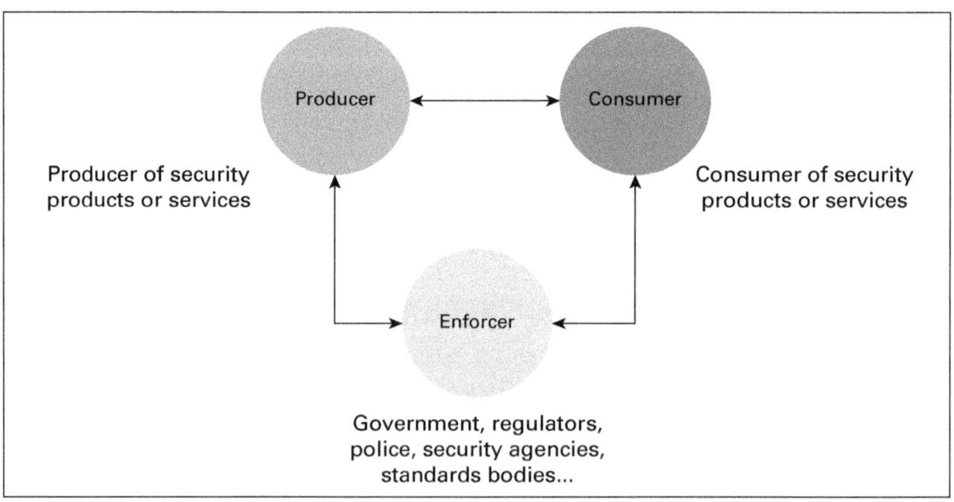

Cyber security consumers

While all organizations are cyber security consumers, it is worth identifying some special subclasses of consumer:

- *Critical infrastructure providers*. These are cyber security consumers who provide services deemed most critical to a nation state. For example, the UK National Protective Security Authority[15] identifies critical infrastructure providers as including those organizations supporting communications, defence, emergency services, energy, financial services, food, government, health, transport and water. Critical infrastructure providers may merit special treatment as consumers, particularly from enforcers, since the impact of a seriously disabling cyber attack could have severe consequences for the lives of citizens.
- *Sectors*. It can sometimes be helpful to consider groupings of cyber security consumers within specific sectors, such as banking, charities, education, media, retail, etc., since these may have common cyber security needs or be subject to common regulatory requirements. Many of these sectors also support themselves through sector-specific cyber security information sharing initiatives.
- *Size*. Another differential between cyber security consumers is size (in terms of both employees and turnover). In general, small organizations are less likely to have internal cyber security expertise or be able to afford expensive services from cyber security producers. This means they may need particular types of support from cyber security enforcers.
- *Individuals*. We, as individuals, are special cyber security consumers, in our various roles as citizens, customers and humans going about our everyday lives. We are arguably the most vulnerable subclass of cyber security consumers and require special support and protection.

Note that cyber security consumers do not just receive support from cyber security producers and enforcers, they often provide important information that producers and enforcers use to improve their services. For example, many businesses gather data that supports threat intelligence models and individual consumers often contribute to improvement of cyber security producers' services by reporting unwanted incidents such as phishing and spam.

Cyber security producers

Cyber security is a big business area and there is a wide range of cyber security producers.[16] We can classify these very roughly by business type:

- *Manufacturers/vendors.* These are the creators of cyber security products. Some of these are very large and provide a wide range of cyber security products, such as Cisco Systems, IBM, Microsoft, etc. Others are much smaller and supply niche products, including cyber security start-ups seeking to launch new concepts into the market.
- *Distributors/resellers.* While some vendors interact directly with consumers, others operate through distributors and resellers who may support multiple vendors and provide additional services such as installation and maintenance.
- *System integrators.* These play an important role since many cyber security consumers do not have the expertise or resources to design and implement cyber security solutions. System integrators fill this niche, which often requires combining products from multiple cyber security vendors.
- *Consultancies.* Consultancies provide independent advice and expertise on any aspect of cyber security, including governance, compliance and design of technical solutions. Consultancies often conduct audits and help to streamline existing processes. Large consultancies such as Deloitte, KPMG and PwC provide a range of cyber security support, while smaller cyber security consultancies provide more specialist services.
- *Managed service providers.* These take on outsourced responsibility for certain operational aspects of cyber security. This might include the running of core components of a business, such as IT services, or handling special cyber security operations, such as disaster recovery services (see Chapter 6).
- *Service providers.* These are providers of specific digital services that themselves need to be secure. This includes providers of internet services, telecommunication and cloud computing.

Again, this producer classification is simplified. Many cyber security producers fit more than one of our business types. Further, this classification hides the fact that many cyber security producers rely on a supply chain of other cyber security producers.

When considering the range of cyber security producers that a cyber security consumer may come to rely on, it is worth recognizing the complexity of the trust relationships upon which cyber security often depends. This, in turn, creates many challenges for effective cyber security enforcement.

Cyber security enforcers

A wide range of organizations play different roles as cyber security enforcers. These operate primarily to benefit cyber security consumers, although much of their work may be through working with cyber security producers to ensure quality of provision. Cyber security enforcers tend to focus on the following areas:

- *International and national security.* This includes international bodies such as the United Nations, which deals with international counter-terrorism, and national security agencies who act on behalf of national governments.
- *Law.* This includes international bodies such as Interpol, regional bodies such as Europol and national police agencies, many of which have dedicated cybercrime units.
- *Regulations.* International organizations responsible for relevant cyber security regulations govern many sectors. For example, the Payment Card Industry Security Standards Council (PCISSC)[17] produces cyber security regulations relating to handling card payments that must be complied with. In many countries, there may be parts of government responsible for specific aspects of cyber security regulation. For example, in the UK the Information Commissioners Office[18] deals with data protection and related regulations. Other organizations, including many consultancies, provide cyber security compliance audits and issues certifications.
- *Advice.* Various organizations support cyber security consumers and producers by providing advice concerning cyber security. These include regional bodies such as the European Union Agency for Cybersecurity (ENISA)[19] and national bodies such as the Canadian Centre for Cyber Security[20] and the UK National Cyber Security Centre (NCSC).[21] Cyber security standard bodies discussed earlier, such as NIST, are also good sources of cyber security advice. There are also a range of independent sources of advice, such as the UK's Get Safe Online website,[22] maintained by a partnership or organizations from a range of both public and private cyber security consumers, producers and enforcers.
- *Professional development.* A number of organizations enforce cyber security indirectly through development of cyber security skills and professionalism. These include universities, training providers and professional bodies. A number of international cyber security professional bodies are very active worldwide, including the International Information System Security Certification Consortium (ISC2),[23] Information Systems Audit and Control Association (ISACA)[24] and the Information Systems Security Association (ISSA).[25] In the United States, Cyber Seek[26] supports cyber security careers through identification of pathways, training opportunities and open positions.

KEY POINTS

- Cyber security involves protecting all aspects of our digital environments, including data, technology and human and societal aspects.
- The goals of cyber security include realization of fundamental security services, such as confidentiality and data integrity.
- Cyber security enables the management of risks to digital assets by means of considering threats and adversarial capabilities.
- Many sources of guidance on cyber security exist, including cyber security standards and adherence to general cyber security principles.
- The cyber security ecosystem consists of cyber security producers offering products and services to cyber security consumers, with both communities supported in different ways by cyber security enforcers.

EXERCISES

1. Take a moment to reflect on all the different digital environments (at home, at work and when out and about) that you engage with on a typical day. For each one, from your own personal perspective, write down the worst security incidents that could occur (for example, data that it would be embarrassing to expose, digital functionality that it would be disastrous not to have available, etc.).
2. For each of the security services we outlined in this chapter, explain whether or not (and why) you would require these services when:
   a. checking an online bank balance from a mobile phone
   b. using a home Wi-Fi network
   c. submitting an online tax return
   d. voting in an online election
3. The CIA triad is often used to represent the goals of cyber security. In your opinion, what are the advantages and disadvantages of using this concept as a framework for discussing cyber security?
4. Consider your personal home digital environment:
   a. What are the main assets?
   b. What are the main cyber security threats?
   c. What cyber security controls are in place?

5 By means of an internet search or otherwise, give at least two examples of reported cyber attacks that have been (or are strongly believed to have been) conducted by:

   a. interpersonal offenders
   b. career criminals
   c. hacktivists
   d. nation states

6 Ransomware is an example of a common cyber attack. Describe in more detail the typical phases (flow) of a ransomware attack. You may wish to base this on a case study of a real attack that has been reported (or that you have experienced).

7 In this chapter, we gave a short list of cyber security standards bodies and discussed their work. Identify a number of other standards bodies (these can be national, regional or sector-specific) that produce cyber security standards and explain what aspects of cyber security they support.

8 For each of our stated cyber security principles, give an example of a bad scenario that could unfold if the principle is not followed. You can either come up with your own example or, even better, find a link to a news article that reports on such an incident.

9 Consider a global jurisdiction that you are familiar with (perhaps where you live or where you work) and identify some organizations that act as cyber security producers and some that act as cyber security enforcers, writing a few lines on each that clarify the main roles they play in their regional cyber security ecosystem.

10 One important concept that we did not discuss explicitly in this chapter, but will consider throughout this book, is that of *trust*. Discuss the extent to which you believe that cyber security facilitates trust, and also the extent to which you believe trust is necessary to facilitate cyber security.

FURTHER READING

- Anderson, R (2021) *Security Engineering: A guide to building dependable distributed systems*, 2nd edn, Wiley
- National Initiative for Cybersecurity Careers and Studies (2023) Explore terms: A glossary of common cyber security words and phrases, https://niccs.cisa.gov/cybersecurity-career-resources/vocabulary (archived at https://perma.cc/D8XQ-DUNH)

- National Institute of Standards and Technology (2023) Cybersecurity, https://www.nist.gov/cybersecurity (archived at https://perma.cc/66C5-43FB)
- National Institute of Standards and Technology (2020) *Security and Privacy Controls for Information Systems and Organizations*, NIST Special Publication 800-53 Revision 5
- Spafford, E, Metcalf, L and Dykstra, J (2023) *Cybersecurity Myths and Misconceptions: Avoiding the hazards and pitfalls that derail us*, Addison-Wesley
- Stallings, W and Brown, L (2018) *Computer Security: Principles and practice*, 4th edn, Pearson
- Taylor, A, Alexander, D, Finch, A and Sutton, D (2020) *Information Security Management Principles*, 3rd edn, BCS Learning and Development

Notes

1 National Cyber Security Centre (2023) What is cyber security? https://www.ncsc.gov.uk/section/about-ncsc/what-is-cyber-security (archived at https://perma.cc/6DUS-WF6T)

2 NIST Computer Security Resource Center (2023) Cyber attack, https://csrc.nist.gov/glossary/term/cyber_attack (archived at https://perma.cc/FF5R-8UMX)

3 For a thoughtful commentary on the challenges of defining cyber security, see: Computerphile (2023) Defining Cybersecurity with Gene Spafford, https://www.youtube.com/watch?v=olgGZmkkooU (archived at https://perma.cc/6CL8-JA78)

4 Rescorla, E (2018) The Transport Layer Security (TLS) Protocol Version 1.3, Internet Engineering Task Force (IETF) Request for Comments: 8446, https://datatracker.ietf.org/doc/html/rfc8446 (archived at https://perma.cc/W26L-XQHF)

5 Stringhini, G (2021) Adversarial Behaviours Knowledge Area, Version 1.0.1, https://www.cybok.org/knowledgebase1_1/ (archived at https://perma.cc/A8XB-QWTQ)

6 The most high-profile attack model is the Lockheed Martin kill chain proposed in: Hutchins, E M, Cloppert, M J and Amin, R M (2011) Intelligence-driven computer network defense informed by analysis of adversary campaigns and intrusion kill chains, *Leading Issues in Information Warfare and Security Research*, 1 (1)

7 ISO (2023) ISO: Global standards for trusted goods and services, https://www.iso.org/home.html (archived at https://perma.cc/E3EM-VC2M)

8 National Institute of Standards and Technology (2023) https://www.nist.gov/ (archived at https://perma.cc/2QML-SEWW)

9 Internet Engineering Taskforce (2023) https://www.ietf.org/ (archived at https://perma.cc/E3MT-23PT)

10 ETSI (2023) Welcome to ETSI, The Standards People, https://www.etsi.org/ (archived at https://perma.cc/6924-ETS5)

11 OASIS Open (2023) https://www.oasis-open.org/ (archived at https://perma.cc/JG8F-WJHW)

12 Homomorphic Encryption Standardization (2023) https://homomorphicencryption.org/ (archived at https://perma.cc/EZ8K-5ELJ)

13 A good overview of cyber security principles can be found in: Martin, A, Rashid, A, Chivers, H, Schneider, S, Lupu, E and Danezis, G (2021) Introduction to CyBOK Knowledge Area, Version 1.1.0, https://www.cybok.org/knowledgebase1_1/ (archived at https://perma.cc/GCB9-6EVX)

14 CyBOK (2023) The Cyber Security Body Of Knowledge, https://www.cybok.org/ (archived at https://perma.cc/NFU6-74LF)

15 National Protective Security Authority (2023) Critical National Infrastructure, https://www.npsa.gov.uk/critical-national-infrastructure-0 (archived at https://perma.cc/MQS6-EUDW)

16 The UK produces an annual analysis of the UK cyber security producer sector. For example, see: Donaldson, S, Crozier, D, Martorell, S, McLaren, I, Douglas, J and Shah, J (2022) UK Cyber Security Sectoral Analysis 2022, https://www.gov.uk/government/publications/cyber-security-sectoral-analysis-2022 (archived at https://perma.cc/58KF-FU9Z)

17 PCI Standards Security Council (2023) https://www.pcisecuritystandards.org/ (archived at https://perma.cc/WP8W-SM5N)

18 Information Commissioner's Office (2023) https://ico.org.uk/ (archived at https://perma.cc/ASX4-DSEM)

19 European Union Agency for Cybersecurity (2023) https://www.enisa.europa.eu/ (archived at https://perma.cc/324A-TE2F)

20 Canadian Center for Cyber Security (2023) https://www.cyber.gc.ca/en (archived at https://perma.cc/F9LG-8YZ4)

21 The National Cyber Security Centre (2023) https://www.ncsc.gov.uk/ (archived at https://perma.cc/CSL5-F2ZE)

22 Get Safe Online (2023) https://www.getsafeonline.org/ (archived at https://perma.cc/M6TB-XS3A)

23 ISC2 (2023) https://www.isc2.org/ (archived at https://perma.cc/QZ76-NWS3)

24 ISACA (2023) We're working together to build a better digital world, https://www.isaca.org/about-us (archived at https://perma.cc/D2UN-ANKU)

25 Information Systems Security Association (2023) https://www.issa.org/ (archived at https://perma.cc/D6Z8-25PN)

26 Cyber Seek (2023) Hack the Gap, https://www.cyberseek.org/ (archived at https://perma.cc/TC37-ATCS)

02 Cryptography

The toolkit of fundamental digital security mechanisms

This chapter explores the fundamental role of cryptography in supporting cyber security. We explain the core functionality of the most-used cryptographic tools and how to decide which cryptographic tools are appropriate to deploy in specific settings, illustrating this by considering regularly used applications of cryptography. We also explore the wider infrastructure surrounding cryptography and how this impacts the security cryptography provides. Finally, we consider several important societal issues arising from use of cryptography. Although cryptography is based on mathematics, this chapter focuses on what cryptography does and how to use it, not on technical details of specific cryptographic tools.

LEARNING OBJECTIVES

- An explanation of the precise role cryptography plays in the security of digital systems.
- Identification and comparison of the most-used cryptographic tools.
- Selection of appropriate cryptographic tools for specific applications.
- Assessment of the security of the wider system within which cryptography is deployed.
- Awareness of societal issues arising from use of cryptography.

The cryptographic toolkit

Cryptography can be considered as a toolkit of mechanisms enabling the provision of core digital security services. In this section we first discuss the role of cryptographic tools in supporting cyber security. We then introduce some of the most widely used tools and explain the different functions of cryptographic algorithms and cryptographic keys. Finally, we identify two classes of cryptographic tool and discuss practical implications of their different features.

The role of cryptography

If we consider providing cyber security as a blend of human, organizational and technological controls, then cryptography lies at the heart of this, providing the fundamental techniques from which security technologies can be constructed. Security for the likes of digital networks, messaging services, payment systems and internet-enabled technologies would be inconceivable without using cryptography. Indeed, cryptography is fundamental to many technologies we later discuss relating to computer systems (Chapter 3), networks and infrastructure (Chapter 4), applications (Chapter 5) and privacy (Chapter 8).

Cryptography provides tools for enabling core digital security services, the most fundamental of which were introduced in Chapter 1. Cryptographic tools are rarely considered in isolation, for several reasons. First, most security technologies have complex security requirements that often necessitate a combination of different digital security services, hence a combined use of different cryptographic tools. Secondly, many cryptographic tools have multiple purposes and their use depends on context (a good example is hash functions, which we discuss later). Thirdly, some cryptographic tools can be used in different ways (for example, block ciphers have different modes of operation). Finally, the security enabled by cryptographic tools depends on the wider digital system in which they are deployed, and its potential vulnerabilities, which is something we discuss shortly.

Cryptographic tools manipulate data, and their design is based on mathematical concepts. We will not explore the mathematical ideas underpinning the details of the most common cryptographic tools because there is no real need to do so. Assuming that well-respected cryptographic tools are deployed, what matters most from a cyber security perspective is what these tools achieve and what issues need to be considered when deploying them. For those interested in exploring the mathematics behind cryptography, we provide suggestions in the further reading.

Cryptographic tools

Although the toolkit of cryptographic mechanisms is extensive, only a handful of cryptographic tools are widely used. This chapter introduces the most important of these, which can be classified as:

- Confidentiality tools: we will discuss several encryption mechanisms, including some special techniques for confidentially exchanging a cryptographic key.
- Integrity tools: we will discuss various integrity mechanisms, including tools for providing both confidentiality and data integrity simultaneously.

One important cryptographic service, entity authentication, is not typically provided by any dedicated cryptographic tools. As we will see, entity authentication is both supported and facilitated by deploying confidentiality and/or integrity tools in different ways.

There are dozens of other cryptographic tools that we will not discuss. Some are designed to achieve more fine-grained outcomes, such as encryption mechanisms that only permit decryption under special conditions. Others offer extended functionality, such as digital signature schemes that enable groups of signers to sign data collectively. Yet others provide different, sometimes more sophisticated, security services, including some of the privacy-enhancing technologies discussed in Chapter 8.

Note that cryptography can do little on its own to support availability. Indeed, some might argue that cryptography creates unavailability, since lost keys or malicious use of encryption can lead to inaccessibility of data. However, a more constructive argument is that prudent deployment of cryptography supports availability since most digital systems could simply not be made available without it!

Cryptographic algorithms and keys

We now take a closer look at the components of a typical cryptographic tool. We use the term 'tool' generically to describe a family of cryptographic mechanisms that offer similar functionality. For example, a block cipher is a cryptographic tool that provides confidentiality and works in a particular way. However, the term 'block cipher' is no more concrete than the term 'hammer'. If you walk into a hardware store you will see different hammers on the shelf, all of which have the same functionality – which one should you buy?

A *cryptographic algorithm* is an instantiation of a cryptographic tool. A block cipher is not something that a developer could implement (it's just an idea), but a block cipher algorithm, such as AES, is. There are many different block cipher algorithms to choose from, each of which specifies the precise process by which data input to the algorithm is transformed into output data. The purpose of the output data varies, depending on the tool the algorithm instantiates. For example, the output of an encryption algorithm is scrambled data intended to disguise the meaning of the input data. On the other hand, the output of a digital signature algorithm is a short digest computed from the input data, designed to enable a verifier to check that the signer committed to that input data.

We assume that the details of a cryptographic algorithm are publicly known. Indeed, most are, since development of standardized cryptographic algorithms enables expert scrutiny and supports compatibility. This means that a cryptographic tool still needs something that distinguishes the capability of a legitimate user from that of an adversary. This is the role played by a cryptographic key.

A *cryptographic key* is an additional piece of relatively short data that is input to a cryptographic algorithm. If two different cryptographic keys are input to the same cryptographic algorithm (and all other inputs are identical) then the resulting output should be different. We can thus use cryptographic keys to associate outputs of cryptographic algorithms with particular users or devices. Consequently, we could regard cryptography as a means by which the challenge of securing data is transformed into the, arguably more manageable, challenge of securing cryptographic keys.

Two types of cryptography

Most cryptography is deployed in situations where a *creator* applies a cryptographic tool, while a *consumer* uses the same tool to obtain some security guarantees. For example, a creator might encrypt data in such a way that only a specific consumer can decrypt it, or a creator might digitally sign some data in such a way that any consumer can verify whether the signature is valid. Note that while creators and consumers are often associated with people and organizations, the actual entities involved in the cryptographic exchange are likely to be computing devices. Some cryptographic tools involve coordination between multiple creators and/or consumers, and sometimes creator and consumer are the same party (for example, when encrypting data for local storage). To keep things simple, we focus on the two-party case depicted in Figure 2.1.

In Figure 2.1, the creator inputs raw data requiring protection and a *creator key* into a *creation algorithm*, generating *crypto output*. This crypto output is cryptographically protected data and is not assumed to be secret – it could, for example, be sent over an unprotected network. A consumer inputs data and a *consumer key* into a *consumption algorithm*, generating output. As we will see, the nature of the consumer input and output data varies across different cryptographic tools.

Creation and consumption algorithms are clearly related. For some tools they are identical, while in others they are slightly different, albeit mathematically intertwined. More significant is the relationship between creator and consumer keys. For some tools these are identical, hence such tools are described as *symmetric*. In symmetric cryptography, the identical creator and consumer key is necessarily secret. A challenge in deploying symmetric cryptography is thus how to securely distribute this key to both creator and consumer.

Figure 2.1 Generic cryptographic model

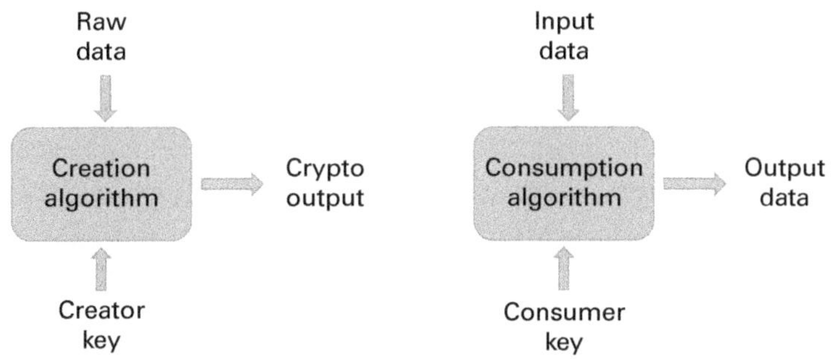

Other tools have different creator and consumer keys, enabling either the creator or consumer key to be publicly known. Cryptographic tools of this type are referred to as *asymmetric*, or more commonly as *public-key* tools. A major advantage of public-key tools is the lack of need to coordinate distribution of the same secret key to different system components. Public-key cryptography also enables a creator and consumer who have not previously had any formal relationship to use cryptography, since one can easily make their public key available to the other (which one depends on the tool). However, public-key cryptography still presents significant key management challenges, as we discuss later in the chapter.

Cryptographic systems

Cryptography plays a fundamental role within a digital system, but we must keep the wider system surrounding cryptography in mind when assessing the effectiveness of cryptographic tools. To demonstrate this, we now consider some of the components of such a system and reflect on what could go wrong that might lead to cryptography failing to provide the intended security.

Cryptographic algorithms

Since cryptographic algorithms define the precise processes used to manipulate data, it would be tempting to regard a cryptographic algorithm as the most vulnerable component of any cryptographic system. While technical weaknesses in an algorithm could be catastrophic, normally such weaknesses are of least concern because most cryptographic deployments use a limited set of well-scrutinized, highly respected cryptographic algorithms. Although this does not guarantee weaknesses will never be found, the chances of such weaknesses arising are relatively low. Of course, this argument does not apply to the risky practice of deploying non-standard algorithms, which is generally not recommended.

One limitation on the security of any cryptographic algorithm is the *key length*, which relates to the total number of possible keys (most cryptographic algorithms either have a fixed key length, or a range of recommended key lengths). One theoretical attack against an encryption algorithm is for an attacker to try out every possible key. For example, an attacker who has intercepted some encrypted data could try decrypting it with every possible decryption key until the data appears to make sense. This process, known as *exhaustive key search*, can only be defended against by having so many possible decryption keys that such a search is deemed infeasible in practice. Fortunately, making an exhaustive key search practically infeasible is not difficult. For example, most symmetric algorithms use a key length of at least 128 bits (the key consists of a string of 128 ones or zeros). Since there are two choices for each bit, there are 2^{128} (2 multiplied by itself 128 times) possible keys. This is so enormous that the most powerful supercomputer would take millions of billions of years to try every key.

The goal of designers of symmetric algorithms is for there to be no obvious means of attacking the algorithm *other* than exhaustive key search. If the key length is believed sufficient, then the algorithm is deemed secure. On the other hand, the security of public-key algorithms is based around a computational problem that is believed to be hard to solve on a computer. For example, the RSA public-key encryption algorithm is built around the perceived difficulty of factoring large numbers – so long as computers struggle to factor large numbers, RSA is deemed secure. For public-key algorithms, key length (which tends to be much longer than for symmetric algorithms) is only indicative of security since exhaustive key search is not the benchmark attack.

The respected cryptographic algorithms in use today have all been designed extremely conservatively to protect against attackers with unimaginably powerful conventional computers. However, there is a potential computing revolution on the horizon which could see development of an entirely new class of *quantum computers* with quite different capabilities. While the development of powerful quantum computers remains highly uncertain, designers of new cryptographic algorithms now assume that such computers *might* exist sometime in the future (even if they never do).

There is mixed news regarding the current suite of well-used cryptographic algorithms with respect to the threat presented by quantum computers. The good news is that while quantum computers might be capable of faster exhaustive key searches, the anticipated improvement is not dramatic. It is widely believed that a doubling of current symmetric key lengths will be more than sufficient. Hence, doubling the currently favoured 128-bit symmetric keys to 256-bit keys should provide post-quantum security. Notably, AES (the most commonly deployed block cipher) already supports 256-bit keys, so upgrading systems using AES should be relatively straightforward. The less good news is that quantum computers might be able to make more progress in solving the hard computational problems around which the most commonly deployed public-key algorithms are based, meaning that such algorithms will probably need replacement.

The potential threat presented by quantum computers should not be ignored, but neither does it diminish our claim that cryptographic algorithms are the least vulnerable component of any cryptographic system. The algorithms used today are highly regarded. Future migration to post-quantum algorithms should ensure that so, too, will be the algorithms we use in the future.

Cryptographic protocols

Most digital systems comprise multiple entities between which there are a range of different security requirements. Cryptographic algorithms are thus deployed as components of *cryptographic protocols*, which specify exactly how algorithms are used during the interactions between different system entities. For example, the TLS protocol (introduced in Chapter 1) specifies interactions between a client and a server, during which they negotiate which cryptographic algorithms they will use, establish entity authentication of the server, undertake a key agreement process that results in shared symmetric keys, and then creates a secure channel that enables confidentiality and data origin authentication of exchanged data. During TLS, a range of different cryptographic algorithms are utilized in a very specific way in order to achieve these various security objectives.

Secure cryptographic protocols are notoriously hard to design. A weak cryptographic protocol, even if it uses strong cryptographic algorithms as components, will not deliver its intended security objectives. In the past, design of cryptographic protocols often relied on informal application of expertise. This proved problematic, since protocol weaknesses are often unintuitive. For example, TLS 1.2 was believed to be secure until a range of unanticipated attacks were discovered. Today, formal modelling tools are used to aid cryptographic protocol design, some of which informed the redesigned TLS 1.3.[1] Use of formal tools alongside extensive (preferably public) expert scrutiny normally results in strong cryptographic protocols that prove robust to attack. Applications deploying such protocols, ideally standardized ones, have less risk of protocol failure because the development process is based on systematic analysis as well as incorporating the views of experts throughout the world.

Implementation of cryptography

Respected cryptographic algorithms used within a sound cryptographic protocol should provide the intended security guarantees, at least on paper. However, in order to build a real cryptographic system, theory needs to be converted into lines of code and/or hardware circuits. Implementation of cryptography thus relies on a secure development process.

Secure development is discussed in much more detail in Chapter 5, but it suffices to note here that cryptography is particularly prone to development failures. This is largely because cryptography itself is sensitive, since tiny changes to the specification of a cryptographic algorithm or protocol can lead to serious security vulnerabilities. The risk of such failures manifesting is sometimes increased by developers lacking an understanding of cryptography and its sensitivity.

While some development failures arise from developers making errors, others can arise when developers are not given adequate instruction. As an example, consider implementation of a cryptographic protocol that specifies data needs to be kept confidential using symmetric encryption. As we will discuss shortly, implementation still requires several decisions to be made. Should a stream cipher or a block cipher be used? Which algorithm should be selected? If a block cipher, which mode of operation should it use? Such decisions should not be left to developers who may lack the expertise to make appropriate choices.

Side-channel attacks on cryptographic systems provide further illustration of how critical implementation of cryptography is.[2] These attacks exploit different aspects of implementation. For example, an attacker with access to a cryptographic device can use *timing attacks* to make detailed measurements of how long the device takes to conduct specific operations in order to deduce information about the key. Similarly, *power-analysis attacks* measure power use when specific operations are being undertaken. Different implementations may be more or less prone to such attacks. While cryptographic algorithms are designed today with an awareness of side-channel attacks, some defences against them can only be made during implementation.

Management of keys

The security cryptography provides is only as good as the security of the keys on which cryptography depends. Cryptographic keys undergo an entire lifecycle, as depicted in Figure 2.2. Keys are initially *generated*, then need to become *established* within a cryptographic system, where they must be *stored*, then *used*, and ultimately *destroyed*. Many systems also require mechanisms enabling keys to be *changed*. *Key management* governs the entire lifecycle of a cryptographic key since failure at any single stage could have serious consequences.

Figure 2.2 Key management lifecycle

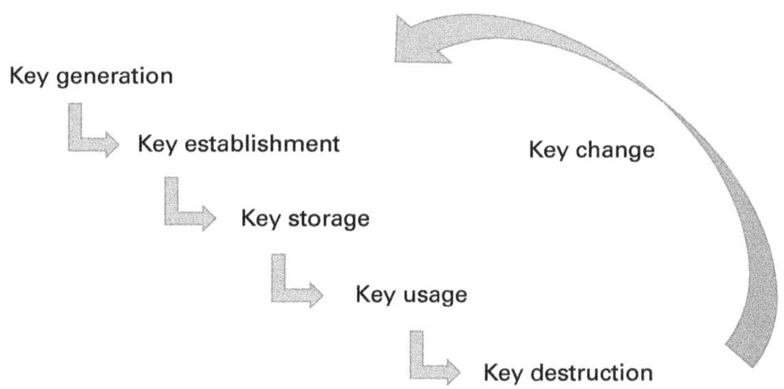

Key management is challenging because it is an aspect of a cryptographic system that is less straightforward to put into practice than, say, selection of an algorithm. While guidance and good practice concerning key management can be provided, key management needs to be suitable for the systems (and organizations) in which cryptography is deployed. We devote an entire section later in this chapter to a more detailed discussion of key management.

Endpoint security

Lastly, it is vital to recognize that there are clear limitations to the security cryptography provides to data. For example, cryptography provides confidentiality from the point of encryption to the point of decryption, but does not protect data at the endpoints both prior to encryption and following decryption. This rather obvious statement reinforces why cyber security requires a holistic approach. Securing endpoints requires knowledge about the security of the computers these endpoints reside on (Chapter 3), the networks and wider infrastructure on which they might arise (Chapter 4), the applications on which they might manifest (Chapter 5), how data at these endpoints might be governed (Chapter 6) and how the users with access to these endpoints might behave (Chapter 9).

Providing confidentiality

The best-known security service that cryptography enables is confidentiality, and tools for providing confidentiality are known as *encryption* mechanisms. While encryption can be used for local storage, we will consider the more complex setting where encryption is used to protect data in transit over a communication channel, as depicted in Figure 2.3. In this case a sender deploys an *encryption algorithm*, which inputs *plaintext* and an *encryption key*, and outputs *ciphertext*. This ciphertext is sent over the communication channel, where any attacker who observes it should not be able to deduce anything meaningful about the underlying plaintext. The legitimate receiver then inputs the ciphertext and the corresponding *decryption key* into the *decryption algorithm*, which outputs the plaintext. Since the encryption and decryption algorithms are closely related, they are often synonymously referred to as the 'encryption algorithm'.

We first consider symmetric encryption, where the encryption and decryption key are identical. We then discuss public-key encryption, where the encryption key is public and the corresponding decryption key is a different (related) secret value. Finally, we explore cryptographic mechanisms for enabling confidential exchange of a symmetric key.

Figure 2.3 Encryption for communication model

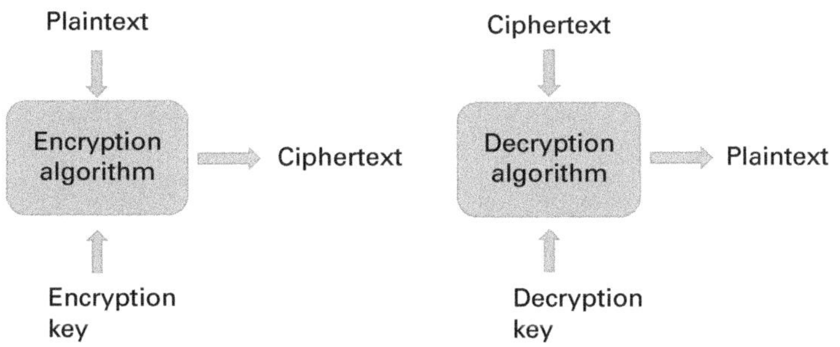

Stream ciphers

A *stream cipher* is a symmetric encryption algorithm that encrypts plaintext bitwise (one, or at most a few, bits at a time). A sender uses the stream cipher to first convert the symmetric key into a pseudorandom string of bits known as the *keystream*, which is then combined bitwise with the plaintext (typically using the XOR operation) to produce ciphertext. The receiver uses the same key to generate the same keystream, which is then combined with the ciphertext to recover the plaintext.

In a stream cipher, the main effort for both the encryption and decryption algorithms is to generate the keystream, which could be done in advance of processing the plaintext (for encryption) or ciphertext (for decryption). The remaining processing for both encryption and decryption involves the simple XOR operation, so stream ciphers are particularly suited to applications where speed is a priority.

Another important property of stream ciphers is that noise arising in the communication channel has limited impact. If one bit of ciphertext is flipped due to noise (for example, a one is corrupted into a zero), on decryption this damaged ciphertext bit only impacts the corresponding single plaintext bit. Stream ciphers are thus well suited to environments where noise can be expected.

This combination of speed and efficient error handling means that typical uses of stream ciphers include digital streaming, military field communications, emergency service radios and mobile telecommunications, all of which involve real-time communications over potentially noisy channels. An example of a stream cipher algorithm is SNOW3G, which is used to protect mobile telecommunications.

Block ciphers

A *block cipher* is a symmetric encryption algorithm that encrypts plaintext in *blocks* of bits at a time, where a typical block size is 128 bits. Block ciphers are much more commonly used than stream ciphers, since they are more versatile and flexible (stream ciphers can be thought of as special encryption mechanisms designed for specific environments). In a block cipher, the encryption algorithm scrambles a block of plaintext and a symmetric key into a block of ciphertext, while the decryption algorithm unscrambles the ciphertext using the same key to recover the plaintext.

The most widely deployed block cipher is the Advanced Encryption Standard (AES), which has a block size of 128 bits and supports key lengths of 128, 192 and 256 bits. The AES encryption algorithm, in common with most block ciphers, involves repeating a sequence of scrambling operations a set number of times, where each sequence is referred to as a *round*. Decryption involves unscrambling each round until the plaintext is recovered. The AES is the 'default' mechanism for providing symmetric encryption, and is used by a vast range of technologies to provide confidentiality, including TLS, Wi-Fi, most virtual private networks, messaging services such as Signal and WhatsApp, and most file encryption software.

While stream cipher encryption requires generating sufficient keystream to encrypt the entire plaintext, what is less self-evident is how a block cipher should encrypt large quantities of plaintext. The obvious approach is to partition the plaintext into blocks, then encrypt each block independently. The problem with this approach is that identical plaintext blocks will be encrypted into identical ciphertext blocks, leaking patterns that might aid an attacker (for example, databases so encrypted would reveal which entries were identical). To avoid this, block ciphers are used in *modes of operation*, which specify how blocks of plaintext should be encrypted in order to avoid basic block repetitions.

There are many different standardized modes of operation, each of which provide different properties, thus demonstrating the versatility of block ciphers.[3] In cipher block chaining (CBC) mode, a plaintext block is first combined with the previous ciphertext block before encryption. In counter (CTR) mode, a counter is used to vary each plaintext block encryption (more precisely, the counter is encrypted before being XORed to the plaintext). There are dedicated modes of operation for tasks such as file encryption and key encryption. Arguably the most important modes of operation are authenticated-encryption modes, which both encrypt plaintext and generate an integrity check value (see later). A recognized mode of operation must be specified before using a block cipher and this should almost never be independent block encryption, which is sometimes referred to as electronic codebook (ECB) mode.

Public-key encryption

While there are many symmetric encryption algorithms, relatively few public-key encryption algorithms are known. Public-key encryption needs to be based around a specific computational problem that is deemed to be hard for a computer to solve in general, but which can be made easy to solve if a special trapdoor value is known. This trapdoor forms the private decryption key that enables the genuine receiver to decrypt the ciphertext. It is not easy to find suitable hard problems with this type of functionality.

The most famous public-key encryption algorithm is RSA, which is based around the computational difficulty of factoring the product of two large primes. An RSA public key consists of two values, one of which is the product of two primes. Whoever knows the two primes is able to compute a separate value, which forms the private key. Anyone else cannot deduce this private key from the public key. The only known way of defeating RSA is to find an efficient means of factoring. Since no such means is known, RSA is deemed secure. Another well-known public-key encryption algorithm is elliptic-curve encryption. This is based around a different hard problem concerning the difficulty of computing discrete logarithms. A major advantage of elliptic-curve encryption is that its key lengths are shorter than RSA. For example, the security provided by an RSA key of length 3072 bits can be provided by an elliptic-curve key of length only 256 bits. Almost all established deployments of public-key encryption use either RSA or elliptic-curve encryption.

While both RSA and elliptic-curve encryption protect data against a conventional adversary, it is possible that an adversary possessing a future quantum computer might be able to break both algorithms. For this reason, a major international effort is ongoing into designing new post-quantum public-key encryption algorithms.[4] These are necessarily based around different computational problems believed to be hard for quantum computers to solve, and tend to have significantly larger key lengths than RSA. An example is Kyber, an algorithm based on a problem related to algebraic lattices, which has been selected by NIST for standardization.

Key exchange

One problem that all public-key encryption algorithms share is that they are computationally inefficient compared to symmetric encryption, making them too slow to use for general data encryption. Consequently, almost all data requiring confidentiality is symmetrically encrypted. Before this can happen, both sender and receiver need to share a symmetric key. While there are many techniques for doing this (see our later discussion on key management), sometimes the only viable option is to use public-key encryption. Such situations typically arise in internet applications such as secure browsing (TLS) and secure messaging applications, where the sender and receiver do not necessarily have a prior relationship around which an alternative symmetric key-sharing process could be designed.

There are two methods by which public-key encryption facilitates symmetric key exchange:

1 In *key encapsulation*, the sender encrypts a symmetric key using the receiver's public encryption key. The receiver then uses their matching private decryption key to decrypt this symmetric key.

2 During a *Diffie-Hellman key exchange*, both sender and receiver exchange their public keys. Each now combines their own private key with the public key of the other. The public and private keys involved in Diffie-Hellman have a special property that results in these two combination processes outputting the same value. Sender and receiver now use this common value to derive a common symmetric key.

While key encapsulation can be used with any public-key encryption algorithm, Diffie-Hellman key exchange relies on algorithms with keys of a special form. One example is elliptic-curve encryption, which results in the widely used ECDH key exchange technique.

Providing data integrity

Data integrity is an important security service because data is easily modified in cyberspace. Unlike confidentiality, which is either provided or not, different strengths of data integrity are available, depending on what degree of modification is to be defended against. As a result, there are a range of cryptographic tools for providing data integrity. In all data integrity settings, as depicted in Figure 2.4, we consider a data *originator* who inputs raw data and an (optional) *integrity key* into an *integrity algorithm* to create an *integrity digest* value (normally much shorter than the original data), and a data *verifier* who uses a *verification algorithm* (often, but not always, the same algorithm used by the originator), an (optional) *verification key* and knowledge of the integrity digest to verify whether the data has been modified.

We first consider hash functions, which on their own only detect accidental data modification. We then introduce message authentication codes, which provide the stronger security service of data origin authentication. Next, we discuss tools

Figure 2.4 Data integrity model

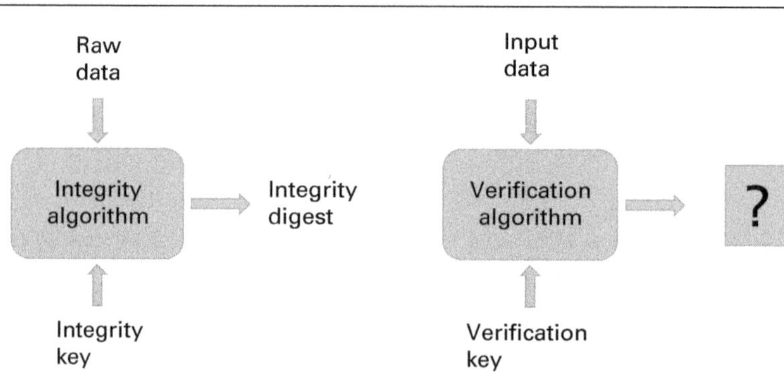

designed to offer both confidentiality and data origin authentication. Finally, we introduce digital signature schemes, which provide the yet stronger security service of non-repudiation.

Hash functions

A *hash function* is a cryptographic algorithm that inputs raw data and outputs an integrity digest value called a *hash*. The hash essentially serves as a short, randomized representation of the input data. Hash functions are designed to ensure that nothing about the original data can be deduced from the corresponding hash, hence are sometimes referred to as *one-way functions*. They are also designed to be *collision-resistant*, meaning that it is extremely hard to find two different data inputs that result (collide) in the same hash output. Note that many such collisions will exist, since hash values are much shorter than the input data, but a hash function is designed to make these practically impossible to find.

Hash functions are unusual cryptographic algorithms because they do not involve keys. This limits them to protection against accidental data modification. Consider an originator who hashes some data, then sends the data alongside its hash to a verifier. The verifier inputs the received data into the hash function and re-computes the hash. If the locally computed hash matches the hash sent by the originator, the verifier can be confident the data was not accidentally modified in transit. What the verifier *cannot* be sure about is whether an active attacker intercepted the data, modified it, replaced the original hash with a new hash computed from the modified data, then passed on the modified data alongside its modified hash. This lack of a key means an attacker can use a hash function just as effectively as both the genuine originator and verifier.

This situation can be improved by deploying hash functions only as part of a data integrity process. In the previous example, if the original hash is protected in some way then the attack described might not be possible. For example, the hash could be communicated from originator to verifier by means of a secure channel, such as a telephone call. Indeed, some software distribution websites display a hash of the software (typically using the MD5 hash function) on their websites, deploying software security techniques to protect the displayed data from modification (see Chapter 5). We shortly discuss how hash functions are also used as components of both message authentication codes and digital signature schemes, each of which provide stronger data integrity.

While hash functions do support data integrity, they are general-purpose cryptographic support tools with a wide range of different uses. These include, for example, being used as sources of pseudorandom output and for binding data items together. Perhaps the most notable example of the latter is the use of hash functions to construct large data structures known as *blockchains* (see also Chapter 8). These offer data integrity by being open, distributed and immutable. They include clever mechanisms for ensuring that the distributed versions of the blockchain are aligned, while the one-way property of hash functions forms the basis for their immutability.

Examples of standardized hash functions in widespread use include SHA-256 and SHA-3.

Message authentication codes

A *message authentication code* (MAC) is a cryptographic algorithm for providing data integrity that is not dissimilar to a hash function except for the additional input of a symmetric key shared by both originator and verifier. The originator inputs the raw data and the key to a *MAC algorithm*, which outputs a *MAC digest*. The data and MAC digest are then sent to the verifier, who re-computes the MAC digest from the raw data and the key, then checks whether the locally computed MAC digest matches the one sent by the originator.

A MAC improves on the strength of data integrity provided by a hash function since a MAC also protects against an active attacker – unlike for a hash function, because they do not know the key an attacker cannot compute a valid MAC digest on any data that they modify. In addition to stronger data integrity, a MAC also provides the verifier with data origin authentication, since a valid MAC digest can only have been computed by an entity possessing the MAC key – in a simple two-party setting, from the verifier's perspective the only other party knowing the MAC key is the originator with whom the key was shared.

While some dedicated MAC algorithms exist, the most widely deployed MAC algorithms are constructed from other cryptographic tools. The most popular construction is arguably HMAC, which is a means of converting a hash function into a MAC. Another well-known construction is CMAC, which is a means of converting a block cipher into a MAC. While MACs are still in widespread use, their popularity as isolated tools for providing data origin authentication is slowly fading for reasons we now explain.

Authenticated encryption

A significant number of uses of cryptography, including the likes of TLS and Wi-Fi, require both confidentiality and data origin authentication. Note that symmetric encryption alone does not provide the latter service. As an extreme example, consider a sender who symmetrically encrypts a random number and sends the ciphertext. Suppose an attacker intercepts this ciphertext and modifies it, before forwarding to the genuine receiver, who decrypts this modified ciphertext to recover a random number. This will, however, be the *wrong* random number, but how will the receiver know?

A natural solution is for the sender to additionally apply a MAC. A subtlety of implementation now arises. Should the sender of a plaintext encrypt then apply a MAC to the plaintext, or encrypt then apply a MAC to the ciphertext, or apply a MAC to the plaintext and then encrypt both the plaintext and the MAC? It is simply not clear. All of these solutions are also relatively inefficient and, it turns out, some have non-obvious security issues. Since inexperienced developers are sometimes left to make such decisions (as we discussed earlier), many traditional uses of cryptography, including older versions of TLS, ended up with unexpected security vulnerabilities.

An *authenticated encryption* mechanism is a symmetric algorithm designed to provide both confidentiality and data origin authentication at the same time. Many authenticated encryption mechanisms are special modes of operation of a block cipher. Examples include counter with CBC-MAC (CCM) mode and Galois Counter (GCM) mode, both of which combine CTR mode encryption with the integrated computation of a MAC digest. Other authenticated encryption mechanisms are constructed from different components, including ChaCha20-Poly1305, which combines a stream cipher and a MAC. Most authenticated encryption mechanisms also enable some of the data to be authenticated but not encrypted, which is useful in situations where confidential data needs to be associated with non-secret data, such as data relating to network routing.

Modern applications of cryptography typically deploy authenticated encryption mechanisms. For example, the Wi-Fi standard WPA3 adopts AES in both GCM (for enterprise) and CCM (for personal) mode, and TLS 1.3 now mandates use of either AES in GCM mode or ChaCha20-Poly1305.

Digital signature schemes

Both MACs and authenticated encryption mechanisms are symmetric tools that enable a verifier to confirm the integrity of data sent by an originator and, in addition, be confident that the originator is as claimed. However, the symmetric nature of these tools means it is hard for either originator or verifier to convince anyone else of this, since anyone acting as a verifier requires knowledge of the secret symmetric key. Further, since both originator and verifier share the key, it is hard for anyone else, even given the key, to determine which party was the true originator of the data.

A *digital signature scheme* is an asymmetric algorithm that enables a verifier to confirm, undeniably, who is the originator of some data. Digital signature schemes thus provide non-repudiation, an even stronger form of data integrity than data origin authentication. In a digital signature scheme, the originator deploys a *signature algorithm* to sign the data using a private *signature key* known only to them. The resulting integrity digest is known as a *digital signature*. The verifier uses a related *verification algorithm* and the corresponding public *verification key* to verify the digital signature. In contrast to symmetric integrity tools, since the verification key is public, this enables anyone to act as a verifier.

Unsurprisingly, digital signature schemes are closely related to public-key encryption. Indeed many public-key encryption algorithms give rise to a related digital signature scheme. These include the RSA digital signature scheme, the Digital Signature Algorithm (DSA) (related to the ElGamal public-key encryption algorithm) and ECDSA (related to elliptic-curve encryption). Like public-key encryption, digital signature schemes are computationally inefficient. To improve efficiency, hash functions are typically used to compress data before it is digitally signed.

Digital signature schemes are most commonly deployed in internet applications where strong integrity is required but it is not possible for originator and verifier to share a key. Examples include secure messaging (including email) and for signing Diffie-Hellman key exchange parameters (for example in TLS 1.3). We will see later that another major use of digital signature schemes is to sign public-key certificates.

Providing entity authentication

In any live interaction in cyberspace, whether accessing a Wi-Fi network or digitally opening a door, the need to establish entity authentication is arguably the most important security service – other aspects of security are often only meaningful once entity authentication of communicating parties has been established. In an entity authentication scenario, a *prover* provides evidence of their identity to a *verifier*, normally to establish whether the prover holds rights to access a particular resource or service (see Chapter 3). There are no dedicated cryptographic algorithms for providing entity authentication, but many cryptographic algorithms we have already discussed form crucial components of cryptographic protocols that can be used to achieve entity authentication.

We begin by reviewing mechanisms for establishing when a communication sent in cyberspace is 'new', something necessary for realizing entity authentication. We consider how cryptography can be used to support a widespread, but weak, entity authentication mechanism, the password. We then discuss how stronger entity authentication can be achieved by means of cryptographic protocols.

Freshness mechanisms

A strong notion of entity authentication relies on two aspects. The first is something uniquely associated with the prover, such as an identifier, password or cryptographic key. The second relates to prevention of *replay attacks*, where an attacker observes and records a genuine entity authentication attempt, then later replays it with the intention of deceiving the verifier. This second aspect requires something indicative of an authentication attempt being new, rather than a replay. We refer to such techniques as *freshness mechanisms*.

The most obvious freshness mechanism is clock-based time. If a prover incorporates the current time into an authentication attempt, a later replay should be detected since the time will be invalid. Of course, clock-based freshness requires both prover and verifier to have access to an agreed notion of time and to maintain synchronization.

An alternative to relying on a clock for freshness is to maintain *sequence numbers*. Rather than incrementing every second, sequence numbers increment with each authentication attempt. Both prover and verifier first agree on a starting sequence number and a rule for incrementing. The prover then includes the current sequence number during an authentication attempt, and the verifier checks the submitted sequence number against their local record to determine whether the authentication attempt is fresh. Both prover and verifier increment their stored sequence numbers at the end of the authentication process. A later replay by an attacker should be detected because the sequence number will be invalid. Use of sequence numbers avoids the need to rely on a synchronized clock, but still requires the maintenance of synchronized sequence numbers.

Use of freshness mechanisms based on synchronized values (whether clock-based or sequence numbers) makes sense in tightly integrated systems such as mobile phone networks. However, synchronized freshness is less suited to open distributed systems, such as the use of TLS to support secure web browsing. An alternative to relying on synchronization is to base freshness around the use of freshly generated random numbers, often referred to as *nonces*. Later in this section we will discuss nonce-based freshness more explicitly.

Passwords and cryptography

The most widespread entity authentication technique is the use of passwords, a subject discussed in more detail in Chapter 3. Passwords, deployed on their own, offer very weak entity authentication since only strongly generated passwords are likely to be unique, and most passwords are static, meaning they are readily replayed. This is why password databases are such a desirable commodity in the world of cybercrime (see Chapter 7). Where passwords are used as a basis for providing entity authentication, it is thus common to supplement their use by relying on other entity authentication factors, as discussed in Chapter 1. While passwords on their own are not cryptographic mechanisms, there are three ways in which passwords and cryptography interact.

First, passwords are normally protected using cryptography. As discussed in Chapter 3, passwords themselves are not stored in password databases, since this would expose them both to system administrators as well as any attacker who breaks into the system. Rather, password databases contain password digests computed from passwords using a cryptographic mechanism. A candidate cryptographic mechanism for password protection is a hash function, but most systems prefer to use a special hash-like cryptographic mechanism designed to deliberately slow down an attacker who is conducting a dictionary attack (see Chapter 3).

Secondly, passwords could be excellent entity authentication mechanisms if they were uniquely chosen and guaranteed to be fresh. This would require a prover to randomly generate a new (strong) password every time they made an authentication attempt to a verifier. Cryptography can be used to build systems with this *one-time password* feature. These most commonly manifest in systems where provers are issued with authentication tokens, or install authentication apps on their phone, which share a symmetric cryptographic key with the verifier system that they wish to authenticate to. Some such systems involve synchronization, requiring the prover's token to encrypt (or cryptographically derive) the time or the latest sequence number and send this as a one-time password to the verifier, who locally conducts the same computation and checks to see if the outputs match. Other systems are nonce-based, and rely on the principle of challenge-response, which we shortly discuss.

Thirdly, passwords themselves are often used to derive cryptographic keys. We discuss this further when we look at key management later in this chapter.

Challenge-response protocols

When synchronization of freshness is hard to establish, the most common means of establishing strong entity authentication is to base it on a nonce-based *challenge-response* protocol. In this case, freshness relies on use of a freshly generated random nonce. The core principle is that if a nonce is generated using a strong random number generator then, for all practical intents and purposes, the nonce is a unique value never generated before and will thus be strong evidence of freshness.

In a challenge-response protocol, we assume that prover and verifier share a symmetric key, or the prover possesses a private key whose use the verifier can affirm by means of the corresponding public key. Assuming the former scenario for simplicity, the prover inputs the freshly generated nonce and the key into a cryptographic algorithm, then sends the output to the verifier, who repeats the same computation locally and checks whether the locally computed output matches that sent by the prover. Use of the key indicates that the output was sent by the prover, and use of the nonce indicates that the authentication attempt is fresh.

One critical aspect of challenge-response concerns who generates the nonce. If the prover generates the nonce then, regardless of how fresh it is, the verifier (who is the one making the entity authentication decision) will not have assurance of freshness since they do not have visibility of its generation. Hence, in a challenge-response protocol it is the verifier who freshly generates the nonce and sends it to the prover (the nonce forms the *challenge*). The prover is then invited to compute a cryptographic output (the *response*) based on this challenge. Since the verifier knows the challenge was fresh, a valid response based on this challenge should also be fresh and thus support strong entity authentication.

Entity authentication and key establishment

While entity authentication is occasionally the only security service required, such as in a secure electronic door entry system, in most cases entity authentication is just one of a number of desired security services. Most uses of cryptography also require freshly generated keys. In open applications such as TLS, fresh symmetric keys need to be established since the communicating entities do not already possess a shared symmetric key. Even in closed applications such as mobile phone networks, where symmetric keys are typically pre-distributed, the actual keys used to protect a communication are session-specific keys and still need to be freshly generated, albeit with the aid of the pre-distributed key. Clearly there is little value in establishing a key unless the communicating entities have some assurance of with whom they are establishing the key. As a result, it is common for real-world cryptographic protocols to require both entity authentication and key establishment.

There are many different protocols combining entity authentication and key establishment since this depends on many other features, including whether an application is symmetric or public-key based, whether key encapsulation or Diffie-Hellman key exchange is preferred, whether entity authentication is unilateral or mutual, and which other security services are required as part of the wider protocol goals.

Key management

As discussed earlier, sound key management is a crucial aspect of the security of any system deploying cryptography, with Figure 2.2 displaying the typical lifecycle of a cryptographic key. Poor key management of any single stage of this lifecycle could have very serious consequences. In this section we consider each of the stages in turn, discussing some of the more popular management approaches and related issues.

Key generation

Failure to securely generate keys is responsible for many compromises of real-world applications of cryptography. Put simply, the security that cryptography provides is only as good as the quality of the randomness used to generate its cryptographic keys.

True randomness, the strongest form of key generation, needs to be based on physical sources such as coin tosses, white noise, radioactive decay and quantum processes. Most true randomness can only be extracted from hardware sources. Consequently, true randomness is expensive to generate. Neither can true randomness be replicated in more than one place – it is, after all, truly random! The problem is that in cryptography we often want the same (random) key to be established at different system locations. If we generate such a key in one location using true randomness then we need a secure means of transporting it to any other locations where it is required. This is not impossible, as we will shortly discuss, but it means that generating keys from true random sources tends to be reserved for high-security applications or long-lived master keys, rather than everyday session keys.

An alternative approach is to extract randomness from local activity on a computer such as mouse movements or internal system data. While these are relatively unpredictable, they are not as random as hardware sources, hence not as secure. Keys generated in this way still require transportation if they are needed on devices other than the one on which they were generated.

Most keys are *pseudorandomly* generated by means of an algorithm. Pseudorandom number generators are designed to output values that appear random, even though they clearly cannot be, since inputting the same values into such an algorithm normally results in the same pseudorandom output being generated. This apparent disadvantage is their primary benefit, since pseudorandom numbers can be generated cheaply in more than one location if the same input values are submitted independently to the same algorithm. A specific class of pseudorandom number generators designed to output cryptographic keys are known as *key derivation functions*. These are designed to derive keys from input values such as passwords or other cryptographic keys. Thus, for example, an application can preinstall a master key on, say, a smartcard and a central server. This master key and some session-specific data can then be submitted to a key derivation function in order to generate a single-use session key. This is broadly the process used to generate keys to protect the likes of mobile phone calls.

Key establishment

Key establishment is the process of getting keys to the places in a system where they are needed. We consider the most basic, and common, scenario of a system where two different communicating entities (sender and receiver) require a copy of the same symmetric key. There are several approaches to addressing this challenge.

The first approach is to arrange for sender and receiver to obtain the same key by means of some manual process. This is not as clumsy a solution as it sounds, since many cryptographic keys are installed into devices at manufacture. Customers acquire the key when they purchase the product, and it is often the manufacturer, or allied service provider, with whom the customer wishes to securely communicate. An example is mobile phones, where keys are preinstalled by network operators on SIM cards that customers receive when they join the network, relying on a manual process such as entering a store in order to purchase the key (SIM card). Users of a Wi-Fi network often manually type a password from which the network key is then derived. Master keys in high-security applications are sometimes manually established by means of elaborate key ceremonies, where senior members of an organization gather and jointly enter data into hardware security modules.

When manual key establishment is not desirable or possible, a second option is for the sender to generate a key, encrypt it, then send it to the receiver. This requires sender and receiver to have a means of doing so. Sometimes they already share a symmetric key that has been manually established. Systems often deploy key hierarchies of this type, where (for example) master keys are manually installed, key-encrypting keys are transported by encrypting them using master keys and session keys are transported by encrypting them using key-encrypting keys. Another option, and the only one for many open internet applications, is to use public-key cryptography, either in the form of key encapsulation or Diffie-Hellman key exchange to securely establish a symmetric key.

A third approach is to piggyback onto a previous key establishment process and derive keys from pre-existing keys. We previously mentioned that mobile phones use this approach to establish session keys to protect specific calls. Another example is TLS, which first establishes a common secret value between sender and receiver using public-key encryption and then derives the required symmetric keys from this established secret.

A further, radically different, approach to key establishment is much less frequently used. This is to deploy *quantum key distribution* (QKD), which can only be used if sender and receiver are connected by means of a quantum channel (such as an optical fibre connection) and have compatible hardware devices. In QKD, the sender generates keying material and transmits it across the quantum channel in the clear. In a normal communication channel this would be crazy, but a quantum channel enables the receiver to detect if anyone else was monitoring the channel, since attempting to read quantum data modifies its state. Quantum key distribution is an expensive solution that only lends itself to special quantum-connected environments.

Key storage

Once keys have become established they need to be stored as securely as possible. Since keys are just special data items, all general data storage issues and techniques also apply to storage of keys (see also Chapter 3). By far the best storage medium is hardware, ideally within a dedicated *hardware security module* that deploys a range of physical protection controls to protect against intrusion. For many uses of cryptography a more pragmatic approach is to store keys within lightweight hardware that still offers a degree of protection, such as a secure enclave on a mobile phone, a trusted platform module, a portable drive or a chip on a smartcard.

Storage of keys in software is not recommended, unless keys themselves are stored in encrypted form. When a key is stored in encrypted form then a different key-encrypting key is needed to decrypt the first key. One not uncommon approach is to avoid storing the key-encrypting key anywhere by deriving it, on demand, from a user-entered password. Of course, this reduces the security provided by the key-encrypting key, and thus of the key it is protecting, to that of the strength of the password.

Key usage

While keeping secret keys confidential is an obvious goal of key management, a more subtle key management objective is to ensure that keys are only used for correct purposes (sometimes called *assurance of purpose*). A guiding principle of key management is to practice *key separation*, meaning that keys are only used for specific purposes (an encryption key, say, is only used for encrypting data). However, assurance of purpose also often involves making sure that keys are only used within their defined *key lifetimes* (since many keys come with an expiry date beyond which they should not be used), ensuring that keys are only used by entities with whom they are associated, and that data integrity of a key has been confirmed before use.

If a key's lifetime has expired, or it has become compromised in some way, then the key should no longer be used. In most cases the key should then be destroyed using a secure process (see Chapter 8 for a general discussion on data sanitization processes). If necessary, a key change process should then be undertaken by generating and establishing a new key. Such key change operations have the potential to become highly complex in large systems, so design of a key management system needs to take this into account.

Public-key management issues

Much of what we have already discussed applies to management of cryptographic keys supporting both symmetric and public-key cryptography; however, there are several specific issues worth noting with respect to the latter.

Concerning key generation, while public-key pair generation does normally involve generating randomness, it is not only about this since public-key pairs need to be mathematically related. Further, asymmetric keys are generally longer than symmetric keys. Consequently, public-key pair generation is a more complex and time-consuming process than for symmetric keys.

A more subtle, but significant, difference concerns assurance of purpose of public keys, which are normally widely disseminated, indeed often publicly distributed.

This means it is necessary to explicitly provide assurance of purpose since, without this, someone could obtain a public key without knowing to whom the key belongs. The most common technique for binding a public key to data relating to assurance of purpose is by means of a *public-key certificate*. This contains the public key, name of key holder, expiry date and fields describing other relevant assurance-of-purpose data, all digitally signed by a trusted *certificate authority* whose role is to check the relevant data and vouch for its accuracy. Before relying on a public key, the digital signature on the public-key certificate should be verified and the fields of the certificate should be checked.

An additional complexity with respect to public keys concerns key change. Since a public-key (certificate) is normally public, it is impossible to determine who currently knows the key and is intending to rely on it. Management of public keys thus requires a process for withdrawing an apparently valid public key should a situation arise where this becomes necessary (for example, the associated private key becomes compromised or the public-key owner leaves the organization). The most common approach is to maintain *certificate revocation lists* (CRLs), which are CA-maintained lists of public-key certificates that appear valid, but have in fact been withdrawn. Before relying on a public key whose certificate seems valid, a user should additionally check whether the certificate is on the relevant CRL, the address for which is normally one of the certificate fields.

Societal issues relating to cryptography

Having focused most of this chapter on how cryptography helps to secure digital systems, we close by considering two societal issues concerning use of cryptography. We also reflect on potential barriers to uptake of cryptography.

Problematic cryptography

Cyber security is impossible to establish without cryptography, but there are several aspects of use of cryptography that can, in certain situations, be problematic. Of course, system designers sometimes regard cryptography as problematic because it introduces overheads. What we consider problematic here is wider societal challenges created by use of cryptography, not merely implementation difficulties.

The main cryptographic tools that lead to societal challenges relate to encryption. This is because encryption protects secrets, and secrets are contentious since not everyone agrees what information in society should be kept confidential. We will shortly look at two separate problems arising from use of encryption. The only other service enabled by cryptography that presents societal challenges is anonymity, a topic explored in more detail in Chapter 8. However, many technical tools for supporting anonymity rely on encryption, so our discussion here also speaks to some of those tensions.

Ransomware

The primary objective of encryption is to restrict access to data to only those who have the decryption key. This is a noble objective if encryption is conducted by a genuine data owner, but potentially catastrophic if someone else performs the encryption. This is precisely what happens during a *ransomware* attack, when an attacker gains access to a system and encrypts data in such a way that only the attacker can decrypt the data. This enables the attacker to hold the genuine data owner to ransom.

Ransomware presents a serious threat to digital systems since it is powerful and potentially disabling. Ransomware is a straightforward use of encryption, so everything we have discussed in this chapter concerning the effectiveness of encryption also applies to ransomware, albeit from a negative perspective. An attacker can make ransomware more effective by choosing a strong encryption algorithm, selecting appropriate key lengths and sensibly managing the decryption key. Just as for benign uses of encryption, many examples of ransomware deploy public-key encryption to transfer symmetric keys that are then used for bulk data encryption. And, as we have discussed for wider uses of cryptography, some examples of ransomware have proved ineffective because developers made mistakes such as embedding the decryption key in software.

There is nothing cryptography can do to prevent its misuse through the likes of ransomware. Defences against ransomware rely on preventing attackers from getting ransomware onto systems in the first place, which concerns issues discussed in almost every other chapter of this book. Broader approaches to dealing with cybercrime are discussed in more detail in Chapter 7.

Encryption control strategies

Another major societal issue concerning use of encryption relates to enforced access to encrypted data. Essentially, under what circumstances might it be reasonable to enable a party other than an intended recipient to have access to data that has been encrypted? Such a party could be a national security agency, a cybercrime investigator or even a senior manager of an organization. In all of those examples, situations could arise where the confidentiality provided by encryption becomes undesirable, such as when the targets of an investigation are using an encrypted messaging service or an employee leaves encrypted company files on their computer when they depart the organization.

The challenge with providing enforced access is that any such means also represents a weakness in the security provided by encryption that could be exploited by others. While some authorities feel strongly that enforced access should be facilitated under certain circumstances, many users of cryptography object strongly to both the ethics and risks behind enforced access. As a result, enforced access creates political tensions that regularly flare up, such as hostility towards technology companies providing encryption services following terrorism incidents.

Strategies for facilitating enforced access essentially map onto the layers of a cryptographic system that we discussed earlier in this chapter. Enforced access could be provided at the algorithmic layer by introducing a *backdoor* weakness into a cryptographic algorithm or its implementation that only accessing authorities know about. This is a highly undesirable approach, since it exposes users of the algorithm to risks if this backdoor becomes more widely discovered. Enforced access could be enabled through exploitation of some aspect of key management, such as restricting key lengths (an approach widely adopted last century through export controls on cryptographic devices), giving authorities copies of decryption keys (*key escrow*) or legally demanding that such keys be handed over under warrant. Enforced access is arguably most effectively enabled by targeting endpoints, such as demanding cryptographic service providers decrypt data on demand, or finding a means of accessing data on user devices after it has been decrypted.

It has proved very hard for national governments to come up with widely accepted and adopted enforced access solutions, and occasionally some have even resorted to placing bans on use of encryption, or engaging in controversial practices. In closed organizations, solutions are arguably easier to find, usually through some sort of key recovery service. Just as for ransomware, the core problem is that encryption works, so demanding that it ceases to work under certain circumstances creates a dilemma that is very hard to resolve.

Usability of cryptography

Finally, while cryptography is fundamental to cyber security, it is also true that most users do not understand cryptography or know how to use it. By far the most effective way of implementing cryptography is thus to design it into systems in such a way that users are unaware cryptography is there. This has been done for the likes of banking and mobile phone networks, whose use of cryptography is hidden. Other uses of cryptography require some limited user interaction, such as requiring passwords from which keys are generated or having to decide how to proceed when presented with an invalid public-key certificate. However, dedicated cryptographic software has traditionally been hard for ordinary users to deploy. We will merely acknowledge this here, and defer to Chapter 9 for a more detailed discussion on cyber security and usability.

KEY POINTS

- The role of cryptography is to provide a range of tools for enabling the core security services that underpin cyber security.
- Cryptographic algorithms enable the problem of securing data to become focused on the problem of securing cryptographic keys.
- Cryptography is deployed within a system that includes algorithms, protocols, implementation, key management and end points, all of which must be considered when assessing cryptography's effectiveness.
- Selecting a cryptographic tool for a specific service involves consideration of several aspects including security strength, efficiency and how necessary keys will become established.
- There are several different phases of key management, each of which must be carefully considered if cryptography is to be used securely.
- Use of cryptography, particularly encryption, provides several significant societal challenges.

EXERCISES

1 Identify six different everyday uses of cryptography, justifying in each case whether there is a need for public-key cryptography or whether it suffices to use symmetric cryptography.

2 A government agency decides to design its own encryption algorithm for securing communications between itself and its international counterparts. Discuss whether this decision is justifiable, including an analysis of the various positive and negative implications.

3 You wish to build a new cryptographic application which will require support for block cipher encryption, key exchange, digital signatures and key derivation, at security levels that should protect data for the next 10 years. Recommend a suitable suite of cryptographic algorithms and appropriate key lengths.

4 Hash functions are one of the most versatile cryptographic tools. Compile a list of potential uses of a hash function, both discussed in this chapter and elsewhere.

5 TLS is the protocol used to secure web communications between a browser and a web server. Explain why the latest 1.3 version of this protocol:

   a. allows communicating entities a (limited) choice of encryption algorithms

   b. mandates the use of authenticated encryption

   c. mandates the use of Diffie-Hellman key exchange

6 Compare digital signatures and handwritten signatures, including consideration of differences in their functionality, security, reliability, usability and deniability.

7 Find a link to an online news story that describes an attack on a use of cryptography that exploits:

 a. a weak cryptographic algorithm
 b. a weak key generation process
 c. inappropriate use of a block cipher mode of operation
 d. a weakness in implementation of cryptography
 e. a weakness in public-key certificate management

8 Your boss has read an article that claims quantum computers are coming soon and that they will render all digital business activities insecure. Not surprisingly, your boss is panicking. Write a brief to your boss that explains your own perspectives on this issue, suggesting actions that your organization should take, both now and in the future.

9 National governments have been known to hold concerns over the use of end-to-end encryption:

 a. What is meant by end-to-end encryption?
 b. Why might governments be concerned by use of end-to-end encryption?
 c. What are your (justified) personal views on whether national governments should possess a capability to have enforced access to data protected by encryption, and what do you suggest they should do regarding citizens' use of end-to-end encryption?

10 Cryptography is discussed early in this book because it underpins cyber security and has connections with each subsequent chapter. For each of the topics of later chapters in this book, explain how cryptography might relate to that topic and any important cryptographic issues that you expect to see discussed there.

FURTHER READING

- Aumasson, J-P (2018) *Serious Cryptography: A practical introduction to modern cryptography*, No Starch Press
- Ferguson, N, Schneier, B and Kohno, T (2010) *Cryptography Engineering: Design principles and practical applications*, Wiley
- Levy, S (2002) *Crypto: How the code rebels beat the government, saving privacy in the digital age*, Penguin

- Martin, K M (2017) *Everyday Cryptography: Fundamental principles and applications*, 2nd edn, Oxford University Press
- Martin, K M (2020) *Cryptography: The key to digital security, how it works and why it matters*, W.W. Norton
- Paterson, K G (2021) Applied Cryptography Knowledge Area, Version 1.0.0, https://www.cybok.org/knowledgebase1_1/ (archived at https://perma.cc/Y4FV-S9BK)
- Piper, F and Murphy, S (2002) *Cryptography: A very short introduction*, Oxford University Press
- Singh, S (2002) *The Code Book*, Fourth Estate
- Stinson, D R and Paterson, M B (2023) *Cryptography: Theory and practice*, 4th edn, CRC Press

Notes

1. See, for example: Paterson, K G and van der Merwe, T (2016) Reactive and Proactive Standardisation of TLS, Security Standardisation Research, *Lecture Notes in Computer Science*, 10074, 160–86
2. A good introduction to side-channel attacks is: Zhou, Y and Feng, D (2005) Side-Channel Attacks: Ten years after its publication and the impacts on cryptographic module security testing, IACR Cryptology ePrint Archive 2005:388
3. NIST maintain a list of approved block cipher modes of operation at: NIST (2023) Block Cipher Techniques: Approved Block Cipher Modes, https://csrc.nist.gov/projects/block-cipher-techniques/bcm/current-modes (archived at https://perma.cc/5T8K-4W7V)
4. This effort is being driven by NIST, with the latest information on the selection process available at: NIST (2023) Post-Quantum Cryptography: Overview, https://csrc.nist.gov/Projects/post-quantum-cryptography (archived at https://perma.cc/SN73-TPEK)

03 Computer system security

Securing core digital technology

In this chapter we discuss computer system security, which concerns both the protection of digital resources on a computer and protection of data residing on a computing device. We begin by describing what a computer system is and the attack surface it presents. We then discuss authentication, which is the means by which users access a computer. This is followed by a look at authorization, which is how a computer determines what a user is permitted to do with its resources. We will also consider how operating systems manage resources. Finally, we take a brief look at several aspects of hardware security.

LEARNING OBJECTIVES

- Identification of the attack surface of a computer system.
- The core security features of a computer system, particularly those provided by the operating system.
- Mechanisms for authentication to a computer.
- How computer systems authorize access to resources.
- Core hardware security functions of a computer.

Introduction to computer systems

We begin by clarifying what we mean by a computer system and then briefly introduce the main elements of a computer system that we will discuss further in this chapter.

What is a computer system?

A *computer system* can be very loosely defined as a group of interacting, interrelated and interdependent digital components (hardware and software) that form a connected whole. This might sound like a rather generic definition that could be used to describe, for example, the whole of the internet! However, in this chapter we will make a narrower interpretation of 'connected whole' to mean the digital components that form a single computing device.

Note that we do not make further restrictions on what we mean by 'device'. This could be a traditional computer such as a desktop or laptop, a mobile phone or, indeed, any object with embedded computing capability such as a modern car or smart domestic appliance. Broadly speaking, all such devices consist of hardware and software, have a central operating system, and thus fall into the scope of this chapter.

As well as largely considering a computer system as an isolated device (which we sometimes refer to simply as a 'computer'), this chapter focuses on the security of core components of a computer system, particularly the operating system. It would thus be reasonable to argue that this is really the first of *three* chapters dealing with computer system security. The material in this chapter is complemented by:

- Chapter 4, which focuses on aspects of security that relate to multiple computer systems communicating within a wider infrastructure;
- Chapter 5, which explores the broader security issues associated with the software and applications that run on a computer system.

We now briefly introduce the core elements of a computer system. Note that this high-level overview of a computer system is intended only to provide sufficient intuition to make sense of the material in the remainder of the chapter. Anyone seeking a deeper understanding of how computer systems work should pursue some of the further resources identified at the end of this chapter.

Hardware

The main hardware elements of a computer system are as follows:

- *Central Processing Unit* (CPU). This is the 'brain' of a computer. The CPU is responsible for executing instructions (programs) written by programmers to run software applications. Most modern CPUs are based on what is known as the *von Neumann architecture*, which comprises:
  - the *control unit*, which is responsible for executing programs and tracking where to move next in a program;

- the *arithmetic logic unit*, which performs the arithmetic and Boolean (binary logic) operations that are critical to executing individual program instructions;
- *memory units*, often referred to as *registers*, which contain the data necessary to run programs.

- *Memory*. This is divided into:
  - *volatile memory*, also known as *random access memory* (RAM), which is the working memory available to running programs while the computer is switched on;
  - *non-volatile memory*, which is the persistent memory that remains even when the computer is switched off. Such memory typically exists on either *hard disk drives*, which use mechanical parts such as spinning disks and magnetic materials to store data, or *solid state drives*, where data is stored in memory cells that do not rely on moving parts and access is managed by a controller chip.

  While there is almost always less volatile memory available than non-volatile, volatile memory is significantly faster to access and process.
- *Motherboard*. This is the main circuit board responsible for connecting all the other hardware components together.
- *Input and output (I/O) interfaces*. These enable different forms of input and output to the computer system, including the likes of keyboards, monitors and speakers.

Other hardware components often form part of a computer system for augmenting specific tasks, such as a network card for facilitating networking and a graphics card for enabling computationally intensive graphics applications.

When first proposed, the von Neumann CPU architecture was revolutionary because data and instructions are stored in the same physical memory. This brought significant benefits in terms of programmability and versatility. However, it also introduced several security concerns, particularly resulting from a lack of memory protection. This meant that any program could access any part of memory, including memory allocated for resource monitoring. This ability to execute arbitrary code ultimately led to *exploits*, which are computer programs that enable a computer system to be attacked. We will see later in this chapter how security protection has been built into modern computer systems in an attempt to control this.

Operating system

Software makes use of the hardware of a computer system to execute instructions. The main software we are focused on in this chapter is the operating system. The security of more general software on a computer system is discussed in Chapter 5.

The *operating system* (OS) is the most important piece of software on any computer system. Examples of OSs include Android, Linux, iOS and Windows. In general terms, the OS is the set of programs and services that enable users of a computer to make effective use of hardware resources (in particular the CPU and memory). One of the most important roles of the OS is to protect computer system resources from abuse (improper or excessive use) and misuse (incorrect or inappropriate use). In order to protect resources, the OS needs to monitor the computer system resources, while also managing requests from users to access and run these resources. The responsibilities of most modern OSs thus include security-related tasks such as:

- enforcing user authentication
- allocating resources to instances of applications (known as *processes*)
- ensuring fair use of computer resources between processes
- enforcing limited or no access to critical OS data
- managing memory
- governing control of inputs and outputs
- starting and stopping programs

We will explore most of these OS tasks in more detail later in this chapter.

The above security and resource management tasks are conducted by the core of the OS, which is sometimes referred to as the *kernel*. Outside of the kernel, the *user space* of the operating system is where resources such as application, libraries and drivers that interact with the kernel reside.

Starting a computer system

When a computer system starts, it initializes a set of functions such as checking memory and making sure that all hardware components are accessible by the OS. The *Unified Extensible Firmware Interface* (UEFI) is *firmware* (software that controls hardware) that plays a crucial role in initializing hardware and *booting* (starting) the OS. One of UEFI's key features, Secure Boot, helps secure the computer system by ensuring that only signed and trusted components are allowed to run. Once the OS is running, it will begin a variety of security measures such as user authentication and authorization.

Trusted computing base

The *trusted computing base* (TCB) of a computer system is the hardware and core OS components (essentially, the kernel) that deliver key security functions. The TCB is the part of the computer system in which absolute trust is placed. This means that the TCB acts as a *root of trust* from which trust in the wider computer system can be derived. Conversely, any compromise of a TCB is extremely serious since the entire trust model for a computer system relies on the TCB being trustworthy and secure.

Core responsibilities of the TCB include:

- *Object isolation:* this prevents interference between objects in memory.
- *Memory protection:* including correctly translating between virtual addresses and physical addresses.
- *Maintaining the file system and drivers:* the latter being the software that interfaces with I/O devices.
- *Authentication:* correctly identifying and verifying legitimate users of the OS.
- *Authorization:* correctly allocating resources to users making access requests.

Later in this chapter we will discuss different hardware components that sometimes serve as part of the TCB.

Security of computer systems

In this section we explain what it might mean to secure a computer system. We begin by identifying the main general goals of computer system security. We then outline the attack surface of a typical computer system. Finally, we briefly discuss security policies, which define the security goals of a computer system more precisely.

General goals of computer system security

Computer systems store and use sensitive data, hence the ultimate goals of computer system security are to support provision of the core cyber security services we discussed in Chapter 1. This is particularly with respect to what we termed in Chapter 1 the CIA triad, which in a computer system security context refers to:

- Confidentiality: Preventing users from reading data stored on a computer system that they are not entitled to.
- Integrity: Ensuring no part of the computer system is modified by an unauthorized entity.
- Availability: Maintaining the computer system services so that they are accessible, on demand, by authorized entities.

Achieving these security goals requires a computer system to have means of strictly controlling and managing its resources through the operating system and hardware.

Attack surface of a computer system

We now consider the different places where a general computer system could be attacked in order to subvert its security goals. Note that the attack surface of a specific computer system is more challenging to quantify because each computer system is fundamentally different. Even if two computer systems seem identical in terms of having the same hardware components, they may well have different versions of software running on them or be configured in different ways.

The general attack surface of a computer system is depicted in Figure 3.1, where squares indicate potential attack points. Proceeding from left to right, an attack could target:

- *Users.* Human users could be manipulated in order to conduct inappropriate behaviour on a computer system by means of exploiting their legitimate credentials and privileges. We discuss the related topic of social engineering in Chapter 7, and human user vulnerabilities more generally in Chapter 9.
- *User interface.* The interface between users and the OS is a potential point of vulnerability that could be exploited to gain access to the computer system. We consider how to secure this interface when we later discuss authentication.
- *User applications and OS services.* The software running on a computer system can be the target of an attack. Later in this chapter we discuss authorization, which attempts to ensure that only the right users get access to the right applications and services. Chapter 5 discusses how to prevent attacks on software more generally.
- *Security countermeasures.* Attacks can arise due to failures or weaknesses in software security countermeasures that result in controls being bypassed. An attacker could, for example, disable monitoring software in order to conceal malware. We discuss some aspects within this chapter, but the design, use and management of security countermeasures is touched on throughout the other chapters of this book.

Figure 3.1 Attack surface of a computer system

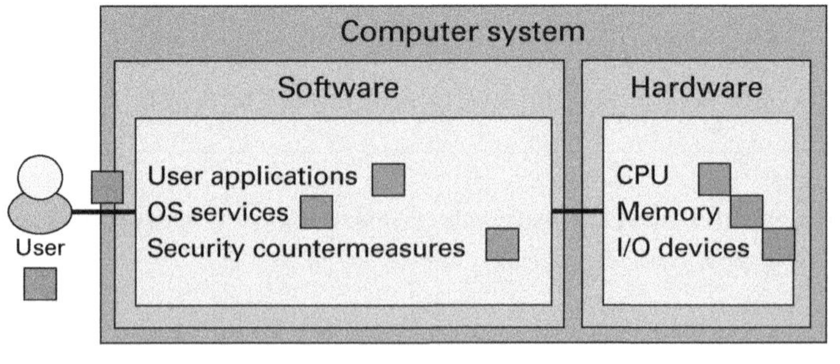

- *CPU*. An attacker can manipulate the management of computer operations in order to control which instruction to execute next. Both Spectre and Meltdown (two examples of critical CPU security vulnerabilities) revealed fundamental design flaws in modern processors' performance-enhancing techniques. They showed that speculative and out-of-order executions, while beneficial for speed, can lead to serious security vulnerabilities if not properly isolated. Despite mitigations, completely resolving these issues without sacrificing performance is challenging, and these vulnerabilities continue to impact the design of future CPU architectures.
- *Memory*. Attacking the memory can lead to privilege escalation and memory corruption. Rowhammer is an example of a vulnerability that exploits the physical properties of memory cells found in DRAM (Dynamic Random Access Memory) chips. In this attack, repeated access to one row of memory can alter the values held in adjacent memory rows.
- *I/O devices*. An input and output device can have its firmware compromised so that the I/O device behaves maliciously. For example, BadUSB is a vulnerability that exploits the firmware of USB devices, allowing them to be reprogrammed to perform malicious activities without the user's knowledge. By targeting the firmware inside the USB device and not the files stored on it, BadUSB makes the attack undetectable by traditional antivirus software or security measures.

Of course, attacks often cascade through different components of this attack surface. For example, an attacker might socially engineer a user in order to gain access to a computer system, then exploit a weakness in the operating system governance to elevate their credentials to those of an administrator, which then enables them to gain unauthorized access to hardware resources of the computer system.

Computer system security policies

The security of a particular computer system relies on a range of security controls, just some of which are discussed in this chapter. One of the most fundamental is the *computer system security policy*, which defines how security controls are applied to the computer system in order to manage the relationship between users and the computer system resources. Such a policy should include, for example:

- how users are authenticated to the computer system (including how this is managed over time, for example by requiring password changes);
- which resources a specific user is granted access to, and what they can do with these resources.

Figure 3.2 Computer system access control

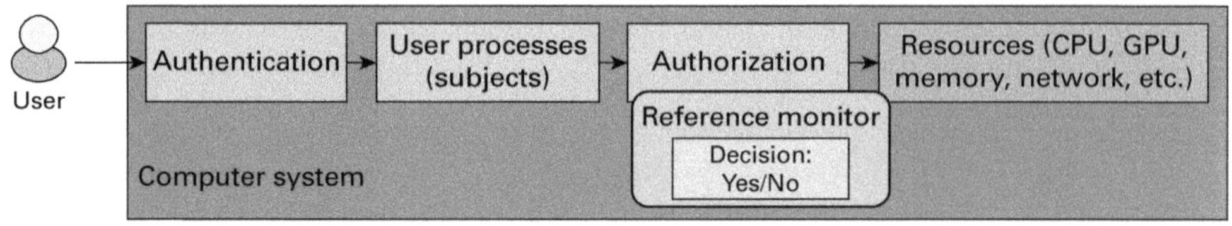

The general process of managing the relationship between users of a computer system and the resources of the computer system is often referred to as *access control* and is depicted in Figure 3.2. This is the subject of the next two sections of this chapter, where we discuss the provision of the two security services that enable this, namely:

- Authentication: Determining whether a user is permitted to access the resources of a computer system.
- Authorization: Determining what an authenticated user can do with the resources on a computer system.

More generally, a computer system security policy might need to align with the broader security policies of the organization in which the computer system is deployed. Organizational security policies are discussed in more detail in Chapter 6.

Authentication

In this section we take a more detailed look at how a user authenticates to a computer system. We will first clarify precisely what we mean by authentication in this context. We then discuss some of the most common techniques for authenticating to a computer system.

Computer system authentication

We first clarify our use of terminology. In this chapter we are using the term 'authentication' to mean what was previously termed 'entity authentication' in Chapters 1 and 2. In Chapter 1 we also flagged the ambiguity behind what an 'entity' was with respect to authentication. In this chapter we will primarily assume that this entity is a human user seeking access to computer system resources (also informally referred to as 'user authentication' in Chapter 1). Note, however, that sometimes:

- the true entity being authenticated might be a device in the possession of a human user;
- an entity seeking authentication to a computer system might be another computer system.

The primary purpose of authentication to a computer system is to distinguish between different users of the computer system, and hence subsequently determine which resources they can access through an authorization process (the subject of the following section of this chapter). Authentication thus acts as the frontline between what was referred to in Chapter 1 as the human and technology layers of a digital system. Without authentication we cannot control what a user can do with the computer system resources and cannot enforce any sense of accountability.

On occasion, it can be helpful to separate authentication into two separate processes:

1. *Identification*. This is the presentation of a claimed identity to a computer system (such as a username).
2. *Verification*. This is the presentation of evidence to support the identification claim (such as a password).

Note that in such cases the real 'work' involved in authentication is being done in the verification step, since identities such as usernames are often publicly accessible. However, some computer systems such as mobile phones have no real need to have a separate identification process since it is generally assumed that there is only one legitimate human user associated with the computer system.

The OS of computer systems with multiple users typically organizes and allocates resources with respect to *user accounts*. The primary purpose of authentication is thus to determine which user account the authenticating user should be linked to.

Password-based authentication

By far the most common means of authentication to a computer system remains the use of passwords. We include in this discussion PINs (which are short numeric passwords) and passphrases (which are long passwords).

As discussed in Chapter 2, passwords are a weak means of supporting authentication (verification) since they tend to be:

- *Poorly chosen*. Many passwords are poorly chosen and easily guessed, even by a human attacker. Even seemingly sophisticated passwords can often be determined by an attacker who exhaustively searches through all possible character combinations, or all likely character combinations (words in a language and/or close variations such as P855word!), by means of a *dictionary attack* until the valid password is found. This type of dictionary attack can easily be automated and is almost guaranteed to find poorly chosen passwords. We will shortly discuss some means by which such dictionary attacks can be deterred (although not prevented).

- *Static.* Basic passwords do not change over multiple authentication attempts. This makes a valid password an extremely useful item of data for an attacker to obtain, hence meriting the investment of significant attack effort. This could be done, for example, by:
  - physical observation of a user entering a password (*shoulder surfing*);
  - placing malware onto a computer system that exploits the user interface in order to capture a password on entry (such as a *keylogger*);
  - conducting a dictionary attack, as just described;
  - extracting a password from a user by means of social engineering, for example through phishing (see Chapter 7);
  - observing network traffic in order to intercept a password in transit between a computer system and an authentication server.
- *Re-used.* Users often deploy the same passwords across multiple computer systems. This increases the potential attack surface that the password is exposed to, as well as reducing the security of the password to that of the weakest computer system within which it is used. It also raises the value of the password to an attacker, creating a single point of failure across multiple systems.

Nonetheless, passwords remain in widespread use because they are familiar to users and relatively easy to use (although see Chapter 9 for an example where passwords are less easy to use).

From a computer system perspective, the basic idea behind password-based authentication is that each user account on the OS is associated with a username and a password selected by the user. During an authentication attempt, the user enters their username (to identify the claimed account) and then their password (to verify the claimed identity). Note that the OS does not store the password itself since this would make the password database a major point of vulnerability and also expose passwords to system administrators. Most OSs use a special cryptographic password-protection function to store passwords. This function has some of the properties of a hash function (see Chapter 2) but, despite often being referred to as a 'hash function', tends to be more sophisticated. When the user enters their password, the OS enters the submitted password to the password-protection function and then compares the output with the one it has stored (which was computed locally when the account was initialized).

Features of OS password-protection functions include:

- *Irreversibility.* It is practically impossible to recover a password from the corresponding output of the password-protection function. In other words, the password protection should be what we termed in Chapter 2 a one-way function.

- *Salts*. As well as inputting the password to the password-protection function, an additional *salt* (a random value associated with the user account) is input. This helps to slow down dictionary attacks, as well as ensuring that two different accounts have different output values even if the same password is used (thus preventing an attacker who manages to access the password database from seeing that two user accounts have the same password).
- *Delays*. Password-protection functions are normally designed to be deliberately slow compared to typical cryptographic functions (for example, they often involve repeated application of a standard cryptographic function). This deliberate delay is designed to have little obvious impact on a single computation during an authentication attempt, but to introduce a cumulative delay that acts as a barrier to an attacker conducting multiple authentication attempts, such as during a dictionary attack.

In addition, some OSs enforce further controls against the likes of dictionary attacks, such as forcing increasing delays between sequential authentication attempts or even preventing access entirely after a certain number of failed authentication attempts.

A computer system security policy should include a *password policy*, which enforces restrictions on password selection and any requirements on frequency of password change. Password policies differ between organizations and best practice has changed significantly over the last decades. Today, a combination of words or use of a passphrase is often recommended because these are fairly easy for a human to remember but difficult to guess or search for (see also Chapter 9). To the frustration of many people, the use of shorter complex passwords remains common practice.

Biometric-based authentication

An alternative to the use of passwords is to utilize measurable human characteristics, known as *biometrics*, to enable authentication to a computer system. Examples of biometrics include facial recognition, fingerprints, hand geometry, iris scanning, keystroke dynamics and voice recognition. Biometrics can offer a stronger means of authentication than passwords and in many cases are easier to use.

The core properties of a suitable biometric technique for computer system authentication are:

1. *Universality*. All people in the user population must possess the biometric characteristic.
2. *Uniqueness*. The biometric characteristic should be unique to any individual within the user population.
3. *Measurability*. The biometric characteristic should be something that can be measured and quantified.

4 *Stability*. The biometric characteristic should remain sufficiently stable to be measured consistently.

5 *Efficiency*. The measurement and verification processes should be efficient to use and not require excessive memory.

6 *Accuracy*. The verification results should be accurate, with low rates of *false negatives* (an authorized user failing to authenticate) and *false positives* (an unauthorized user succeeding in an authentication attempt).

7 *Acceptability*. The member of the user population should be comfortable using the biometric characteristic as a means of authentication.

Biometrics can either be *static*, meaning that they are based on fixed characteristics such as fingerprints, or *dynamic*, meaning that they measure a changeable characteristic such as voice recognition. Some high-security biometric technologies even assess liveness, taking additional measurements such as temperature and blood oxygenation.

When a user registers with a biometric system they need to enrol. During enrolment a *biometric template* is generated, which is the data point that will be stored by the OS of the computer system and subsequently used for verification. The biometric template essentially plays the role of the password in password-based authentication. Note that many biometric systems do not require the equivalent of a username, since the biometric will be used for both identification and verification.

After enrolment, a biometric system's main task is to either identify or verify a user through a matching system. The general process that is undertaken during biometric-based authentication is depicted in Figure 3.3 and is as follows:

- *Data collection*. Sensors on the computer system are used to acquire data concerning the biometric characteristic.
- *Signal processing*. Relevant features are extracted from the sensor data and, where appropriate, cleared or enhanced.
- *Matching*. The processed data is compared with the biometric template that was generated during enrolment and subsequently stored by the computer system.
- *Decision*. The result of the matching is a decision, which is a binary yes or no in the case of verification, and an identity in the case of identification. Note that the decision tends not to be absolute and relies on a preset threshold of tolerance. Designers face a trade-off favouring either strict policies that risk false negatives or permissive policies that tolerate greater risk of false positives.

Figure 3.3 Biometric-based authentication process

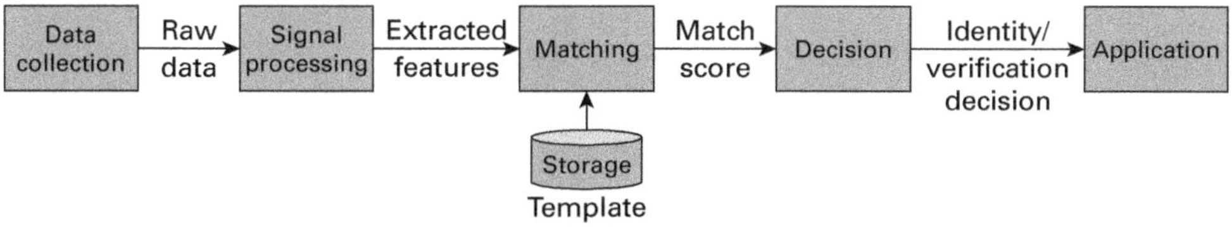

Token-based authentication

Yet another common means of authenticating to a computer system is for a user to demonstrate possession of some sort of token, which is typically represented as a dedicated device such as a smartcard, RFID tag or dedicated authentication token, or an authentication application running on a device such as mobile phone.

Token-based authentication normally relies on some sort of cryptographic protocol that runs between the token and the computer system the user is authenticating to. The computer system will, essentially, seek evidence that the token possesses a cryptographic key that is associated with the user. A common way of doing this is by means of a challenge-response protocol, as discussed in Chapter 2.

Some dedicated authentication tokens use a system clock to encrypt the time and display the resulting ciphertext on a small screen. The user then returns this ciphertext as evidence that the token is in their possession. This is an example of the one-time password systems we discussed in Chapter 2. Note that dedicated tokens of this type are increasingly being replaced by applications running on mobile phones, since phones are cryptographically enabled devices that almost all users already have in their possession.

Multifactor authentication

As observed in Chapter 1, it is common for a computer system to demand a stronger means of authentication by requiring users to combine more than one authentication technique. Hence, for example, a user might be required to enter a password (itself not a strong means of authentication) and then demonstrate possession of a mobile phone by supplying a one-time password code that is generated by an application running on the user's mobile phone. Indeed, such a process is often even further strengthened by the application on the mobile phone requiring activation by means of a biometric. The combination of these authentication techniques provides a much stronger means of authenticating to the computer system than using each technique in isolation.

Authorization

In this section we discuss how a computer system proceeds to allocate resources following a successful user authentication.

Goal of authorization

The goal of authorization is to enforce the part of the computer system security policy that relates to who can do what on the computer system. Indeed, authorization can be regarded as a codification of the security policy that enables a computer system to make access decisions concerning its resources.

The different ways that computer system resources can be used are normally defined as *access rights*, which are sometimes alternatively described as *permissions* or *privileges*. In general, most computer systems define three different access rights, namely:

1. *Read*. This enables the viewing of a resource.
2. *Write*. This enables the modification of a resource.
3. *Execute*. This enables a resource such as a program to be run (note that not every resource, such as a text file, can be executed).

Some computer systems treat these access rights as mutually exclusive, while others may have one dependent on the other. For example, some computer systems demand that in order to execute a program a user must have both read and write access to it.

Note also that different OSs treat the meaning of execute differently depending on the context. For example, in the Unix OS:

- to execute a file, both read and execute must be granted;
- to enter a directory, execute must be granted;
- to list the contents of a directory, read and execute must be granted;
- to create a file in a directory, write and execute must be granted.

The reference monitor

The *reference monitor* is an abstract concept that describes a component of a computer system OS that acts as a guard that mediates access requests to computer system resources, either granting them or denying them.

When considering the role of the reference monitor, we distinguish between three different concepts:

1. *Principals*. These are users (or other entities) who make access requests. Each principal on a modern OS will be associated with their own user account. Principals are capable of creating and destroying subjects.

2 *Subjects*. These are processes running on the computer system that act on behalf of principals to access objects.
3 *Objects*. These are computer system resources such as files, directories, CPU, memory or I/O devices.

Principals thus make access requests for objects through subjects. The reference monitor then makes access request decisions based on what principal is associated with a particular subject making the access request. To keep things simple, we will mainly refer to principals interacting with objects in the subsequent discussion, while technically it is subjects that interact directly with objects.

Note that the reference monitor is an abstract concept that can take many different forms within the software of the OS. In Figure 3.4 we indicate three common placements of the reference monitor.

1 *Stacked*. A stacked reference monitor runs on top of a host operating system or hardware, typically as part of the OS kernel. It monitors access to resources by processes running on the system, ensuring that the operating system enforces access control policies for all applications.
2 *Sandboxed*. A sandboxed reference monitor operates inside a controlled and isolated environment, restricting the actions of the processes within it. Sandboxes isolate potentially untrusted applications or code and restrict their access to the system's resources, with the reference monitor enforcing the security policies in that isolated environment.
3 *Embedded*. An embedded reference monitor operates as part of a program, meaning it is tightly integrated with the system that it is monitoring and enforcing security policies for.

Figure 3.4 Different placements of the reference monitor

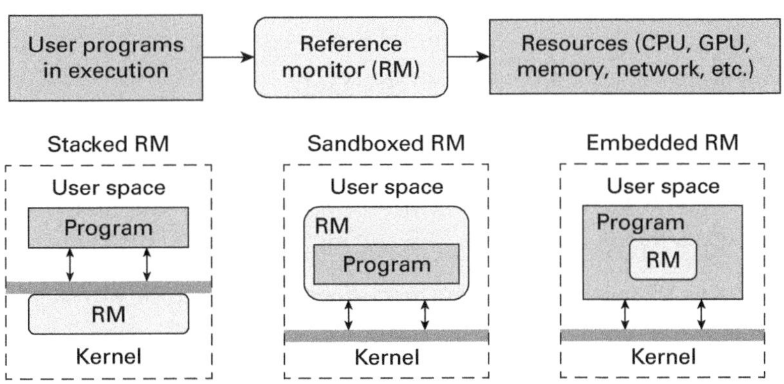

REAL-WORLD EXAMPLE Unix identifiers

To illustrate how authorization concerns more than simple access of resources by individual human users, we will consider how the Unix OS organizes and labels principals.

The Unix kernel has no concept of usernames and works on the basis of identifiers. Unix makes use of several different types of identifiers, including *user identifiers* (UIDs) and *group identifiers* (GIDs). Each user has a unique UID and can be assigned to groups, each of which has its own GID. The UID 0 represents the only privileged superuser on a Unix system, referred to as *root*. UIDs between 1 and 999 are reserved for principals representing specific operating tasks, such as printer services. UIDs greater than 1,000 are assigned to human users. The use of groups enables a scalable approach to be taken to access control. Groups also exist for specific tasks, such as printer administration.

Unix root is almost all-powerful. Root can read or write to any bit of main memory, read or write to any file of any user, and start or stop processes of any user. However, root cannot write to read-only system data in order to protect the OS itself. Root also cannot recover user passwords, although root can reset user passwords.

Unix stores UID/GID information (the mapping between usernames and UIDs) in a file labelled /etc/passwd, which stores essential information for login, including usernames. This is linked to a file that stores the cryptographically protected passwords.

Access control policies

An *access control policy* is the specification of what access rights a given principal has to the objects on a computer system. A range of different approaches can be taken to defining an access control policy.

One separation of policies that is sometimes useful to consider is into access control policies that are:

- *Discretionary*. This means that access rights are assigned on an individual principal basis. In such cases the ownership of resources is typically important in deciding which access rights to assign to an object.
- *Mandatory*. This means that access rights are based on a general classification system rather than on individuals. This is common in government/military systems, where principals fall into preassigned ranks and objects such as data files have ranked classifications (such as top secret, secret, restricted, unclassified, etc.).

Access rights themselves can be assigned on a number of different bases. These include:

- *Role-based*. These are access rights that are defined by, for example, a job function of a principal within an organization. For example, the role of IT support or

Human Resources Manager might be used to determine which access rights to assign to a principal holding such a role.

- *Rule-based.* These are access rights that are defined by policy rules. For example, internal files residing on an organizational computer system might only be available to employee principals during the official working hours of the organization.
- *Attribute-based.* These are access rights assigned on the basis of *attributes*, which are labels associated with a principal. For example, an attribute might relate to a department within an organization, a qualification held by a principal or the age of a principal.

Access control models

Access control policies specify what access rights are assigned to computer system principals. It remains to decide how to make an access control work in practice. One general aid for doing this is *access control models*, which capture different aspects of how to implement an effective and consistent access control policy.

An *access control matrix* is the crudest access control model. This is a simple table consisting of one row for each principal and one column for each object. Each entry in the access control matrix contains the list of access rights that the corresponding principal holds for the corresponding object. An example of a simple access control matrix is shown in Figure 3.5. This shows that, for example, John holds read, write and execute rights to helloworld.sh, while Michael has no access rights to myfile.txt.

Note that an access control matrix is primarily conceptual and not suitable for direct implementation since, unlike our simple example in Figure 3.5, a real access control matrix will be enormous, potentially containing millions of entries, and be extremely sparse, since the majority of entries are likely to be blank. An access control matrix is therefore extremely inefficient to use as a mechanism for conducting access control. In addition, an access control matrix, should it be directly implemented, would also represent a single point of failure since if the matrix became corrupted then access control for the entire operating system would be impacted.

Figure 3.5 An example of a simple access control matrix

Principals \ Objects	song.ogg	helloworld.sh	myfile.txt
John	{r,w}	{r,w,x}	{r,w}
Michael	{r}	{r,x}	

However, access control matrices form the basis for two alternative access control models that are much more practical to use:

1 *Access Control Lists* (ACLs). Using this model, each object maintains a list of all the principals permitted to access it and what rights they hold. This list represents a column of the corresponding access control matrix, meaning that the matrix is essentially distributed amongst the objects rather than existing as a centralized data structure. The ACL model is the most widely adopted access control model amongst modern OSs. One disadvantage of ACLs, however, is that if we want to check the full access rights of a particular principal across all objects (perhaps for auditing reasons) then this requires inspection of every object's ACL, which is very inefficient.
2 *Capabilities*. This is the dual concept to use of ACLs, and corresponds to distributing rows of an access control matrix to principals. A capability is thus attached to a principal and lists all the objects that they have access to, and which rights they hold over them. Capabilities are typically implemented in services and application software such as database applications because they allow us to query permissions or links on a per-principal basis. The main problem with using capabilities is the dual problem to that of ACLs. In this case it becomes very inefficient to determine which principals can access a given object.

One problem that can arise, even with the specification of an access control policy, is that there can be inbuilt inconsistencies. For example, in theory at least, a principal could be given read access to a file but not read access to the folder containing that file, etc. A number of more rigorous access control models have been proposed that enable deductions to be made about the overall consistency of the associated security policy. These are typically associated with mandatory access control policies. Two of the most well-known access control models of this type are:

- *The Bell-LaPadula model* (BLP). The BLP assumes that all principals and objects are organized into hierarchical classification levels, such as those associated with military or national intelligence environments. The goal of the BLP is to maintain consistent confidentiality. Core to the BLP model are the following two rules:
  a. *No read up*. This means that principals cannot read objects at a higher level. This prevents data at high classification levels from being seen by principals who do not have sufficient clearance to access it.
  b. *No write down*. This means that principals cannot write data to objects at a lower level. This prevents data associated with a high classification level from leaking to environments accessible to principals with a lower classification level.

- *The Biba model.* This is similar to the BLP except that it focuses on maintaining consistent integrity, rather than confidentiality. The two main rules are the duals of those of the BLP, namely:
  a. *No write up.* This means that principals cannot write data to objects at a higher level. This prevents data associated with a high classification level from being corrupted by data associated with a lower classification level.
  b. *No read down.* This means that principals cannot read objects at a lower level. This prevents a principal at a high classification level from potentially corrupting their environment by, for example, reading a disk at a lower classification level that might have been compromised by malware (perhaps because systems at the lower classification level have less rigorous security controls).

Both the BLP and Biba are powerful access control models since they provide inbuilt consistency (unlike ACLs and capabilities). However, they do also rely on several fairly impractical assumptions that do not make them suitable for general computer systems. These include:

- the overarching security goal of a system is either confidentiality or integrity
- access rights never change
- there is no risk of insider threats

A range of other access control models exist that apply to particular types of computer system. One example is the *Chinese Wall model*, which segments objects into categories and develops a set of rules that ensures that no principal can ever access objects on the 'other side' of one of these virtual 'walls'. This access control model was motivated by the idea of dynamic *separation of duty* security policies within some organizations, particularly those governing data that is associated with potential conflicts of interest. The *Clark-Wilson model* is another model that also separates duties. It also enforces *well-formed transactions* by ensuring that objects can only be accessed via an intermediary using a set of pre-defined transaction commands. This prevents users from making inappropriate requests.

The OS as a resource manager

We now consider further issues relating to the important security role of the OS as a computer system resource manager.

Motivation for resource management

Appropriately managing resources on a computer system yields many security benefits. As an analogy, consider the management of work desks in an open-plan office. In such an environment, a substantial amount of personal and work-related paperwork might exist on any desk at any given time, much of which might be extremely sensitive. The space on a desk in this type of office has the potential to be disorganized and exposed to both internal employees and external visitors. The disorganization makes it slower for an employee to obtain the relevant information that they need at a time that they need it, thus reducing the efficiency of an employee performing a work-related task. The exposure makes information in documents potentially vulnerable to any threat actor who enters the office to seek sensitive information. Note that such a threat might be internal or external. While the potential shared goal alignment might make a colleague less of a threat than an external party, they nonetheless present a potential risk.

Computer systems share many similarities with this open-plan office scenario. They provide a common platform on which many different operations are conducted, often in parallel and potentially exposed to one another. There is thus a need for the operations running on a computer to be organized for efficiency reasons, and for the visibility of sensitive information to be limited for security reasons. Threats to a computer system can also arise from both internal and external sources. Two of the most important resources on a computer system are memory and CPU time. A major role of the OS is thus to manage these resources efficiently and securely. This includes facilitating the running of multiple computer programs concurrently, while also having them not interfere negatively with one another.

Management of memory and CPU time

Computer programs are compiled from source code and use physical and virtual *addresses* (specifications of precisely where within the memory data can be accessed) to store variables and constants. A large portion of what the OS does is to manage address space usage. Memory changes to be executed are first done in relative terms (virtual memory) and, once the program instructions need to be executed on the computer system, these are translated into a physical memory addresses. Ensuring that memory is managed without external influences is critical to the security of the OS as memory in use is a finite resource and will eventually be overwritten by other future operations.

An OS executes tasks on a computer system by means of *processes*, which encapsulate all the information required to run a program on the CPU. To manage processes, the OS makes use of *process scheduling* to determine which programs should be next in line to use the CPU based on process priority. The OS needs context about a process in order for it to create, terminate, pause or resume its execution. This includes specific information about its execution state, value of the *program counter* (which refers to where in the program it currently is), memory management information and details of precisely which I/O resources it is using. A *dispatcher* assigns the CPU and a time slot to a given process. When a program starts, one or more processes are created and added to a *ready* list. Once a process reaches the top of the ready list and the CPU becomes available, the process will enter the *running* state. A process may then enter the *blocked* state (for example, waiting for I/O to complete), otherwise the process may be interrupted (the time slot ends or a higher-priority process needs the processor) and returns to *ready* state.

The resource management aspect of the OS is responsible for managing both memory and CPU time, as well as forwarding access requests to hardware components. The OS also deploys CPU *interrupts* (instructions to switch tasks) to enable multitasking. Part of this multitasking capability also involves denying inappropriate access requests to access memory. We discuss interrupts more generally later when we look at hardware security.

Integrity of the OS

The integrity of the OS is critically important. Attacks on computer systems may try to bypass the OS's resource management and related security measures by attempting to compromise or side-step its normal activities and access controls. An OS must thus be able to protect itself from such external threats as well as threats posed by itself, such as bugs, errors, data corruption and inappropriate behaviour by processes acting on behalf of the user or OS services. This makes the OS both the arbitrator of access requests and an object of its own access control procedures.

In order to maintain integrity and to act as an effective resource manager, OSs thus need to enforce the following requirements:

- *Separate execution domains*. The OS needs to maintain separate environments in which commands can execute, each with their own set of permissions, in order to protect the computer system's resources from unauthorized accesses. For example, the OS needs to distinguish between different users of a computer system, as well as distinguishing between user commands and those issued by the OS.
- *Process separation*. The OS needs to ensure that different computer processes do not influence one another, except in very limited and controlled circumstances.
- *Memory protection*. The OS needs to maintain strict management of read, write and execute access requests to memory.
- *Input/output*. The OS needs to enforce strict management of what enters and leaves the computer system, while also making sure that such operations are not misused.
- *Robustness*. The OS needs to perform all security functions reliably and at high capacity since OS security is constantly invoked.

We have already seen how the reference monitor and resource management support some of these requirements. We now consider other key OS features that support these requirements.

Privilege levels and controlled invocation

Key to memory management of processes is the concept of *least privilege*. This means that a user, program, indeed anything running on or accessing the resources of a computer system, is only given sufficient capabilities to perform necessary tasks and nothing more.

An OS must be able to distinguish between access requests made by processes on behalf of users and access requests made by the OS's own services. The OS therefore assigns *privilege levels* to processes, which are means of allocating different levels of access to the core system resources. An example of this is the use of *protection rings* in some computer systems to assign four different privilege levels:

- Ring 0. This is the most privileged level, associated with OS kernel services.
- Ring 1. This relates to I/O, associated with components such as drivers that communicate with external components such as mice, keyboards, network cards and hard drives.
- Ring 2. This relates to high-level OS services, for example those associated with networking and the file system.
- Ring 3. This is the least privileged level and is associated with user programs such as web browsers, media players and word processors.

Envisaging these privilege levels as concentric rings centred on Ring 0, the general idea is that processes within each ring can access one another as well as outer rings, but that no process can access processes of inner rings. That said, there are occasions when a low privilege process (say from Ring 3) might need temporary access to the likes of a kernel service (Ring 0). Most OSs thus support *controlled invocation*, which enables a restricted and temporary elevation of privilege level via a *handler*, which is an OS functionality that performs the desired operation on behalf of the low-level process.

Note that this privilege ring concept is also visualized in Figure 3.6, where rings are replaced by layers, hence 'outer' and 'inner' rings refer to 'upper' and 'lower' layers of the figure.

Users and the OS

The role of the OS is largely kept invisible to users of a computer system, who are shielded from the core of the OS in order to prevent them taking actions which might detrimentally impact its performance. This includes, for example, the use of graphical user interfaces (GUIs) to ease the interaction between a human user and the computer system itself. For example, most OSs visually present data to a human user in the form of a file and folder structure, which is an abstract construct enabled by the GUI to help a human user make sense of and engage with the underlying data. Without the GUI helping the human user to interact with the computer system resources in this way, there is a risk that a user would (accidentally) interfere with data associated with critical system functionality.

Security and usability of a computer system sometimes rub against one another. On the one hand, we wish to make a computer system as usable as possible, which might require a rich set of features to be enabled that allow a user to engage in sophisticated ways with the system resources. On the other hand, a more feature-rich computer system has an increased attack surface and may be more difficult to keep secure. The need to carefully design the trade-offs between security and usability of a computer system is a topic we return to in Chapter 9.

Hardware and security

Having mainly focused on operating system security in this chapter, we close with a brief look at some aspects of computer system security associated with hardware. In this section we will discuss some security considerations for hardware, as well as the use of hardware for security purposes.

Beneath the OS

In the last section we discussed the use of privileges levels to capture OS access levels to the resources of a computer system. We considered a conceptualization of privilege levels in terms of three rings, labelled 0–3. It is technically also possible to compromise a computer system 'beneath' the OS, by which we mean outside of the OS at a component level beneath which the OS runs.

Figure 3.6 extends the concept of privilege rings to layers beneath the OS. These can be thought of as rings even more privileged than Ring 0, since an attack that compromises these lower layers can compromise OS services running at Ring 0 privilege level.

In order to maintain the privilege ring concept, and because these layers beneath the OS are essentially privilege rings even lower than Ring 0, we have abstractly labelled these as Rings -1 to -3. In order of sequence, these are:

- Ring -1. This relates to *hypervisors*, which are virtualization technologies. Hypervisors enable multiple OSs to be run on a single piece of computer system hardware, and can create several OSs on the same hardware (often referred to as *virtual machines*). By being responsible for the supervision of different OSs, the hypervisor has an even more elevated privilege level on the computer system than the equivalent Ring 0 (root) privileges of any individual OS.

Figure 3.6 Ring levels of a computer security architecture

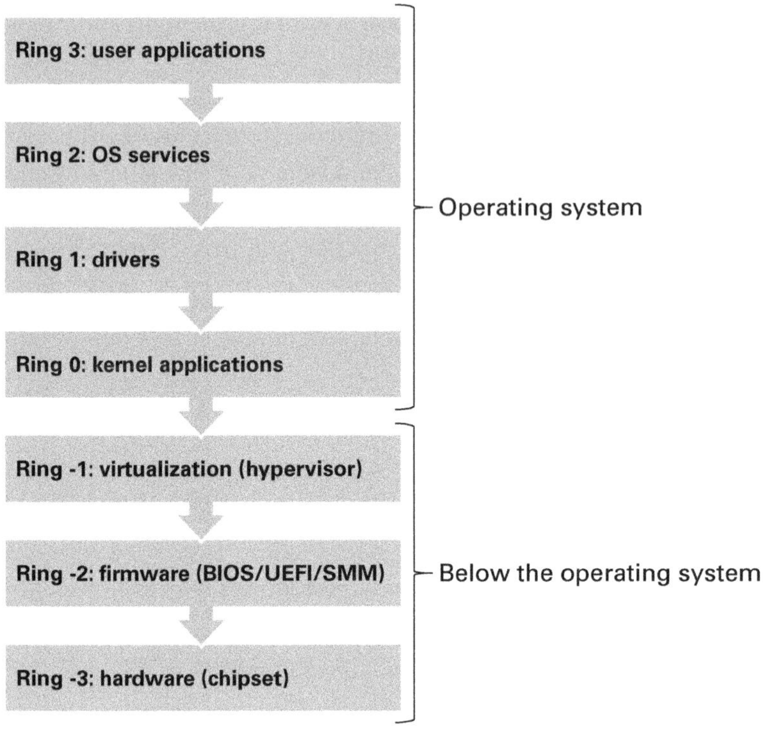

- Ring -2. This comprises the firmware that enables functionality such as computer system startup. It includes *system management mode*, which is a mode of operation of a computer system that enables the hardware to temporarily suspend normal activities, including running the OS. A Ring -2 compromise will impact operation of hypervisors as well as all OS functionality.
- Ring -3. This is the 'bare metal' of the hardware, including the motherboard and associated *chipset*, which comprises the various electronic components that sit on the motherboard. This is the lowest layer of the computer system and represents the most serious layer that could be compromised.

Interrupts

As previously mentioned with respect to memory and CPU time, interrupts are disruptions in the normal execution of instructions on the computer system. This is to allow higher-priority instructions to be executed immediately for safety, performance or security reasons. Interrupts can, broadly speaking, happen due to activity by a user, the external environment or the hardware itself. The execution of the original program then continues once the interrupt instruction has completed. *Asynchronous interrupts* are initiated outside of the normal CPU execution cycle. For example, some peripheral devices (such as a mouse or keyboard) must sometimes communicate with the OS immediately to access system resources. Mouse and keyboard interactions thus trigger asynchronous interrupts because they can be initiated unpredictably at any time. *Synchronous interrupts* on the other hand are generated by the CPU while executing instructions. Examples include preventing a CPU from overheating or avoiding problematic mathematical calculations (such as division by 0). Interrupts are important for the security of computer systems for efficient handling of critical events on the computer system as well as being able to isolate privileged operations.

Hardware for security

Dedicated hardware components also often form part of the core protection of a computer system and lie at the heart of its trusted computing base. These tend to involve shifting the root of trust from the CPU of the computer system to special hardware components existing elsewhere on the motherboard. Examples include:

- *Trusted platform module* (TPM). This is an international standard for a secure cryptography processor. A TPM is a microcontroller designed to secure hardware and software through trusted cryptographic key generation. A TPM is often used to facilitate hard disk encryption, and it can also be used for device attestation that provides evidence about the software state of a platform and confirms it has not been tampered with. A TPM is physically distinct from the rest of the computer system (or emulated as such).
- *Hardware security module* (HSM). This is a physical device used to manage, store and protect cryptographic keys and perform cryptographic operations securely. HSMs are widely used in industries that require high levels of security, such as financial services, healthcare, government and cloud computing to safeguard sensitive data and perform secure transactions.
- *Trusted execution environment* (TEE). This is an isolated execution area in memory that provides additional security features such as facilitating processes that have their own memory, processing resources and I/O capabilities. In other words, a TEE is a secure area of memory that is designed to protect sensitive information and processes from being accessed by untrusted processes. TEEs are often implemented using hardware-based security measures, such as *secure enclaves* (private regions of memory in hardware) that provide an additional layer of protection against physical attacks or tampering. Examples of TEEs include

IBM's Secure Service Container, Trusted Execution Technology and the SGX Software Guard Extensions.

- *Secure element.* This is a tamper-resistant storage unit such as a smart card or SIM card for storing secrets such as cryptographic keys. By using a secure element, we move the root of trust completely outside the core computer system. Secure elements are typically smaller than HSMs. Both serve critical security functions but are targeted at different environments and use cases.

KEY POINTS

- Computer systems have a broad attack surface, with potential points of vulnerability arising in software, hardware and the interface between the computer system and the external environment.
- The processes of authentication and authorization are crucial to ensuring that the computer system resources are used appropriately.
- A range of different approaches can be taken to defining access control policies and implementing access control to computer system resources.
- The operating system is the core software on a computer system and responsible for much of the security functionality, including the management of computer system memory.
- The trusted computing base of a computer system supports the core security functionality and normally consists of a combination of computer system software and hardware.

EXERCISES

1. Select an OS of your choice and read up on its security features. Try to map these features onto some of the topics that we have covered in this chapter.
2. Linux is an example of an OS that is developed through a public open-source process that involves peer review. Explain the extent to which you believe this process makes Linux a more or less secure OS than a closed proprietary OS such as Windows.
3. Suggest some alternative ways of authenticating on a computer system that were not explicitly discussed in this chapter.

4 Propose countermeasures for the following password-related security violations:

a. An online dictionary attack, where an attacker uses a dictionary attack to attempt to log in to a computer system.

b. An offline dictionary attack, where an attacker gains access to a (cryptographically protected) password database and uses a dictionary to find passwords.

c. A phishing attack, where a user is fooled into revealing their current password to an attacker by means of a fake email from a system administrator asking them to reset their password.

d. Multiple reuse of password across different computer systems.

e. A network sniffing attack where an attacker intercepts a password as it is sent across a network.

5 Provide two different examples of a multifactor authentication process. Now discuss what it would take for an attacker to defeat this multifactor authentication and gain access to the computer system (you might want to seek reported examples of real breaches of authentication processes to illustrate this).

6 Compare the use of ACLs and capabilities from the perspective of:

a. determining whether an access request should be authorized during run-time;

b. adding access rights for a new principal;

c. deleting all access rights for an existing principal.

7 Suppose you are in charge of the cyber security of a new company that has just been formed. The company has around 100 employees and sells both devices and services to the public. You have a free hand to design new security processes. Suggest how your company should manage authentication and authorization, both internally and with respect to external customers.

8 Do computer system security requirements differ between an Internet of Things (IoT) device (such as a voice assistant or smart doorbell) and a traditional desktop computer? Justify your answer.

9 Read up on UEFI and BIOS and explain the benefits and drawbacks of each approach with respect to security.

10 Suppose the trusted computing base of a computer system becomes compromised in some way. Suggest what options we might have for recovering the situation to achieve a workable and trustworthy computer system.

FURTHER READING

- Anderson, R (2021) *Security Engineering: A guide to building dependable distributed systems*, 3rd edn, Wiley
- Bell-LaPadula model: http://www.albany.edu/acc/courses/ia/classics/belllapadula1.pdf http://csrc.nist.gov/publications/history/bell76.pdf (archived at https://perma.cc/9EMH-T3K5)
- National Initiative for Cybersecurity Careers and Studies (2023) Explore Terms: A glossary of common cybersecurity words and phrases, https://niccs.cisa.gov/cybersecurity-career-resources/vocabulary (archived at https://perma.cc/98LZ-HEJD)
- Gasser, M (1988) *Building a Secure Computer System* (p. 85), Van Nostrand Reinhold Company
- Goodrich, M T and Tamassia, R (2011) *Introduction to Computer Security*, Pearson
- Gollmann, D (2010) *Computer Security*, 3rd edn, Wiley
- National Institute of Standards and Technology (2020) *Security and Privacy Controls for Information Systems and Organizations*, NIST Special Publication 800-53 Revision 5
- National Institute of Standards and Technology (2023) Cybersecurity, https://www.nist.gov/cybersecurity (archived at https://perma.cc/3SJV-3USG)
- NIST Digital Identity Guidelines: Authentication and Lifecycle management, http://nvlpubs.nist.gov/nistpubs/SpecialPublications/NIST.SP.800-63b.pdf (archived at https://perma.cc/PV2N-T8JU)

04 Network security

Securing the technology backbone

In the previous chapter we considered computer systems largely as standalone devices. In this chapter we discuss network security, which concerns the security of the communication connections between different computer systems. To understand security issues that arise in computer networks, we first introduce the basics of computer networking. We then consider the various layers of a computer network, identifying where points of vulnerability might arise. Next, we discuss a range of techniques that can be used to secure computer networks. These include secure channels, which exist on or between networking layers, and then supporting technologies such as firewalls and intrusion detection systems. Finally, we consider further issues, including the challenge presented by denial of service attacks.

LEARNING OBJECTIVES

- Fundamental networking concepts and points of vulnerability.
- Security issues that can arise at different networking layers.
- Network routing and addressing security.
- Establishment of secure channels.
- Core network security technologies, including firewalls and intrusion detection systems.

Network security fundamentals

Digital environments rarely involve standalone computer systems. Instead, they consist of distributed systems, where digital applications run on multiple interconnected devices (or nodes) across a network. The simplest possible network involves two directly connected devices exchanging data. Most networks, however, are far more complex in structure.

In this section we provide a brief introduction to computer networks. We then consider adversaries in such networks. Finally, we introduce network layering, which provides a framework for considering both the functionality and security issues that arise in computer networks.

How data reaches destination devices

Imagine a network connecting many devices. The first issue we consider is how data sent over a network reaches the network devices for which it is intended. Viewed somewhat simplistically, there are two primary options:

1. *Broadcast.* In this case data is sent to every device on the network. It then becomes the job of every device to figure out whether the data received is relevant to it or not.
2. *Unicast.* In this case the data is accompanied by an instruction to direct it to a specific device. In order to facilitate this, each device needs some form of *address*, which is an identifier that is unique within the network. It is the responsibility of the network to deliver data to the correct device (address).

A hybrid between broadcast and unicast is also possible when *multicast* is used to broadcast to a subset of devices on a network.

Organization of data exchange

The simplest way to exchange data over a network is to send a one-off message, whereby a closed unit of data is transferred from one device to another. However, most data transfers across networks are more complex.

We use the term *session* to describe multiple exchanges of data that 'belong together'. A session can be thought of as a conversation that takes places between two networked devices, often involving data exchange in both directions. Sessions can either be short-lived or last a long time (weeks or months). The data exchanged within a session typically consists of multiple messages, sometimes organized as a continuous data stream.

Network protocols establish the rules of communication between devices on a network, organizing how data is formatted and specifying various processes related to sending and receiving data. Network protocols are used at every level of communication and form the foundations of computer networks.

Types of network

There are many ways to build computer networks based on the types of underlying technology and network configuration. Examples of network types include:

- *Point-to-point.* This describes a simple network consisting of two devices that are directly connected.

- *Bus*. This is a network where multiple devices are connected by means of a single common connection (known as a *bus*).
- *Star*. This is a network where each device is connected to a central device by means of a point-to-point connection.
- *Wireless*. This describes a range of network types that use radio technology to communicate, rather than physical wires.
- *Local area*. This term is often used to describe networks serving a relatively limited geographical area. Common examples are *Ethernet*, which is a set of standards for wired local area networks, and *Wi-Fi*, which is a set of standards for wireless local area networks.
- *Wide area*. This is a network connecting devices that are spread over a large geographical area, such as a corporate network.
- *Internetwork*. This term is sometimes used to describe a large network that interconnects a range of smaller networks. The most famous example, of course, is the *internet*.

Adversaries in networks

In network security, we need to think about where an *adversary* (a malicious actor) might exist with respect to a network, as well as what the adversary's capabilities might be.

Network adversaries can be:

- *Internal*, for example a corrupted device on the network.
- *External*, for example a corrupted device on a different network that is interconnected to a network.
- *On-path* if data exchanged over a network passes directly through a device (or part of a network) controlled by the adversary. A noteworthy on-path adversary is a *machine-in-the-middle* adversary, which controls a device on a network and is capable of modifying data that is passed through it.
- *Off-path* if the adversary is not on-path.
- *Passive* if they simply observe data on the network but do not block or modify it.
- *Active* if they perform actions on network data such as data modification, replay of previously exchanged data or *spoofing* (inserting false data).

In general, we will assume that an adversary potentially controls multiple devices on a network, but not the entire network. Such an adversary might interact with the network in different ways, for example:

- provide fake services to users;
- spoof network management messages to gain control over parts of a network;
- redirect communication so that an initially off-path adversary becomes an on-path adversary (in this way an adversary that initially seems quite harmless might be able to gain capabilities and develop into a strong adversary).

Network layering

Network layering means to simplify complex communications by dividing the problem of device communications into smaller, more manageable 'layers', each with a specific function. These layers interact with the ones directly above and below, making network troubleshooting and implementation easier.

Figure 4.1 depicts the various network layers (sometimes called the *network stack*) in three important models. The first example is the well-known *ISO/OSI model*, which originates from early efforts to structure large-scale computer networks systematically. The ISO/OSI model is based around some of the most fundamental

Figure 4.1 Common layering models for computer networking

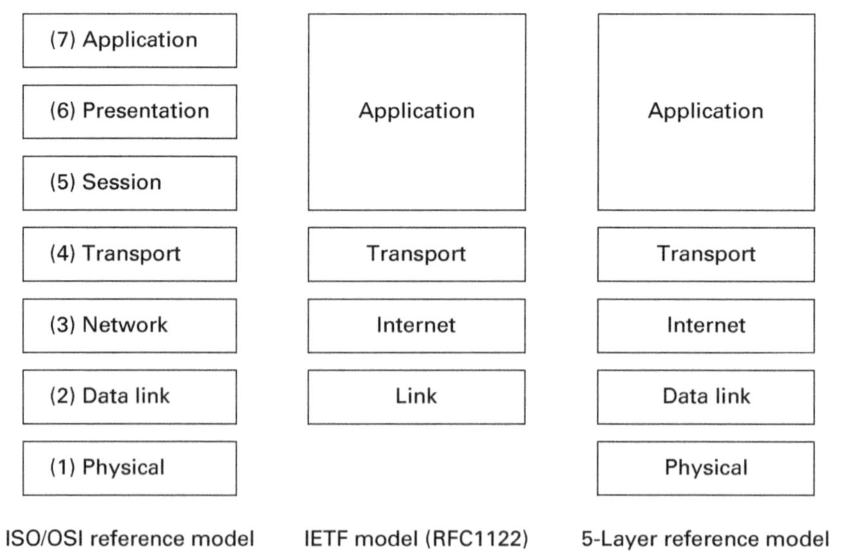

subtasks involved in sending data over a computer network. The layers and their purposes are:

1 *Physical layer.* This manages the physical transmission of raw data (bits) over communication mediums such as cables, wireless channels, etc.
2 *Data link layer.* This ensures error-free data transfer between directly connected devices using *frames* (a way to organize data into smaller units). This layer handles physical addressing (such as MAC addresses, see later) and error detection.
3 *Network layer.* This is responsible for logical addressing (such as IP addresses, see later) and routing data across multiple networks.
4 *Transport layer.* This provides reliable data transfer, ensuring error correction, segmentation and flow control (such as TCP for reliable transfer and UDP for faster, connectionless communication, see later).
5 *Session layer.* This manages sessions between applications, ensuring reliable connection setup, maintenance and termination.
6 *Presentation layer.* This translates data between the previous layers and the application layer, handling encryption, compression and data format translation.
7 *Application layer.* This interfaces directly with end-user applications, providing services such as file transfers, emails and network access (including HTTP and DNS, see later).

Many networks do not strictly follow this approach, in particular regarding the last three layers. The *5-layer reference model* is a simplified version of the ISO/OSI model. This model is especially relevant for teaching and understanding the core functions of network protocols and is aligned closely with the 4-layer IETF model described in RFC1122 by the Internet Engineering Task Force (IETF). The five layers define distinct responsibilities in the process of transmitting and receiving data across networks, from the physical transmission medium to the applications that receive the data. These layers are similar to the OSI model except for the omission of the session and presentation layers, while the network layer is referred to as the internet layer.

We will use the 5-layer reference model to organize the next sections of this chapter, discussing each of the five layers, how they are commonly implemented in practice and what security implications arise.

Physical layer

The physical layer of a network realizes the transfer of bits from one network device to another. How this is implemented varies enormously depending on the technology used (for example, wired or wireless). The primary purpose of the physical layer is data transmission. As a result, security tends not to be provided by default.

This is a powerful layer for an adversary to attack since it is right at the bottom of the network stack and hence everything above depends upon it. A physical layer adversary could be one who is in close physical proximity to a wired communication and can tap a wire, or one who can capture the radio signal of a wireless communication. Such an adversary could either passively eavesdrop or actively manipulate data, including injection of false signals.

Note that adversarial actions do not necessarily require direct access to the physical layer. For example, a copper wire can act as an antenna and emit (weak) electromagnetic radiation that can be used to reconstruct the data exchanged over it. Physical layer attacks on wireless networks are much simpler, since an adversary simply needs to place a commercially available transmitter's antenna within range.

An adversary might also disrupt communication on the physical layer by cutting a wire or *jamming* radio communication by emitting a strong radio signal (noise) that makes regular transmission impossible.

Attacks on wired connections can be mitigated by ensuring strong physical security. However, this is not always possible and might require significant effort (for example, in cases where wires run through public spaces). It is very hard to secure wireless networks from physical layer attacks. Some technologies, such as Wi-Fi, implement an encrypted layer above the physical connection to at least provide confidentiality and integrity for transmissions. However, such measures do not prevent an adversary from disrupting radio communication.

Data link layer

The data link layer builds on the physical layer by introducing functionality to send frames within a single network from one device to another. Implementation of the data link layer depends on the specifics of the physical layer implementation below. This typically includes encoding of frame boundaries, determining whether addressing of frames is necessary (less so in point-to-point networks) and deciding how addressing is realized.

Frames and MAC addresses

We will focus on the high-level concepts employed in Ethernet and Wi-Fi networks, which share similar characteristics because they are interoperable by design.

Both Ethernet and Wi-Fi follow a similar structure for frames that consists of:

1. *Header*. This includes the addresses of the sender and receiver of the frame.
2. *Body*. This consists of the payload (core messaging data) provided by the upper layers.

Addressing is done using *media access control (MAC) addresses*. (Note that this is a different concept to Message Authentication Codes, abbreviated to MACs, that we discussed in Chapter 2.) A networking MAC address is a unique 48-bit identifier of the *network adapter* that connects a device to the network. MAC addresses are typically assigned and hard-coded by a device manufacturer. If a device has multiple network adapters (such as both an Ethernet adapter and a Wi-Fi adapter) then it will have multiple associated MAC addresses.

Modern Ethernet networks deploy *switches*, which are network components that analyse the header of each frame to extract the MAC addresses of the sender and receiver. The switch stores the sender's MAC address along with an internal identifier for the link it received the frame from. By doing so, the switch autonomously learns which MAC address is reachable on which link. To forward a frame, the switch then looks up if it has previously seen a frame sent by the destination MAC address of the current frame. If this lookup is successful, the switch only forwards the frame on that link. If it is unsuccessful, it resorts to broadcasting (called *flooding* in Ethernet terminology).

Data link layer security issues

Since MAC addresses are hardcoded on manufacture, you might imagine that they are unique and non-modifiable. However, the MAC address assigned to a network adapter is just an initialization value, since any network participant is able to change a MAC address arbitrarily. In particular, an adversary in an Ethernet network could assign themselves the MAC address of any other participant.

Recall that switches learn MAC addresses to improve efficiency of transmission. They also have to be able to adapt to topology changes (such as when a network participant moves to a different location and reconnects on a different link to the switch). Hence, switches allow multiple entries for the same MAC address to be associated with different links. An adversary could thus send a frame to the switch containing such a MAC address as its source (a *spoofed* MAC address). The switch would then forward any frames directed to this MAC address to the adversary. Note that the adversary can also employ this technique to not only fool switches, but also other devices on the network.

It is possible to extend a switch with additional functionality to detect attacks of the type just described. Higher-end switches provide functionality such as (centralized) MAC address monitoring or blocking frames from unusual MAC addresses (a feature called *port security*). Another functionality found in such switches is *port authentication*, which requires each device to authenticate to a central authority within the network in order to participate. However, such features need to be present in the network infrastructure, and be properly configured and monitored, which are efforts that only a few network operators undertake.

As we have seen, the data link layer typically operates on trust. Malicious adversaries can just spoof MAC addresses in order to redirect or inject data.

Note, however, that there are certain circumstances where there might be security and privacy reasons for wanting to change a MAC address. These include when ethical hacking (see Chapter 5) and for preserving privacy and anonymity when using public or unsecured Wi-Fi networks (by changing the MAC address periodically we can avoid being tracked or profiled based on the device's identifier).

Internet layer

In this section we consider the role of the internet layer, which is primarily responsible for routing packets of data.

Internet layer addressing

The internet layer introduces global internet layer addresses, which are distinct from the MAC addresses used in the data link layer. Internet layer addresses are administratively assigned by network operators rather than device vendors. This approach allows information about the network to be encoded within the internet layer address.

For the internet (the internetwork known as the internet, not the abstract internet referred to in the internet layer!), such *IP addresses* are not arbitrarily assigned by network administrators otherwise there would be global chaos. Instead, this address space is subject to a form of regulatory control to avoid any assignment conflicts. Internet network operators are assigned a number of addresses to be used by hosts within their networks. There are also private address spaces that can be used in internal networks to avoid any conflicts with addresses on the public internet. This allocation of addresses is maintained by five community-led *regional internet registries* (RIRs), each of which is responsible for a distinct share of addresses.

Common protocols used by the internet layer are the *internet protocol version 4* (IPv4) and the *internet protocol version 6* (IPv6). At a high level both protocols share similarities, but there are some differences in how addresses are defined and how the protocols integrate with the data link layer. Note that while IPv6 is the official successor of IPv4, many networks still operate using IPv4. For now, we focus on IPv4.

In IPv4, addresses are 32 bits long and are often (for human readability) written as four decimal numbers divided by the '.' symbol, while each number represents one byte (eight bits) of the address. Such an address is logically divided into two parts:

1 *Network prefix*. This is an identifier for the local network, which is typically formed by a data link layer broadcast domain and is often referred to as a *subnet*.
2 *Host identifier*. This identifies a device within the subnet.

Local network transmission

Before we describe how packets can be routed across networks, we first consider transmitting packets within a local network, in other words to an address contained within the same subnet (and hence within the same data link layer broadcast domain). We will once again assume that we are using an Ethernet-style network.

Following the standard layering principle, we need to hand data over as payload to the next layer below, the data link layer. To construct a frame, we need to know the MAC addresses of the sender and destination. While obtaining the sender's MAC address is relatively simple (it is known to the network stack on the local device), we need a way to find out the receiver's MAC address based on the destination's IP address. One option would be to distribute such information beforehand to all devices within the network. However, such an approach is not feasible in large dynamic environments.

The solution is to use the *address resolution protocol* (ARP), which provides a simple strategy to obtain the MAC address of the intended receiver. Using the ARP protocol, the sender broadcasts a frame within the local network that requests the bearer of the IPv4 address in question to respond directly to the sender of this message. The intended recipient then sends a response containing its MAC address. Such responses are typically stored in a local cache on the device to avoid further queries for the same IPv4 address.

From a security perspective, this approach is seemingly insecure as any actor within the same network can just spoof IPv4 addresses and ARP responses. In fact, a common attack technique within local networks is for an adversary to become a machine-in-the-middle and re-route all packets to the adversary's device. In particular, the adversary can either wait for an ARP query and try to respond faster than the benign bearer of an IP address or the adversary can proactively send ARP responses for queries that have not yet been sent.

Another issue in local networks is how devices get their IPv4 addresses in the first place. Either each device gets an address manually assigned and configured by an administrator or we can use dynamic allocation and configuration. For the latter, networks typically use the *dynamic host configuration protocol* (DHCP), which uses a server within the data link layer's broadcast domain to take care of assigning addresses. This DHCP server maintains a pool of IPv4 addresses usable for dynamic allocation. Roughly speaking, the DHCP protocol works as follows:

1. When a new host joins the network, it broadcasts a DHCP *discover* message across the network.
2. The DHCP server then responds with an *offer*, containing a currently unused IPv4 address along with some other meta information.
3. The client (the new host) then claims that IPv4 address with a DHCP *request* message.
4. The server confirms with an acknowledgement.

DHCP also contains lifecycle management of such allocations, including regular checks of whether a host is still using an IPv4 address. A server can also be pre-configured with a list of static allocations for certain MAC addresses.

From a security perspective, there are no particular measures in the DHCP protocol itself preventing an adversary from acting as a DHCP server. In fact, the DHCP protocol has been designed with multiple competing DHCP servers within the same network in mind and does not contain any authentication mechanism to differentiate between benign and malicious DHCP messages.

Routing

So far, we have only discussed the transfer of packets within local networks. However, typically such networks do not operate in isolation, but are interconnected to other networks. A *router* is a device connected to two or more networks that takes care of forwarding packets from one network to another.

Consider a simple example. Suppose we have two networks, one running the subnet 1.0.0.0/8 and the other 2.0.0.0/8. Let host A in the first subnet bear IPv4 address 1.0.0.1, host B in the second subnet bear IPv4 address 2.0.0.2, and let router R be connected to both networks, bearing IPv4 addresses 1.0.0.10 and 2.0.0.20 in the respective subnets. When host A wants to send a packet to host B (in other words, a packet from 1.0.0.1 to 2.0.0.2), host A can easily determine that the destination is not part of the same subnet. The sender thus needs to make a routing decision (despite not being a designated router).

Routing decisions on non-router devices are straightforward. Such devices usually have a configuration parameter called *default router* that is set to an IPv4 address within the same subnet. To send a packet to a destination address not within the same subnet, the routing decision is to send the packet to the host bearing this default IPv4 address. Note that the packet's header remains unmodified and still states the final destination address. It is the data link layer addressing that is then used to transfer the packet to that router (in other words, host A resolves the MAC address associated with its default router's IPv4 address 1.0.0.10, typically using ARP, then puts the IPv4 packet in a data link layer frame addressed to that MAC address). When router R receives the packet, it uses the destination address for its routing decision.

In this scenario, the routing decision is simple: the destination address is part of a directly connected subnet. Hence, the router forwards the packet and sends it (inside a data link layer frame) to the intended receiver. The data link layer frame's header states that it is sent from the MAC address of the router's network interface in the second network to the MAC address of host B. The packet's IPv4 header (still) states that it is a message from 1.0.0.1 to 2.0.0.2. One might think that such a message might resemble a spoofing attack (the packet is sent from a MAC address that is not associated with the IPv4 source address), yet this is benign behaviour since the packet was created by the bearer of the IPv4 address 1.0.0.1.

Large-scale routing

The previous example scenario described a simple setting composed of just two networks directly interconnected by one router. In large-scale settings, in particular the internet, source and destination hosts of packets are often not conveniently located in directly adjacent networks. Instead, packets must typically traverse many networks and many routers in order to reach their final destination. While packets will be passed from router to router in a similar manner to our previous example, we now focus on the routing decision process within each router.

Note that interconnections between subnets can be visualized on a piece of paper as a graph of scattered points (subnets) connected by lines (routers). The challenge of efficiently routing packets in such an internetwork boils down to finding an economical *path* of connections (an unbroken line) from source to destination, not unlike the challenge faced by a driver planning a journey on an interconnected road network. In many cases there will be multiple alternative paths that lead from source to destination to choose from.

A naïve approach to this problem would be to analyse this graph in detail and calculate the best paths for each possible connection, either beforehand or at the time when a packet needs to be routed. For smaller internetworks, this might indeed be feasible so long as:

1. The structure of the internetwork is known.
2. There are no changes (or faults) in the network.
3. There is no need to consider balancing the network load on multiple connections to deal with high demand.

Routers typically maintain a *routing table*, which contains entries that each have a destination parameter (a single IP address or a range of IP addresses, typically expressed in the same way as a subnet) and a 'next hop' parameter that states the IP address of another router to which a packet for the destination is supposed to be sent. When the router receives a packet to forward, it simply looks up the entry with matching destination and forwards the packet to the next hop. In a small internetwork scenario, we could just configure these routing tables accordingly and then routing would be straightforward.

In practice, however, internetworks such as the internet are too complex (the structure is unknown), too dynamic and too congested to be guided by manually configured routing tables. Instead, *routing protocols* that run between adjacent routers are deployed to propagate information about the routing structure. The goal of a routing protocol is to calculate effective (dynamic) routing tables for each router that react to changes to the internetwork structure and operational environment. There are different types of routing protocols, with the most important ones being:

- *Distance-vector routing protocols*. These propagate information about the whole internetwork structure and allow each router to obtain a full picture of all connections. Using this information, a router can then calculate a good routing table based on shortest paths. Note that this is always a decision local to the router, and other routers might come to different conclusions.
- *Path-vector routing protocols*. These propagate limited information. In other words, a router announces that it knows a next hop for a particular destination, but not precisely which router this next hop is to or whether it knows alternative next hops. This is accompanied by meta information (such as coarse information about path length) which can be used by routers to determine how to choose between two competing next hops. This limited information approach scales better for large-scale internetworks such as the internet.

A common example of a path-vector routing protocol is the *border gateway protocol* (BGP), which is also the foundation for internet routing. To deal with the scale of the internet, BGP further aggregates subnets that form smaller internetworks into *autonomous systems* (ASs), which also have to be maintained by the same entity. BGP then takes care of exchanging routing information across ASs, while an AS internally might run different routing protocols.

Routing security

A major issue for BGP (and most other routing protocols) is the inherent lack of security. Announcements from other routers are normally trusted without further verification. Neither is information about regulatory assignments of subnets to ASs represented in BGP. This allows malicious ASs to simply announce that they have a good path to certain subnets, luring connected ASs' routers to produce flawed routing tables which direct packets to this malicious AS. Such attacks are known as *BGP hijacking* or *prefix hijacking* attacks.

That said, there are efforts to introduce a security layer to such routing protocols. For example, *BGPsec* is an extension of BGP that introduces cryptographic attestations to BGP announcements, linking each announced subnet back to the AS that got the subnet allocated. To further prove this allocation, BGPsec builds on the *resource public key infrastructure* (RPKI) standard, which introduces public-key certificates issued by regulatory bodies to ASs (see Chapter 2). However, use of BGPsec is not mandatory and not yet widely adopted by ASs.

IPv6

As we have just discussed, IPv4, the most common protocol for the internet layer, does not provide many security guarantees. IPv4 was primarily designed for functionality, not security. While some attempts have been made to retrofit security features, these tend not to be widely adopted, leaving the foundations for internetworks such as the internet rather insecure.

As mentioned earlier, IPv6 is the successor to IPv4. This was primarily designed to increase the available address space (IPv6 uses 128-bit addresses). To enable transition, both protocols can be run in parallel.

Many of the mechanisms previously described for IPv4 have IPv6 counterparts, such as the *neighbour discovery protocol* (NDP) resembling ARP, and BGPv6 providing routing information. While there is also a DHCPv6 protocol, it plays a secondary role in the automatic configuration of devices in local networks. Instead, IPv6 introduces slightly different mechanisms. Routers generally announce their existence with *router advertisements* broadcast over local networks. These router advertisements also inform hosts about which subnet they are located within. Devices are supposed to randomly select a host identifier by themselves. Due to the large address space for host identifiers (typically 64 bit), allocation conflicts are deemed a negligible problem. Furthermore, this mechanism inherently allows multiple subnets to co-exist within the same network.

Transport layer

So far, we have discussed how data is transferred from device to device. However, we typically want to exchange data between applications running on these devices. Since modern computer systems tend to be multi-tasking devices, we also need a way to handle the communication of multiple applications at the same time. Indeed, a single application might communicate with several other applications running on different devices. Further, some applications might want to communicate using continuous data streams instead of single messages and thus require some guarantees about message delivery, integrity and ordering. All of these issues are typically addressed within the transport layer. In this section we discuss the two most widely used transport layer protocols.

User datagram protocol

The *user datagram protocol* (UDP) is primarily designed to achieve two objectives:

1. Addressing applications that are running on the same device.
2. Providing a lightweight integrity guarantee for data.

The general idea behind UDP is for applications to create *sockets* on their host device. A UDP socket can send and receive data and is identified by a *port number*, which is a 2-byte value. Data is exchanged by means of *datagrams*, which are sent from one socket on one device to another socket on a different device. Port numbers are accompanied by an IP address. For example, the address 1.2.3.4:80 is used to define the socket with port number 80 on the device with IP address 1.2.3.4.

Similar to protocols at the lower layers, UDP datagrams consist of a header and a payload. The header contains several fields, including source and destination port numbers. It also contains a *checksum*, which is a value calculated over the payload (and some parts of the header) that provides a simple way for a datagram receiver to check whether the data has been damaged in transit (for example, due to transmission errors). Note that this checksum is *not* a strong data integrity mechanism such as the MACs and digital signatures schemes that we discussed in Chapter 2. Rather, just like the hash functions we also discussed in Chapter 2, the checksum calculation does not involve a secret key and hence could be recomputed by an adversary for any data that they modify. If the checksum for a received datagram is invalid then the recipient should drop (ignore) the datagram.

Transmission control protocol

The *transmission control protocol* (TCP) goes further than UDP by providing mechanisms that provide reliable transportation of data. These include:

- *Sequence numbers*. These provide a mechanism for ordering data. That is, when the sender sends out three sets of data A, B, and C and, due to different routing decisions these arrive in the order C, A, B, using the sequence numbers these messages can be reordered back to their original order.
- *Acknowledgements*. These notify the sender of a successful transfer. If a sender does not receive such an acknowledgement, it will automatically retransmit the data.

Further, TCP introduces the concept of a *connection*, which is a bidirectional communication channel established between two sockets that can be used to send continuous streams of data. In contrast to UDP, sockets in TCP can take one of two roles, often referred to as *client* socket and *server* socket. Essentially, connections are initiated from client sockets, while a connection request is responded to by a server socket. To this end, server sockets need to be created to anticipate connections and listen for such requests. The connection establishment between the communication peers is performed in a *three-way handshake*, which is an exchange of three messages that establishes a reliable connection between two devices (a client and a server).

TCP also includes mechanisms for terminating connections, various strategies to resend messages aiming to improve overall performance and message buffering.

Transport layer security issues

In what must be becoming a familiar message (!), as for the previous layers, transport layer protocols such as UDP and TCP do not aim to establish any security guarantees. We have seen that intercepting data on lower layers is often simply a matter of becoming an on-path adversary. At the transport layer, we are now located above network and internetwork routing. Data delivery to a socket is handled by a host's network stack, typically beyond the control of non-privileged processes and users. In other words, this last routing step can only be compromised by an adversary who obtains privileged control of a computer system. This is a topic that we considered in more detail in Chapter 3.

Similarly, spoofing on the transport layer is essentially a matter of spoofing an internet layer message and then crafting a suitable payload. As there are no inherent security mechanisms, this might appear easy at first glance (and it is for UDP datagrams). However, for TCP datagrams, an adversary needs to deal with the connection mechanism of TCP. While an adversary can still easily spoof the initial message of a connection handshake, for every other message the adversary would need to know some of the sequence numbers maintained for the connection. If the attacker is not on-path or can determine the sequence numbers by some other means (for example, guessing the outcome of a predictable choice of an initial sequence number generator), spoofing messages that will be accepted by the peer is hard as messages with sequence numbers that are unexpected will be dropped. Note that the TCP connection mechanism was not designed for security, yet it happens to make injecting messages into an existing connection hard for off-path adversaries.

Application layer

The previous layers establish the core of the network communication infrastructure. This means that applications can now build upon this infrastructure, often by means of their own protocols.

Hypertext transfer protocol

An example of an application layer protocol is the *hypertext transfer protocol* (HTTP). This protocol provides a framework for serving websites but is also commonly used as a communication framework between applications. Even HTTP can be layered in the sense that inside HTTP messages data is often encoded using the *JavaScript object notation* (JSON) or the *extensible markup language* (XML), which technically adds another (internal) layer to handle data representation.

Application layer sessions

Security is often provided at the application layer. This typically begins with some form of entity authentication (see Chapters 1, 2 and 3) prior to the establishment of a logical session running between two communication partners. While this can be done using relatively weak passwords (see Chapter 3), a session is often established by means of a more sophisticated cryptographic protocol (see Chapter 2).

Applications often build their own session logic on top of the layers we discussed previously. One common approach is to establish a *session identifier* (or *session ID*), which is then used as a token in each data exchange to link to other messages within the same session. An alternative approach is to recognize an underlying TCP connection as the session. However, as we discussed previously, the current communication infrastructure does not provide any guarantees about the confidentiality and integrity of exchanged data. Hence, without employing any further security, for example the use of cryptographic mechanisms, an adversary can easily hijack an existing session by intercepting a message bearing a session ID and reusing this ID in subsequent spoofed messages, or by infiltrating an existing TCP connection. While an application can, of course, employ cryptographic mechanisms to protect messages and sessions in its own proprietary way, it can also build on generic protocols, such as TLS (see Chapter 1 and the next section) to secure its communication.

Beyond layering

Before we conclude our journey through network layering, it is worth mentioning that there are also some mechanisms, which typically provide supportive services, that technically skip some of these layers.

An example for this is the *internet control message protocol* (ICMP), which is a protocol building directly on IP and that provides a means for network testing and error notification.

Also, note that there are sometimes good reasons to deviate from a classical network stack. In the next section, we will discuss virtual private networks, which in some instances run the IP protocol on top of a secure channel, which in turn builds on a TCP connection running on another instance of the IP protocol. Also, some applications maintain their own communication infrastructure on top of the standard network stack, effectively building a virtual overlay network.

Secure channels

Our discussion of the previous layers has clearly shown that, in its basic form, the core network infrastructure is not designed to provide security. This creates a need for additional means of protection for data exchanged over insecure networking infrastructure.

Goals of a secure channel

A common approach to introducing stronger security into the standard network stack is to establish a *secure channel*. At a high level, a secure channel can be an additional network layer that is inserted in between two existing standard layers. The idea here is that this new secure channel layer provides the same means of communication to the upper layer while re-using the functionality of the lower layer. Inside this secure channel layer, we typically employ cryptographic techniques to protect the data that is exchanged.

The main security goals of most secure channels are usually confidentiality and data integrity (most commonly data origin authentication) but can also include other goals such as protection against replays (see Chapter 2). We later discuss how secure channels handle entity authentication.

Types of secure channel

There are various conceptualizations and implementations of secure channels. Some important examples are as follows:

- *Virtual private networks* (VPNs). These are secure channels that are established with the intention of running network infrastructure protocols within their protection. A VPN can, for example, provide some sort of data link connection (often called a *Layer 2 VPN*, referring to the position of the data link layer in the OSI layer model), or just implement a protocol of the internet layer (typically IPv4 or IPv6). Often, the idea is to link (parts of) trusted networks (ones where we assume that there are no adversaries present) over an untrusted network such as the internet.
- *Internet Protocol Security* (IPsec). This defines a set of extensions to IPv4 and IPv6 that build on cryptographic mechanisms to protect data. IPsec can act as a protection layer between the internet layer and the transport layer. This is often used to mask the internal IP addresses of corporate networks and facilitate routing over a VPN connection. IPsec is highly configurable in terms of its security guarantees, with some modes providing confidentiality and data integrity, while other modes only provide integrity guarantees.
- *Transport Layer Security* (TLS). This protocol, which was first discussed in Chapter 1, builds on stream-like connections as provided for TCP. As suggested by its name, TLS can be seen as a layer placed on top of the transport layer. TLS emerged from the earlier *Secure Sockets Layer* (SSL) protocol. Like IPsec, TLS is configurable and can be used in different ways to achieve different security guarantees.

- *Lower layer secure channels*. Another form of secure channel is established by security measures that are sometimes employed by lower layer networking technologies. An example is the family of secure channels facilitated by Wi-Fi standards known as *Wi-Fi Protected Access* (WPA), which protect frames transmitted over the radio interface.

Secure channel entity authentication

To ensure that only authorized entities participate in such secure channels, these often run in combination with entity authentication protocols or even include such mechanisms within their specification.

If this authentication mechanism authenticates only one entity to the other, but not vice-versa, then we call this *unilateral* entity authentication. As discussed in Chapter 1, a common example of a unilaterally authenticated channel is secure web browsing. When a user navigates to a website that employs HTTPS (which refers to the HTTP protocol running on top of TLS), the web server authenticates itself as a web server authoritative for the web address that the user has entered. In TLS, this is done by the web server first presenting a public-key certificate (see Chapter 2) containing the domain name of the web address. This is then either used to securely transfer keying material that is subsequently used to authenticate the server or is used to verify digital signed protocol messages. In either case, the user (or rather, the user's web browser) typically does not authenticate itself to the web server. As a result, the user knows that they are communicating with a legitimate server, but the user is not authenticated to the server. On the web, user authentication is typically performed at the application layer, often by the user entering some credentials such as a password.

A secure channel can also be *mutually* authenticated. In this case, both communication partners authenticate themselves to each other when establishing the secure channel. For example, this is often employed by VPNs to ensure that their virtual network link is established between the correct entities.

While entity authentication is sometimes embedded in the (handshake) of the protocol realizing a secure channel (as is done for TLS), in other cases entity authentication is provided by an entirely separate authentication protocol such as the *remote authentication dial-in user service* (RADIUS). This latter approach is often employed for VPN connections and corporate Wi-Fi networks.

Note that entity authentication does not automatically imply that an authenticated peer is authorized to perform certain actions. Hence, a system establishing a secure channel also needs to implement access control mechanisms that check whether the peer is allowed to access a service or perform any actions over the secure channel. Authorization is discussed in more detail in Chapter 3.

Network security technologies

In addition to the network stack and secure channels, there are other technologies and techniques that provide supporting services. In this section we take a brief look at some of the most important of these.

Domain name system security

In our discussion thus far, we assumed that communication is established based on numerical addresses, such as IP addresses. In practice, however, in the case of the internet, services are often addressed using a *domain name* (sometimes referred to as a *host name*).

Domain names are structured, with the highest-level (root) domain names maintained by the *internet corporation for assigned names and numbers* (ICANN), a non-profit organization. Directly beneath this root are *top-level domains*, including country-code top-level domains (such as .uk) and generic top-level domains (such as .com), each of which is maintained by a different entity. Individuals and organizations can register a domain beneath these top-level domains (subject to top-level specific eligibility criteria) and can then maintain their own name structure beneath their domain.

A domain holder is sovereign over the entries in their domain, while the domain itself is linked to a public controlled structure. A common example for entries in this *domain name system* (DNS) is IP addresses. Consider a holder of the domain example.com who wants clients to use the name www.example.com to connect to its services. This requires an entry for www.example.com pointing to the IP address of the service. When a customer then enters this name, it will be resolved by first looking up .com in the ICANN-maintained root, then example.com in the .com domain, and finally www.example.com within the domain example.com. This is technically solved using the *DNS protocol*, a simple protocol that allows a client to query a server about such entries. Resolving a name then follows the principle previously described, starting with a query to the ICANN root servers, which are available at well-known IP addresses. These then indicate a delegation to .com and provide the IP addresses for the servers authoritative for .com. This delegation principle continues until a server can provide the IP address for the name queried. To speed up this process, clients typically delegate this task to DNS resolvers, which are specialized services often run by internet service providers. A DNS resolver usually caches responses to skip frequent queries and provides the information immediately from their cache.

However, the DNS protocol by itself does not contain any security mechanisms and queries are performed as single, short UDP datagrams, which only contain a short query ID to provide a rudimentary session mechanism. Hence, the system is vulnerable to spoofing attacks in which an adversary simply guesses this query ID (for example by spoofing many messages, each containing a different query ID) and provides false information. Such false information could be about a delegation (effectively directing the delegation of a domain to the wrong DNS servers) or about an IP address for a name.

To prevent such attacks, the *domain name system security extensions* (DNSSEC) have been introduced. Simply speaking, DNSSEC introduces digital signatures (see Chapter 2) on every entry in the DNS system (including domain delegations). The ICANN-maintained root operates as a trust anchor and domain delegations are accompanied with the public key of the delegee. Hence, if you look up example.com and query the ICANN root servers, you get a digitally signed response about the delegation to .com and details of which public key you should use to verify any signature provided in responses from .com servers. The same concept is applied down to the domain of example.com, such that a client querying the example.com DNS servers for www.example.com receives a digitally signed response for the corresponding IP address. Effectively, DNSSEC establishes a public-key infrastructure of signing keys for DNS entries. However, the deployment of DNSSEC is not universal.

Firewalls and segmentation

In our previous discussion about internetwork routing, we implicitly assumed that all messages are forwarded without any restrictions. However, we typically want to control which messages can be sent across network boundaries.

A common scenario, for example, is to restrict access to internal services from public networks. Public-facing services might contain security flaws, which could be exploited by adversaries who then take over the internal system. Hence, the hosts providing such public-facing services should also be restricted in their network communication in order to contain the damage and prevent *lateral movement* (a term describing an attacker's strategy to use such a host as a launchpad to mount further attacks inside the network that then appear to originate from the compromised host).

To restrict the message flow in a network, *firewalls* enable a network administrator to implement an access control policy on network communication. Typically, modern-day routers provide integrated firewall functionality, but it can also be found on regular network devices. A firewall can be a *packet filter*, which is a rule-based system that can block network messages based on header information of the protocols running in the (generic) network layers (data link, internet and transport layer). Such a packet filter can be:

- *Stateless* if it performs a decision based on every packet in isolation by looking at parameters such as source and destination IP addresses, and TCP or UDP ports.
- *Stateful* if it also takes context about connections into account, meaning that it tracks connections and can link subsequent packets to existing connections.

While this approach is straightforward, it cannot account for applications maintaining multiple connections for a single logical session, which then cannot be linked together by the limited view of the packet filter. To overcome this issue, some packet filter implementations resort to *deep packet inspection* (DPI), which inspects packet contents belonging to the application layer. Of course, this is highly application-dependent and requires at least some understanding of the application logic. Also, usage of secure channels typically prevents DPI as it would require the breaking of confidentiality protection.

Packet filters are typically used in a well-structured internetwork topology within the realm of a single entity. Such a structure follows the concept of *network segmentation*, which involves separating services into single networks and isolating these networks using restrictive packet filter policies. A common example is the deployment of a *demilitarized zone*, which involves placing public-facing services onto a separate network that is isolated from internal services to prevent lateral movement.

Finally, an *application firewall* is a firewall that is informed about (some) aspects of the application logic of the system it aims to protect. Such application firewalls then can impose more fine-grained access control as well as detect common attack patterns. A common type of application firewall is a *web application firewall,* which is an application firewall tailored for HTTP-based communication. Such application firewalls typically also act as the endpoint of TLS-secured channels in order to operate on unencrypted data.

Intrusion detection and prevention

It is also important to monitor activities inside a network to detect any sort of attack not otherwise accounted for, or attacks mounted on a previously unknown vulnerability.

This monitoring is provided by *intrusion detection systems* (IDSs), which either automatically check for known attack patterns (*signature-based* IDSs, sometimes known as *misuse-based* IDSs) or check whether activities deviate from previously observed patterns (*anomaly-based* IDSs).

The main distinction between these two approaches is that signature-based IDSs report on, and may help stop, known bad activities, whereas anomaly-based IDSs report on, and may help stop, suspicious activities. Both strategies are also often employed together.

IDSs can also be deployed at different levels. For example, a *network-based* IDS captures and analyses (samples of) network traffic at important points of the (inter) network, while a *host-based* IDS monitors system activities on devices. Network-based IDSs obtain a less granular view of activities as they mainly examine network packets, while host-based IDSs obtain very detailed views of activities from individual devices. Both approaches have their advantages and disadvantages in terms of use and maintenance, and are often employed together.

It is worth noting that *anti-virus software* is a type of host-based threat detection tool, primarily focused on identifying and removing known malware (see Chapter 5), often through signature matching. Modern host-based IDSs go beyond anti-virus software, for example by detecting zero-day threats and monitoring unusual behaviour, thus offering more comprehensive protection.

Security practitioners can also generate *cyber threat intelligence* by analysing network and host-based activities. This can be used to identify patterns of behaviour and *indicators of compromise*, which are items of evidence that strongly indicate a network intrusion.

As an IDS is a passive system, its purpose is primarily to notify and alert network operators about suspicious activities. It is then the task of the network operators to take appropriate action. As this process involves human intervention, it can sometimes be too slow to mitigate a running attack. *Intrusion prevention systems* (IPSs) are IDSs that can also actively take measures to intervene in suspicious activities that they detect. Such intervention can, for example, be adapting a firewall configuration to block suspicious traffic. This approach is often used by web application firewalls, which include some signature-based IPS functionality to block requests containing common exploits.

Security operations centres

Large organizations typically have dedicated organizational functions focused on monitoring their networks and wider systems.

A *security operations centre* (SOC) is a centralized unit responsible for monitoring, detecting, responding to and managing cyber security incidents. An SOC acts as a command centre where a team of cyber security professionals works around the clock to protect the organization's digital assets. Most SOCs deploy IDSs and IPSs among many other tools to detect and respond to attacks.

It is not uncommon for SOCs to be shared across organizations. Also, many nation states maintain national SOCs.

Honeypots, moving targets and deception

A complementary approach to network defence technologies such as firewalls and IDSs is to deploy techniques that are designed to make life much harder for an attacker

One such network defence strategy is to employ *honeypots*, which are services that mimic real services but do not provide any business-related functionality. The only purpose of a honeypot is to lure adversaries into interacting with them in order to detect the attacker's presence and subsequently analyse their behaviour. These decoy services are often placed in isolated environments and help practitioners to obtain insights into adversarial tactics and techniques.

More generally, *moving targets* are dynamic defence strategies where the attack surface is constantly changed or reconfigured. The idea behind this approach is to make it more difficult for attackers to exploit a system, as the system's overall structure and behaviour are continuously evolving. This, in turn, increases the complexity and cost for attackers because their strategies and tools must adapt to the changing environment, making it harder to find and exploit vulnerabilities.

More broadly, we can categorize different approaches to deceiving adversaries into various types. These include:

- *Concealment*. This approach involves hiding valuable assets by presenting them as innocuous while redirecting attackers toward honeypots, thereby wasting their time and resources.
- *Camouflage*. This technique masks assets through dynamic creation and removal of resources, utilizing technologies such as software-defined networks to enable virtualization as part of this deception strategy.
- *Disinformation*. Attackers can be deliberately fooled by providing inaccurate information, such as false error messages or inaccurate claims regarding file accessibility, ensuring that the misinformation cannot be easily disproven.
- *Displays/ruses*. Introducing counterfeit resources, including false credentials and decoy activities, can mislead attackers without disrupting legitimate users, thus minimizing false positives and bandwidth usage.
- *Feints*. These can be used to simulate vulnerability to one form of attack, while obscuring a secondary, more subtle, defence mechanism.
- *Unpredictability*. This approach disrupts an attacker's focus by deliberately making the network defence behave (seemingly) erratically.

Further issues

In this final section we reflect on one network security issue that is difficult to defend against and indicate other network types not covered in this chapter.

Denial of service

Thus far we have mostly focused on confidentiality and integrity network security goals. Another important aspect, however, is availability of services. A common and widespread class of attacks aiming to break availability of services are *denial of service* (DoS) attacks, which typically aim to exhaust the resources necessary to provide a service. Such resources can, for example, be the necessary network bandwidth to provide the service, or the computational power or memory space of the host providing the service.

A simple DoS attack strategy is to congest the necessary network link (or links) to reach the host. Naïvely, this can be achieved by sending a vast quantity of network messages directed to the address of the host. These messages do not need to have any meaningful content as their only purpose is to congest the network.

If an adversary sends these messages from its own network or host directly, the amount of network bandwidth is obviously limited by the capabilities of the adversary's own internetwork connections, as well as the capacity of the internetwork transporting these messages to the victim. To make such attacks more effective, an adversary could lure other (benign) systems to also send messages to the victim. To this end, the adversary could exploit services that send large responses to small requests and send such requests with a spoofed source address (the one of the victim). This approach is often referred to as an *amplified DoS attack*.

A similar strategy is *distributed DoS* (DDoS), where an adversary first infiltrates many other computer systems (called *bots* or *zombies* in this context) by exploiting system vulnerabilities to form a malicious network of attack devices known as a *botnet*. Each bot then connects to a *command-and-control* (CnC) service operated by the adversary. To attack a victim, the adversary instructs the botnet using the CnC service to send messages to the victim simultaneously, which very likely will overwhelm the victim's network resources.

In general, these types of DoS attack are relatively hard to prevent as they do not exploit explicit vulnerabilities in the victim's infrastructure, but rather the capacity of its network. Mitigations need to be implemented at the victim's internetwork peers, such as filtering requests at high-capacity routers before these enter the bottleneck of the network infrastructure. *Load balancing* helps protect against DDoS attacks by distributing incoming network traffic across multiple servers, preventing any single server from becoming overwhelmed. Having failover redundancies (redirecting traffic to other, still operational, servers) and built-in network traffic filtering (for example, based on geographical distributions) can also help.

Another type of DoS attack exploits issues in a victim's network stack. An example is *TCP SYN flooding*, where an adversary sends many TCP connection requests to the victim. The victim then assumes that these messages are legitimate requests and consequently starts its part of the TCP connection handshake. The victim needs to maintain state and track the connection initialization, which requires (a small amount of) memory. However, TCP implementations typically only reserve a limited amount of space for connection tracking, resulting in quick exhaustion of this memory space. As a consequence, the victim is then unable to process any further connection requests, rendering its services unavailable. This particular issue can be mitigated by the use of *SYN cookies*, a strategy which avoids the need to store information about incomplete handshakes by including cryptographically protected information in the handshake response.

Attacks on availability are amongst the hardest to defend computer networks against. There is no single solution that can be used to defend against them. Implementing the good security practices outlined in this chapter and throughout this book arguably provides the best means of defence.

Other networking environments

There are three areas of networking that we would encourage readers to further explore. These are:

- *Application layer and above*. There are many different application frameworks that sit on top of the standard network stack, and which raise different types of security issues. For example, although we have briefly touched on web security, there is a great deal more that could be discussed. Note that some aspects of web security are explored in Chapter 5.
- *Critical infrastructure networks*. Our focus on standard networks has meant that more bespoke networking environments have not been discussed at length. These include the many network-controlled cyber-physical systems that underpin critical infrastructure, such as power grids and industrial control systems.
- *Emerging network technology*. New networking technologies are emerging, including software-defined networks, Internet of Things (IoT), edge computing, fog computing, multiprotocol label switching and network function virtualization. These have potential to change the ways that network infrastructure is constructed and are likely to present new challenges to the standard network layer models since boundaries between traditional layers may become blurred.

KEY POINTS

- Computer networks come in a variety of shapes and sizes, each presenting its own set of distinct challenges from both maintenance and security perspectives.
- Network layering provides models for separating the different functionality of a network and enables different security issues, such as those related to address and routing, to be systematically defined and addressed.
- Standard network technologies such as network protocols were mainly developed to provide data transmission functionality and have very little in-built security or privacy.
- Security measures can be introduced at different layers of the network stack, as well as through the establishment of secure channels between layers.

- A range of security technologies further support network security, including firewalls and intrusion detection systems.
- Security services such as confidentiality, data integrity and entity authentication can be introduced to strengthen network security, but attacks on network availability are much harder to defend against.

EXERCISES

1 Suppose you are in a team designing the digital infrastructure for a new business that sells goods online. Your role in this team is to cover aspects of network security.

   a. First, imagine that you are an external adversary who wants to either disrupt the business services or steal customer data. In what different ways might you try to attack the business networks?

   b. Now provide a range of general network security design recommendations that will help to defend the business against such attacks.

2 Tin-can telephones are simple toys that transmit speech over pieces of string. Imagine building a communication (inter)network using tin-can telephones with human operators as routers (one human operates a number of tin-can telephones connected to other operators).

   a. How might human operators run such a network in terms of managing addressing, routing and forwarding messages, etc.?

   b. How might attackers intercept or spoof messages sent over such a network?

   c. How might an attacker attempt to disrupt the availability of this network?

   d. What security measures could we introduce to help prevent attacks on this network?

3 Wireshark (https://www.wireshark.org) is a widely-used software that can be used to monitor and analyse network messages. Install this tool on one of your devices and record network traffic while you are browsing the web. Now try to draw connections between what you observe and some of the concepts discussed in this chapter. For example, you should be able to identify the use of some of the network layer and infrastructure protocols that we discussed, such as ARP, IP and TCP.

4 As we have seen, data transfer being routed over the internet can be easily manipulated. Imagine that almost every external network connection is under attack. To what extent can an internal network be defended against such a hostile external environment?

5 TLS typically relies on a public-key infrastructure to authenticate communicating peers. Web browsers come with a number of certification authorities (CAs) pre-registered, which serve as trust anchors to authenticate TLS connections (see also Chapter 2). Connect to a website using TLS (make sure the URL starts with https://). Most web browsers now enable you to view some details about the current TLS connection.

   a. Find out which CA has issued (digitally signed) the current connection's certificate.
   b. Which digital signature scheme did they use to sign the certificate?
   c. Which cryptographic scheme is the public key contained in the certificate designed for and what key length does it have?
   d. What other information is contained in this public-key certificate?
   e. What certificate chain (a hierarchical series of certificates) links the website certificate to the root CA certificate pre-installed in your browser?
   f. Which other CAs have root certificates that are pre-installed in your web browser?

6 Secure channels can be established at different layers in the network stack. For each layer of the 5-layer network stack:

   a. Discuss the advantages and disadvantages of establishing a secure channel above (or on) that layer.
   b. Give an example of a type of secure channel (or protocol enabling a secure channel) operating above (or on) that layer, as well as a potential use case for such a channel.

7 Your boss (who is not a security expert) has just invested in some new firewall technology and is proudly telling the board that your company's networks are now completely secure from external threats. Write a memo to your boss that outlines the extent to which you agree with their sentiment, explaining how the firewall can be used to improve security but also outlining the limitations of a firewall.

8 Suppose your job is to design a new network stack for the internet from scratch, with security in mind as well as functionality.

   a. What would your overall security goals be?
   b. Suggest a possible network stack (if you reuse any existing layers then explain why).

9 Network segmentation is sometimes employed to prevent lateral movement.

   a. Give an example of such lateral movement.
   b. What common patterns are used to structure a network into segments?
   c. Explain how virtual local area networks (VLANs) can be used to implement network segmentation.

10 Frames in the data link layer typically are limited in size, depending on the network technology used and its configuration. Hence, if a message is routed into another network, it might exceed the limit of this second network. IP provides a solution to deal with this issue: the datagram is split into smaller chunks called *fragments*, each becoming a separate IP packet. To what extent does IP fragmentation potentially create security issues?

FURTHER READING

- Kaufman, C, Perlman, R and Speciner, M (2022) *Network Security: Private communication in a public world*, 3rd edn, Prentice Hall
- Peterson, L and Davie, B (2011) *Computer Networks: A systems approach*, 5th edn, Morgan Kaufmann
- Rossow, C and Jha, S (n.d.) Network Security Knowledge Area. Version 2.0.0. Cyber Security Body of Knowledge (CyBoK), https://cybok.org (archived at https://perma.cc/A3XD-R6FP)
- Stallings, W (2018) *Network Security Essentials: Applications and standards*, 6th edn, Pearson
- Tanenbaum, A, Wetherall, D and Feamster, N (2020) *Computer Networks*, 6th edn, Pearson

05 Software and application security

Securing computer programs

In the previous chapters we looked at the security of computer systems and how they are connected. In this chapter we turn our attention to the software and applications that run on a computer system. After introducing fundamental concepts, we begin by looking at the wide range of vulnerabilities that can occur in software. We discuss how to classify vulnerabilities and then review a range of common vulnerabilities. Next, we consider how secure programming can be used to try to prevent vulnerabilities arising, followed by a discussion about how vulnerabilities can be managed once they have arisen. Finally, we take a step back and consider the more general process of secure software design.

LEARNING OBJECTIVES

- Classifying software vulnerabilities.
- Examples of common software vulnerabilities.
- How to develop secure computer programs.
- Management of vulnerabilities in a computer system.
- How to develop and design secure software.

Fundamentals of software security

In this section we introduce a range of fundamental concepts required for processing the rest of this chapter. This includes some aspects of computer memory management and an introduction to vulnerabilities and malware.

What software security involves

In general terms, *software security* is the practice of designing, developing and maintaining software that protects it (and related components of computer systems) from unauthorized access, misuse or other attacks. Note that in this chapter we will use several pieces of terminology at times synonymously, although they are technically different:

- *Software.* This is a generic term for any set of instructions that informs a computer system how to conduct a task. We will commonly use this term when considering such instruction sets in generality. Software is created using a programming language, which codifies the instruction set.
- *Program.* A computer program is a piece of software designed to perform a specific task. We will tend to use this term when referring to a particular item of software or when considering programming (sometimes referred to as *coding*), the creation of software.
- *Application.* This is software that is designed to provide tasks that are of direct benefit to users or organizations. Applications are thus user-facing (such as an online banking application). This distinguishes them from system software that operates on behalf of users but runs more in the background. An important example of software that we would not normally refer to as an application is an operating system, which is software we discussed in detail in Chapter 3.

For many years software security was not considered as seriously as some of the other aspects of cyber security explored in this book. This was partially due to a general failure to appreciate the risks presented by software, but also because the principles behind secure software design had not yet been adequately recognized and formalized. Today, the importance of software security is much better understood, largely due to the sheer extent of problems that have arisen from software *insecurity*.

Software security aims to identify and mitigate security issues that can arise within software to ensure software operates securely in potentially hostile environments, whether this be a local device or on a broader network. Software security is thus mainly about understanding how to write and manage software to minimize opportunities for malicious actors to gain access to assets and systems we wish to protect. In this chapter we consider what security problems software can present, how to manage these problems, and how to create secure software in such a way that security problems do not arise in the first place. This is far from easy to achieve, but we will discuss many useful techniques and best practices.

Process memory management

Before proceeding, we need to understand a few concepts that are important for our later discussions on what security problems can arise within poorly designed software. This discussion builds on the material presented in Chapter 3.

In what follows, we will use the term *program* to describe a static instruction set (the code that the programmer wrote) and the term *process* to describe the execution of this program in the memory of a computer system. In other words, the program is the recipe and the process is the cooking of it!

A *binary* is a file that is encoded in a machine-readable format (intended to be processed by a computer) as opposed to human readable text. This could be data embedded in a file or a program in the form of a *binary executable*. Once loaded by the operating system (OS), binary executables are instantiated as processes.

Once an OS runs a process, it *allocates* memory to the process. As part of this memory allocation, the OS can utilize two areas of memory:

1 *Heap*. This is a readable and writable memory segment that dynamically stores allocated data. The heap is primarily for short-term data and blocks of memory are allocated and subsequently released in an arbitrary, non-methodical manner.
2 *Stack*. This is a readable and writable memory segment that allocates memory in a structured fashion. The stack follows a *last-in, first-out* (LIFO) model for memory access. This is somewhat akin to the idea of a stack of paper on a desk. Items are *pushed* (added) to and *popped* (removed) from the top of the stack. For example, if the main() function of a program first invokes the function a(), which in turn invokes the function b(), then b() will eventually return control to a(), which in turn will return control to the main() function.

The operation of the stack is critical to understand when it comes to vulnerabilities since several common vulnerabilities arise from manipulation of the stack's predictable operational nature. These vulnerabilities often relate to incorrect memory handling or exploitation of the stack's LIFO behaviour (see later).

Vulnerabilities and exploits

In Chapter 1 we defined a vulnerability to be a weakness in a digital environment that could threaten the security of an asset. In this chapter we will refine this definition slightly given our software security context. Hence, for our current discussion, a *vulnerability* is a flaw in software, hardware, network or a wider process that can be exploited by an attacker to gain unauthorized access, cause damage or otherwise disrupt operations. We will be particularly interested in software vulnerabilities, or vulnerabilities that enable undesirable interactions with software.

Vulnerabilities can arise in many ways, including poor design, coding errors, misconfigurations or inadequate security practices. Once a vulnerability is identified, malicious actors may use it as an attack vector for stealing sensitive data, injecting malicious code or gaining control of systems. Vulnerabilities in software arise due to a variety of factors, including:

- *Mistakes*. At least for now, most software is designed and created by humans. As we discuss in more detail in Chapter 9, humans are prone to making errors for many varied reasons. Hence, software is often flawed simply because its human programmers have made mistakes. This is particularly common when designing complex software systems that are challenging to fully understand, making it likely that certain use cases that can subsequently leave a system vulnerable are accidentally overlooked.

- *Insecure programming practices*. As we will discuss later, vulnerabilities can also arise from poor programming practices. These are not quite the same as errors, since these are practices that can, and should, be outlawed. Common examples include failing to check or *sanitize* (remove unsafe) user inputs or storing sensitive data in unencrypted form.
- *Ignorance*. Vulnerabilities often arise simply from a lack of knowledge or awareness of security. Some programmers have little background expertise in security and will thus write insecure software without realizing that the resulting code is prone to vulnerabilities, or the implications of this.
- *Misconfigurations*. A system can be misconfigured in such a way that vulnerabilities are introduced. We later discuss such an example involving firewall misconfiguration.

As noted in Chapter 3, an *exploit* is a computer program that uses a vulnerability to cause incorrect or undefined behaviour in a computer system. This behaviour could lead to almost anything untoward, including unauthorized access, privilege escalation, data disclosure or disruption of system operations. The term *exposure* is sometimes used to describe an actual incident where an exploit is used. Put more simply, a vulnerability is a 'disaster waiting to happen', an exploit is a mechanism by which an undesirable event occurs due to a vulnerability and an exposure is such an event happening.

Malware

One of the most common means of conducting an exploit (exploiting a vulnerability) is using *malware* (a portmanteau of 'malicious' and 'software'). Malware is software that has been created for malicious purposes, such as to extract sensitive data, manipulate the integrity of data or disrupt the functionality of a computer system.

There are many different types of malware. These include the following examples:

- *Virus*. This is a computer program that infects files and then spreads to other computer systems when transferred (either by a user or software) and executed. Viruses were amongst the first examples of malware that arose and, due to the mass and unpredictable target range, tend to focus on disruptive activities such as data corruption and blocking of services.

- *Worm*. This is a self-replicating computer program that can spread between different computer systems without any direct user interaction. Worms are particularly dangerous in highly connected networks, where they can spread quickly and extensively. One of the earliest examples of malware was the 1971 Creeper worm, which had a harmless payload but served as a precursor for the more insidious malware that we see many examples of today.
- *Trojan*. This term is used to describe malware that is disguised as legitimate software, enabling attackers to gain access to a computer system once the trojan is installed. The etymology of this term comes from the mythical wooden Trojan horse used by the Ancient Greeks to gain access, and ultimately conquer, the city of Troy.
- *Ransomware*. As discussed in Chapter 2, ransomware is a type of malware that encrypts a victim's data, then communicates a payment demand for its release. As noted in Chapter 7, the use of ransomware is a widespread criminal business practice and ransomware attacks are even offered 'as a service' by criminal groups. For large organizations, ransomware represents a particularly serious threat, leading to ransomware becoming one of the most significant global cybersecurity concerns.
- *Spyware*. This is malware designed to secretly monitor user activities and steal sensitive information without the user's knowledge. Spyware can be targeted at specific organizations to seek commercially sensitive data or can be deployed at scale to seek credentials or financial data. Spyware represents a threat to user privacy, which is a subject we discuss in Chapter 8.
- *Keylogger*. This is a type of spyware that records a user's keystrokes and can thus be used to capture sensitive data such as passwords and financial data. A keylogger also enables an attacker to capture unencrypted data at the point of entry, circumventing protection such as end-to-end encryption.
- *Rootkit*. This is a particularly problematic type of malware that is designed to take control of all or part of a computer system. The objective of a rootkit is to obtain access to a component of a computer system that is otherwise unauthorized, ideally a privileged component (see Chapter 3). A rootkit typically conceals its presence. Once installed, however, the rootkit can be used to modify other software and potentially gain command of the victim's computer system.
- *Logic bomb*. This is malware that installs itself on a computer system and then remains dormant until triggered by a specific event or condition. Logic bombs are typically components of more sophisticated attacks. For example, a logic bomb could be used to trigger members of a botnet to conduct a distributed denial of service attack (see Chapter 4).
- *Cryptojacker*. This is an example of malware with a very precise function, in this case to hijack a victim's computing resources to mine cryptocurrency (a highly intensive process) without the user's knowledge.

As we can see from this (incomplete) list of diverse types of malware, the breadth of damage that malware can cause is highly concerning, which is why malware is deemed a significant threat to computer systems. It is also worth noting that sometimes malware is the direct means by which malicious activity is undertaken (as is the case for ransomware), while at other times malware is used to prepare the ground for a later attack (as is the case for logic bombs).

Classifying vulnerabilities

In this section we consider why it is important to be able to classify vulnerabilities and discuss some common mechanisms for doing so.

Why classify vulnerabilities?

Most attacks on computer systems arise from vulnerabilities. However, as we will see later in this chapter, the full range of different vulnerability types is extensive. Making sense of the vulnerability landscape is thus extremely challenging.

Organizing and categorizing security vulnerabilities based on certain criteria helps us better understand the nature, impacts and risks presented by vulnerabilities. In turn, this helps to prioritize and manage vulnerabilities more effectively, making it easier to prevent, detect and mitigate the potential threats that they represent.

Vulnerability classification typically involves grouping vulnerabilities according to their causes, impacts, exploitability or any other attributes that define how they behave and the risks that they represent. By doing so we can subsequently implement targeted security controls, improve software development practices and allocate resources more efficiently for mitigation. Before we look at vulnerability classification, it is worth clarifying some related terminology that is relevant to the subsequent discussion:

- *Bug*. This is a word often used to describe a flaw in the design or implementation of a computer system and its software that leads to undefined or incorrect behaviour. Bugs typically cause functional problems such as crashes, incorrect results or performance issues, but bugs do not necessarily pose a security risk. That said, some bugs can lead to security concerns if they create conditions that can be exploited by malware or malicious actors.
- *Vulnerability*. As we defined earlier, a vulnerability is a specific flaw that can be exploited by a malicious actor. Vulnerabilities always represent security risks, which is not the case for bugs. That said, vulnerabilities often arise because of bugs.
- *Weakness*. This is a broader term that is used to refer to a defect in the design, development or configuration of software or systems that could, in turn, lead to bugs or vulnerabilities arising. While a weakness might not always be directly

exploitable, it can increase the likelihood of exploits manifesting themselves. Unlike bugs and vulnerabilities, weaknesses tend not to be immediately fixable, largely because they result from more general design issues.

Vulnerability classification methods

We now look at some of the most common mechanisms for classifying vulnerabilities (we are using this term in generality here because, as you will see, one of these classifications addresses weaknesses).

First, we consider three mechanisms for considering specific vulnerabilities (weaknesses):

- *Common vulnerabilities and exposures* (CVE). This is a standard for cataloguing publicly disclosed security vulnerabilities and exposures in software and hardware. Each CVE entry is assigned a unique identity in the format [CVE-YEAR-NUMBER] to facilitate common referencing and to track a specific vulnerability across multiple occurrences on different platforms over time. A CVE entry typically includes a brief description of the vulnerability, its potential impact, and references to further details (such as advisories, patches or more in-depth analyses). However, CVE entries do not include technical fixes or detailed exploit code. CVEs are commonly used in security tools, vulnerability databases such as the *national vulnerability database* (NVD), patch management systems and reporting frameworks, thus helping to standardize vulnerability management.
- *Common weakness enumeration* (CWE). This is an effort, like CVE, to catalogue software and hardware security flaws, design errors or issues in software architecture that could lead to vulnerabilities. Unlike CVE, which focuses on specific instances of vulnerabilities, CWE focuses on the underlying weaknesses that enable those vulnerabilities to exist in the first place.
- *Common vulnerability scoring system* (CVSS). This assigns a numerical score to vulnerabilities that helps security practitioners to assess vulnerabilities based on their potential impact and exploitability. The CVSS score ranges from 0.0 (no impact) to 10.0 (critical impact), allowing different vulnerabilities to be ranked and prioritized for mitigation.

Next, we provide examples of two (out of many) mechanisms for classifying vulnerabilities more generally. These are:

- *Adversarial tactics, techniques and common knowledge* (ATT&CK). This is a framework that focuses on categorizing vulnerabilities and attack methods based on adversarial tactics (goals) and techniques (specific methods used to achieve those goals). Rather than providing a list of specific vulnerabilities, ATT&CK enables the identification of key security gaps that need to be addressed.

- *Common attack pattern enumeration and classification* (CAPEC). This is a hierarchical catalogue of attack patterns. It provides detailed descriptions of how attackers exploit system vulnerabilities, aiding an understanding and ability to defend against these methods. CAPEC focuses on classifying attack techniques, including their goals, prerequisites and typical impacts. It is used for threat modelling, security assessments and building defensive strategies by identifying patterns in attack behaviour.

Common software vulnerabilities

To indicate the diversity of vulnerabilities that can arise in software, in this section we introduce some of the most common types of vulnerability. We stress that this list consists of examples and is by no means a comprehensive capture of the full range of potential software vulnerabilities out there.

Ambiguity

One common source of security vulnerabilities arises from ambiguities in code. Just as for life in general, if the instructions within a piece of software are imprecise then it is possible that there are undesirable consequences.

One example of an ambiguity arises with respect to *signed* and *unsigned integers*. Put simply, these represent two different formats that enable binary numbers to represent both positive and negative integers. Ambiguity can arise if it is not made clear which format is being used. An example of a problem that could arise is if an unsigned integer is used as a counter and is allowed to decrease below zero. If this is not interpreted correctly, the counter might then be interpreted as a very high number, leading to further vulnerabilities such as buffer overflows (see later).

Other types of ambiguity can arise if the data type of a program variable is not made clear. An example is when a program expects one specific data type (such as an integer) but in fact accepts *any* data type (such as a string of characters). This could arise if the program is a web application expecting numerical user identities to access profile information. The ability of an attacker to inject arbitrary strings instead of user identities could result in many different forms of incorrect application behaviour. More generally, vulnerabilities arising from an application failing to properly check all inputs or operations before acting upon them are sometimes referred to as examples of *incomplete mediation*.

Broken access control

In Chapter 3 we discussed the importance of access control in ensuring that only authorized users can conduct computer system operations. We also saw how complex it can be to define a consistent access control policy.

A potential source of vulnerabilities is through broken access control, where 'broken' means that an attacker can access part of a computer system that they should not be allowed to. This then enables the attacker to potentially perform actions or access resources that they should not be permitted to.

Rootkits provide an extreme example of broken access control, since they generally involve defeating the intended access control protection and enabling an attacker to gain elevated privileges on a computer system.

Broken cryptographic implementations

As we discussed in Chapter 2, cryptography is particularly sensitive to implementation failures and hence represents a significant source of potential vulnerabilities. Just some of the many vulnerabilities that could arise from 'broken' cryptographic implementations are:

- *Custom cryptography*. As we noted in Chapter 2, it is wise to deploy standardized cryptographic mechanisms. It is extremely likely that any developer choosing to design their own custom cryptographic solutions is likely to be introducing inherent vulnerabilities arising from the likelihood that the cryptography itself is not fit for purpose.
- *Custom key generation*. While many developers choose to use standardized cryptography, they often fail to appreciate the importance of strong key-generation processes. As we saw in Chapter 2, strong cryptography becomes weak cryptography if the underlying keys are in any way predictable. Weak key generation techniques thus present serious vulnerabilities.
- *Poor key management*. More generally, any weaknesses in key management (see Chapter 2) have the potential to lead to vulnerabilities. For example, poor protection of keys in storage (such as storing within software), weak key distribution processes and failures to handle efficient key revocation all represent vulnerabilities.
- *Inappropriate handling of sensitive parameters*. As well as keys, many cryptographic mechanisms involve inputs such as initial variables and random numbers. If these are not handled within an implementation sensitively then they can become a source of vulnerability. For example, an unpredictable initial variable that is replaced by a counter or a random number that is replaced by a password, are both vulnerabilities.

- *Failure to conduct critical actions*. Cryptography is carefully designed as a process involving critical actions which, if not conducted, potentially lead to vulnerabilities. An example is verification of public-key certificates (see Chapter 2). If one entity presents its public-key certificate but this is not fully verified by the recipient, then the recipient has no guarantees of who they are communicating with.

Buffer overflows

A *buffer overflow* occurs when a program puts more data into a region of temporary memory (a *buffer*) than it can handle, thus causing the computer system to overwrite to nearby memory. This might sound harmless, but buffer overflows can be cleverly designed to cause significant harm.

The main risk comes from the fact that buffer overflows can be used to push undesirable code into unintended areas of a computer system's memory. This undesirable code might be malware, which can then run and release its impact upon the computer system, or the undesirable code might simply disrupt code that was supposed to be running on the computer system. The consequences of a buffer overflow can thus be almost anything, from data corruption and system crashes to the execution of almost any type of malware.

Buffer overflows are amongst the oldest types of software vulnerability and remain a cause for serious concern due to the many ways in which they can arise. An example of a common source of buffer overflows is insufficient *bounds checking*, which involves checking whether a variable in a computer program lies within a predefined range.

Code injection

Code injection is an attack in which malicious code is inserted into a vulnerable application, causing it to execute unintended commands. This often arises because of an application improperly handling user input (for example, through previously discussed incomplete mediation). This then allows an attacker to insert their own instructions. A common class of code injection vulnerability is *SQL injection*, where attackers manipulate database queries that are managed using the *Structured Query Language* (SQL).

Code injection can lead to dire consequences such as data breaches, system compromise and loss of trust in a computer system. Preventing such attacks requires validating and sanitizing user input, using parameterized queries to separate code from data, and following best security practices such as the principle of least privilege (see Chapter 3). These measures help to ensure that malicious code cannot be executed by the application.

Cross-site request forgery

Cross-site request forgery (CSRF) allows attackers to fool users into executing unwanted actions on web applications in which they are already authenticated. These typically occur after a user has logged on to a site and then subsequently visits a malicious web page that sends requests to the legitimate site using the user's credentials. As the web browser includes the user's authentication cookies or tokens with the request, the web application assumes that the request is legitimate, potentially leading to unauthorized actions such as changing account settings, transferring funds or submitting forms without the user's consent.

To mitigate the risk of CSRF attacks, programmers can, for example, enforce *same site* cookie attributes, which restrict how cookies are sent alongside requests.

Cross-site scripting

Cross-site scripting (XSS) enables attackers to add harmful code to websites, which can impact users by stealing their data or taking control of parts of the site. This occurs when a web application accepts user input without proper validation or sanitization, enabling an attacker to embed harmful JavaScript code into the content served to unsuspecting users. When these users load the compromised web page, the malicious script executes in their browsers, potentially leading to various attacks such as stealing session cookies, redirecting users to phishing sites (see Chapter 7) or manipulating web content.

Insecure legacy functions

Programming languages tend not to be statically specified, but rather evolve over time. This means that certain functionality may eventually become obsolete or deprecated. This can arise for any reason, including the fact that more efficient or more secure functionality is brought in to replace the old code. However, the obsolete functionality often remains accessible and might continue to be used, leading to potential vulnerabilities.

An example is *gets()*, which is a legacy function in the C++ programming language. This poses a significant threat to software security due to an inherent design flaw that does not check whether an input fits within the allocated size of the relevant buffer. This can lead to a buffer overflow. Attackers can then intentionally provide oversized input to overwrite critical memory regions, such as the return address in a program's stack. Once this happens, attackers can inject malicious code and hijack the execution flow of the program.

Memory mismanagement

Mismanagement of memory in software can lead to security vulnerabilities by allowing unauthorized access to memory. One notable example is the *use-after-free* vulnerability, which occurs when a program continues to use a *pointer* (a variable that stores a memory address) after the memory it points to has been *deallocated* (the content that existed at that address no longer exists). This can result in accessing memory that may be reallocated for other purposes, potentially allowing an attacker to overwrite it with malicious instructions. Such manipulation can lead to arbitrary code execution, data corruption or program crashes, creating significant security risks.

Software and security misconfiguration

Misconfiguration of software and security features (due to errors or oversight) can leave a computer system vulnerable to many types of attack. System usage can then lead to inadvertently exposing sensitive information, providing unauthorized access or leaving core protection mechanisms disabled by mistake.

A good example is a misconfigured firewall (see Chapter 4). Recall that a firewall's primary function is to filter incoming and outgoing traffic based on predefined security rules. However, if misconfigured, a firewall could end up exposing the network to security risks. Examples include:

- *Brute forcing open ports.* Port 22 is the network port (see Chapter 4) for *Secure Shell* (SSH), which is a protocol that enables secure connection to remote devices. If port 22 is misconfigured so that it remains open to the entire internet without restriction, then an attacker can launch a brute force attack (for example a dictionary attack against a user password) to gain unauthorized access.
- *Incorrect rule prioritization.* Firewalls work by processing rules in a particular order. If the rules are set up inappropriately, critical protections can be bypassed. For example, an administrator may accidentally place a permissive rule (such as allowing all traffic) higher in the rule list, overriding more restrictive rules meant to secure specific services.
- *Disabled logging and monitoring.* Firewalls typically have logging features to monitor suspicious activities or breaches. If logging is disabled, security incidents may go unnoticed.
- *Default settings.* Many firewalls come with default configurations that are meant to be adjusted according to the organization's specific security needs. Leaving default settings in place can expose the system to known exploits. For example, if a firewall is left with the default administrative credentials (such as username and password

admin), attackers can easily guess such credentials and gain control over the firewall. This then allows them to modify firewall rules or disable security features.

- *Excessive permissions*. Firewalls should operate on the principle of least privilege, where only the necessary traffic is allowed and everything else is denied by default. If the firewall is configured to allow more permissions than necessary, this widens the potential attack surface.
- *Failure to segment networks properly*. As discussed in Chapter 4, firewalls can be used to enforce network segmentation, which isolates distinct parts of a network to limit the spread of an attack. If the firewall is not configured to properly segment the network, a breach in one area can easily spread across the entire network.

Race conditions

A *race condition* happens when the behaviour of a system depends on the timing of uncontrollable events, leading to potentially insecure outcomes. Specifically, more than one process or thread could attempt to access a shared resource (for example, memory) and the timing of their accesses enables one of the processes to bypass an access control.

For example, if a program checks whether a specific user can access a specific file, an attacker could manipulate the system between the access request and the action taking place. This is known as a *time-of-check, time-of-use* (TOCTOU) vulnerability and can result in unauthorized actions, data corruption or privilege escalation.

Secure programming and mitigation

Thus far in this chapter we have painted a bleak picture of the myriad things that can go wrong with the design, development and implementation of software. Now we begin consideration of how to engage in practices that reduce the risk of such problems arising in the first place. We start by discussing *secure programming*, which is the practice of creating software with security in mind, ensuring that applications using that software can resist and mitigate malicious attacks.

It is quite natural to design software from a constructive viewpoint, making sure that the software does the right things when the right things happen. When the wrong things happen, however, many software developers do not consider carefully enough how the system is likely to respond. In this section, we review a range of common good practice approaches, many of which involve consideration of how a system will handle unexpected situations.

Input validation and sanitization

Many of our previously discussed vulnerabilities arise from situations where computer programs encounter unexpected inputs and fail to respond in a safe way. *Input validation* is the practice of ensuring that the data input by users or external sources to a program is both correct and expected. Input validation involves checking that input data adheres to predefined rules or constraints before being processed. The purpose is to reject invalid or potentially malicious data before it enters the system and causes problems.

There are several different approaches to conducting input validation. These include:

- *Allowing lists (whitelisting)*. Using this approach, a software system only accepts known, approved input types and rejects all other inputs. This is considered a good approach from a security perspective because it involves explicitly stating what is acceptable and, if designed well, means that allowed data types have each been evaluated before being added to the list.
- *Denying lists (blacklisting)*. This is the opposite approach, where a software system rejects known, potentially harmful values and accepts everything else. This approach enables known issues to be countered but is less secure than whitelisting because there remains a risk that inputs relating to new, unknown issues could bypass the blacklist and lead to vulnerabilities.
- *Format validation and well-formedness checks*. This practice involves ensuring that a software system checks that an input matches the anticipated format. This might be, for example, the format of an email address, date or phone number. This reduces the risk that such inputs are replaced by malicious data.
- *Range validation*. Most numerical inputs are likely to fall within an expected range. Using this approach, a software system checks whether input values lie within an anticipated range (for example, an adult age input falls between 18 and 100). Inputs outside the expected range can either be rejected or flagged.
- *Length validation*. Many inputs to programs have anticipated or permitted minimum and/or maximum lengths. Using this approach a software system checks the length of an input to ensure that it does not fall below, or exceed, permitted lengths.

A complementary process to input validation is *input sanitization*, which is the cleaning or modifying of input data to make it safe for a software system to process. This involves, for example, removing harmful characters or data strings that might enable the injection of malicious code or otherwise disrupt the software's functionality.

Exception handling

Exception handling ensures that a software application responds to unexpected conditions in a controlled, secure and predictable manner. Such exceptions can arise in different ways, including from programming errors, inappropriate inputs or communication disruptions. Part of exception handling is managing any resulting error messages. If exceptions are not effectively handled, consequences can include exposition of sensitive system data, leaving software in an unstable state, or providing attackers with valuable information that enables them to exploit other vulnerabilities.

Examples of good practices related to exception handling include:

- *Generic error messaging*. By ensuring that only generic error messages are shown to users (for example: 'An error occurred, please try again later'), an application reduces the risk of revealing information that could later aid an attack. Detailed error logs that contain information relating to the specific problem that occurred should be restricted to authorized personnel responsible for system management.
- *Maintaining stability*. Exception handling should ensure that when unexpected issues occur, an application either recovers or safely terminates without compromising security. One approach is the use of *try-catch blocks*, which involve placing potentially problematic sections of code (ones where exceptions are anticipated) in an isolated *try block*, which is immediately followed by a *catch block* designed to safely manage the exception.
- *Input validation and sanitization*. The approaches we previously discussed for input validation and sanitization all help to manage exceptions that might arise from inappropriate inputs.

Safe memory management

Safe memory management is a critical aspect of secure programming, since poor memory handling can lead to vulnerabilities such as buffer overflows, memory leaks and use-after-free errors, which attackers can exploit. Just some of the many good practices include:

- *Use of an integrated development environment* (IDE). In recent years, it has become increasingly popular to write programs in simple code editors and run programs without inspecting them. Learning how to properly debug code is a crucial skill for the writing of reliable, safe and secure code. An IDE is a software application that provides tools to facilitate debugging, performance analysis and other auditing functionality.

- *Use of automatic memory management.* Where possible, programming languages should be used that automatically manage memory (for example, those that make use of *garbage collection* that frees up computer memory after it has been used). This can help reduce the risk of errors such as memory leaks and *dangling pointers* that point to areas of deallocated memory.
- *Avoidance of legacy functions.* The use of deprecated functions known to be insecure or unsafe when handling memory must be avoided.
- *Checking the result of memory allocation.* Whenever memory is allocated, it is essential to check whether the memory allocation was successful before using it.
- *Freeing deallocated memory.* Allocated memory should be deallocated when it is no longer needed. This prevents memory leaks or memory resources becoming exhausted.
- *Using safe memory management libraries.* Memory management libraries (see also discussion of secure libraries) help track memory leaks, bounds errors and other common issues.
- *Memory zeroing.* When dealing with sensitive data such as passwords or cryptographic keys, it is important to ensure that the memory storing the data is overwritten (for example, zeroed out) before it is freed. This helps ensure that sensitive data is not left lingering in memory after it has been used.
- *Using modern compilers and enabling security features.* Modern compilers support memory protection features such as stack canaries (see later). Enabling security features also adds an extra layer of protection against common memory-related vulnerabilities.

Avoiding unprotected secrets

One relatively straightforward practice that eliminates a range of vulnerabilities is to avoid storing secret values either within software or as outputs of software. This might seem an obvious suggestion, but it is surprising how often poor software development practices result in sensitive data such as passwords, security tokens, authentication identifiers and cryptographic keys being left unprotected (in the clear).

The most obvious mitigation is to ensure that appropriate cryptographic techniques such as encryption or hashing are used to avoid such data exposure. Further details of such mechanisms can be found in Chapter 2.

Use of secure libraries

As noted at the start of this chapter, software security is much better understood today than it was in the past. One part of this better understanding has been the recognition that certain aspects of software development, particularly relating to security, are so difficult to get right that it is better to use libraries of code that have been well scrutinized and deemed safe to deploy.

The result of this has been the establishment of well-tested, security-hardened, external code libraries that supply code performing common security functions such as cryptographic operations, input validation and memory management. These libraries are typically maintained by security experts, regularly updated to patch known issues, and designed to follow best practices, ensuring safer implementations of critical functionality compared to custom-built software. By using code from such libraries, developers significantly reduce the likelihood of introducing vulnerabilities.

Model checking

Model checking is the use of mathematics to prove or disprove the correctness of a software system's design or implementation against specified requirements, ensuring that it behaves as intended in all possible circumstances. Systematically checking all execution paths in this way helps to uncover issues that other testing processes might miss. This ensures that software behaves as expected under every condition, reducing the chances of rare but critical security flaws manifesting themselves.

Model checking is particularly useful for the development of safety-critical systems where software flaws could have extremely serious consequences, such as loss of life.

Code reviews

A secure programming practice that is relatively easy to implement is *code reviews*, where other programmers scrutinize code and deploy a peer review process that can help to verify the correctness and secure implementation of software. This use of 'many eyes' mitigates the risk of a lone developer making a mistake in isolation.

Code reviews can also help to foster a culture of shared responsibility for security amongst peer developers, prompting programmers to think critically about potential threats. Software developers can also exchange best practices and thus develop better secure programming techniques through an environment of mutual learning and support.

To an extent, placing developed code into open-source repositories or contributing to libraries also facilitates code review, since such code can (at least in theory) receive wide scrutiny.

Static and dynamic analysis

A range of general analysis techniques are available to help programmers evaluate the quality and behaviour of software during the development process. These can be very helpful for assessing issues relating to security. Analysis techniques often fall into two broad classes:

1 *Static analysis* involves examining code without executing it. This type of analysis is performed during the development stage, typically using automated tools to inspect the code for potential issues such as syntax errors or security vulnerabilities. Static analysis helps to ensure that the code follows best practices and adheres to relevant coding standards. Since it does not require running the program, static analysis is often the best way of catching errors early in development.
2 *Dynamic analysis* involves examining programs while they are running. This focuses on run-time behaviour, checking how the software performs under various conditions. It can be used for assessing, for example, memory usage and response times. Dynamic analysis is necessary for revealing issues that are only evident when the code is executed, such as memory leaks, race conditions and runtime exceptions. Dynamic analysis is also helpful for identifying bugs and vulnerabilities that relate to the environment within which the software will be run, or those that arise through interaction with different components during real-time execution.

Software security testing

It is good practice to test any type of software for core functionality, as well as security. It is important to ensure that programs behave as intended before deployment. Testing techniques range in scope, from testing a single component (*unit testing*) through to testing the integration of an entire system.

There are also specialist approaches to testing software specifically for security issues. These include:

- *Fuzz testing*. This involves providing unexpected, random or malformed inputs to a computer program to expose vulnerabilities and bugs that may lead to security issues.
- *Black box testing*. This involves the tester evaluating the functionality of a system without having knowledge of its internal workings, source code or architecture. The focus is thus on examining the input-output behaviour of the application, ensuring that it meets the required specifications and performs as expected.

Binary hardening

Binary hardening is the process of strengthening compiled binary executables, making them less vulnerable and more resistant to exploitation by attackers. This involves adding security mechanisms to binaries to prevent common attacks. Binary hardening can be applied either during the software compilation process or afterwards through additional tools. Some example techniques include:

- *Stack randomization*. This changes the location of memory addresses used by core components of a program (such as the stack, heap and libraries) each time the program is run. This makes it difficult for attackers to predict where specific code or data resides in memory, reducing the effectiveness of attacks such as buffer overflows.
- *Executable space protection*. This marks certain areas of memory, such as the stack and heap, as non-executable for certain conditions. This prevents code that resides in those regions from being executed.
- *Stack canaries*. These are specific values placed on the stack to detect and prevent buffer-overflow attacks. When a function is executed, a small, random value (the *canary*) is placed between the buffer and the control data (such as a return address). If the buffer overflow occurs, the canary will be overwritten and the program will detect this and terminate, preventing the attack.
- *Control flow integrity*. This ensures that the program's control flow (the order in which functions are executed) follows a legitimate path. This prevents attacks where an adversary tries to manipulate the execution flow.

Vulnerability management

While secure programming techniques help to reduce the risk of vulnerabilities, it is almost impossible to prevent vulnerabilities from existing. In this section we consider several topics that relate to the need to learn to live with vulnerabilities and minimize their impact.

Vulnerability lifecycle

It is worth being aware of the background lifecycle that most vulnerabilities go through:

1. *Discovery*. Every vulnerability begins life by being discovered. This might be by those studying systems, such as researchers, practitioners or programmers, or by attackers of systems seeking opportunities to exploit.
2. *Disclosure*. The next stage tends to be disclosure, whereby the wider community is informed about the discovery of a vulnerability. The ethical principle of *responsible disclosure* makes it a duty of parties discovering a vulnerability to first disclose it to relevant vendors (and perhaps national authorities), allowing time to

fix the vulnerability before disclosing the details. This process ensures that vulnerabilities can be addressed before malicious actors exploit them, minimizing the risk to users and organizations. Of course, an attacker who discovers a new vulnerability is unlikely to disclose it. The term *zero-day exploit* is sometimes used to describe an exploit that is based on a vulnerability that has been discovered but not disclosed by such an adversary.

3. *Patching*. Once disclosed, programmers often work to create a *patch*, which is a repair that mitigates (or removes) the vulnerability. The patch should then be widely disseminated.
4. *Patch implementation*. The patch should be implemented by those relying on the software impacted by the vulnerability.

The timings and tightness of the vulnerability lifecycle significantly determine the potential impact of a vulnerability. In an ideal world, vulnerabilities are discovered, disclosed, a patch is found and disseminated, and the patch is then rapidly implemented, before any damage is caused. However, the time between a vulnerability being discovered and a patch being implemented presents an opportunity for an attacker to exploit that vulnerability. Indeed, one of the biggest issues with vulnerability management is that many systems fail to implement patches long after a vulnerability has been disclosed and a patch disseminated.

Patch management

The sheer frequency and scale of vulnerability discoveries makes it very difficult for those running systems to keep up with the many vulnerability lifecycles that are in play. For this reason, it is extremely important to have good *patch management*, which is the systematic obtaining, testing and implementation of patches to vulnerabilities.

Patch management is part of the general process of managing security software updates. Some good practices for patch management include:

1. *Automate where possible*. Using automated patch management tools to regularly scan systems for necessary updates makes it easier to stay in control of patching. Required patches should then be implemented promptly. Automating as much of this process as possible reduces the risks of dangerous delays in patch implementation.
2. *Prioritize critical patches*. It is good practice to focus on applying security patches for critical vulnerabilities first, especially those actively being exploited in the wild. The previously discussed vulnerability classification schemes such as CVSS can help with such prioritization.

3 *Test before deployment.* Although patches represent solutions to potential problems, they still represent software that requires safe integration into an existing system. Patches should thus always be tested within a controlled environment before any wider implementation.
4 *Create a patching policy.* To ensure that patches are applied in a controlled and methodical way, a patch management policy should be established that outlines the processes involved for identifying, testing, approving and deploying patches. This policy should include timelines for patch deployment based on severity levels.
5 *Regularly monitoring.* It is crucial to stay informed about new vulnerabilities by using vulnerability scanning tools and by subscribing to security advisories. Doing so will help to prevent critical patches from being overlooked.
6 *Backup and recovery plans.* Before applying patches, it is important to ensure recent system backups are available. In the event a patch implementation results in issues, backups allow for quick system restoration.
7 *Schedule routine patch cycles.* Establishing a regular patching schedule for non-critical updates makes it easier to keep software up to date and secure, while minimizing disruption to normal business operations.

Vulnerability scanning

Vulnerability scanning is the process of using automated tools to identify potential security flaws in software, networks or systems by scanning for known vulnerabilities. These tools assess configurations, software versions and exposed services to detect issues such as outdated software, missing patches, misconfigurations or known exploits.

Vulnerability scans produce scan summaries that highlight areas of concern, allowing vulnerabilities to be addressed before attackers exploit them. Vulnerability scans provide a broad overview of potential issues and are useful for continuous background monitoring.

Penetration testing

While patch management and vulnerability scanning are ongoing processes that provide effective day-to-day vulnerability management, occasionally a more serious audit of the security of a system is merited.

Penetration testing (sometimes referred to as *ethical hacking*) involves skilled experts attempting to breach a system's defences using techniques similar to those that might be deployed by a malicious attacker. The goal of penetration testing is to identify vulnerabilities before real-world attackers can exploit them, thus strengthening the security of a system.

Penetration testing can be very useful for exposing any of the vulnerabilities discussed in this chapter, since penetration testers are trained to think like an adversary. Indeed, penetration testing is not just about software security since penetration testing can be used to assess the entire security infrastructure of an organization.

System hardening

More generally, the best approach to building systems that are secure against vulnerabilities is to apply good security practices with respect to all the various aspects of cybersecurity that we discuss in this book. With respect to computer systems themselves, the term *system hardening* is sometimes used to describe the process of securing a computer system or network by reducing its overall surface of vulnerability, which includes the software running on it.

System hardening is generally achieved by seeking to minimize the number of potential entry points that an attacker might have to a computer system. Examples of system-hardening processes include:

- removing unnecessary software and services
- patching and keeping systems up to date
- disabling unused ports and protocols (see Chapter 4)
- enforcing strong entity authentication mechanisms (see Chapter 3)
- limiting access and privileges (see Chapter 3)
- enforcing secure configurations
- installing and enabling security tools (see Chapters 3 and 4)
- encrypting sensitive database entries (see Chapter 2)
- enabling logging and monitoring (see Chapter 6)
- enabling backups and recovery processes (see Chapter 6)

Reverse engineering

Lastly, we discuss a technique that can occasionally help with vulnerability management. *Reverse engineering* is the process of analysing a system (software or hardware) to understand its design and functionality without access to the original source code or documentation.

Reverse engineering has both defensive and offensive implications in software security. In terms of defence, it can help ethical hackers and researchers discover flaws and create patches for vulnerabilities. Reverse engineering is a particularly useful technique for analysing and combating malware. However, attackers can also use reverse engineering to find and exploit vulnerabilities, or to bypass licence protections. Programmers sometimes obfuscate their code to protect it from this type of unauthorized analysis.

Secure software development

While secure programming techniques help to design specific pieces of software in a secure way, the wider processes around software development also play a significant role in software security. In this section we discuss a range of general software development issues that contribute to security of software. These are all based around an overarching principle that software should be *secure by design*, meaning that security should be embedded in systems from the outset, not as an afterthought (see also Chapter 1).

Software development models

Software development models apply a structured and systematic approach to building software, aiming to ensure efficiency and quality by guiding development through distinct stages such as requirements gathering, design, development, testing, deployment and maintenance. Different software development models provide various frameworks for managing the complexity of software development, balancing speed, quality and flexibility.

Adhering to a software development model also benefits security, since by including security requirements at an early stage, security can be built into software and evaluated throughout the development process. A range of different models exist, each reflecting different strategies for managing software development. These include the somewhat rigid *Waterfall* and *V* models, while the *Agile* and *Test-driven* development models offer greater flexibility and iterative improvement.

The *Microsoft security development lifecycle* (SDL) is a security-focused development framework that integrates security best practices into each phase of software development, aiming to reduce vulnerabilities and strengthen security throughout the development lifecycle. During design, threat modelling (discussed next) is performed and secure coding practices are enforced throughout development. Penetration tests and code reviews are conducted before deployment to catch potential risks at an early stage.

Threat modelling

Threat modelling is a systematic process to identify, assess and address potential security threats, vulnerabilities and risks in software systems. The primary goal of threat modelling is to anticipate and mitigate potential security issues before they can be exploited by malicious actors. Threat modelling helps security teams and programmers to better understand the attack surface of a system and proactively implement security measures to protect critical assets.

Common threat modelling frameworks include:

- *STRIDE*. This model's name arises from a mnemonic designed to remind development teams of the main attack vectors they face, namely: Spoofing, Tampering, Repudiation, Information disclosure, Denial of service and Elevation of privilege.
- *DREAD*. This is a quantitative risk assessment model that again uses a mnemonic to help prioritize threats according to core features, namely their potential Damage, Reproducibility, Exploitability, Affected users and Discoverability. This model helps development teams assign a numerical risk score to threats, enabling them to determine which ones to address ahead of others.
- *Attack trees*. These models represent potential attack paths that an adversary might take to compromise a system. Each branch represents a step in the attack, and the overall structure indicates how different attack methods relate to one another.

Secure software development design principles

A few design principles can be used to guide secure software development. Some are general software development principles that are particularly relevant to security, while others are security focused. Useful principles include:

- *Defence in depth*. This design principle is inherited from the military strategy of the same name. It reflects the fact that software tends to be deployed in hostile environments exposed to many attack vectors. The core idea behind defence in depth is that effective security is layered, with a secure system using many (independent) layers rather than relying on any single layer to provide adequate defence.
- *Loosely coupled, highly cohesive*. Loose coupling refers to a system having little or no knowledge of other separate components and thus being able to operate fairly independently. High cohesion refers to designing components that have a well-defined purpose and will work well with other sub-components of the wider system. The combination of these two design approaches aims to reduce system complexity and create systems that are robust, reliable, reusable, as well as easy to understand. In turn, such systems are likely to be simpler to modify and audit, and demand fewer resources, making them more straightforward to keep secure.
- *Minimum viable product*. This is an engineering paradigm that encourages controlled growth in complexity of a system's design in tandem with the developer's capacity. This controlled growth forces programmers to carefully consider which features are strictly necessary at any given time, and only implement those. This focused approach to software design means that more emphasis can be placed on keeping software as simple as possible, making security more manageable (at least in principle).

- *Saltzer and Schroder's principles.* These attempt to aid programmers who develop secure systems. Saltzer and Schroer proposed eight security design principles (many of which have been raised in our previous discussions and some of which were mentioned more broadly in Chapter 1). These are:
  - *Economy of mechanism.* A system should be as simple as possible, making vulnerabilities easier to discover and the software easier to maintain.
  - *Fail-safe defaults.* Unless explicitly authorized, access to resources should be denied by default.
  - *Complete mediation.* Every attempt to access resources must be intercepted and evaluated.
  - *Open design.* The strength of a protection mechanism should be independent of knowledge about it (the opposite principle to the much-maligned notion of *security by obscurity*, where security relies partly on hiding the detailed workings of a system – a dangerous approach since security becomes compromised if such details are subsequently discovered).
  - *Least privilege.* A program should only have access to the resources it strictly needs to perform a task.
  - *Least common mechanism.* Use of shared resources (program and data) should be minimized.
  - *Separation of privilege.* Critical tasks should be divided amongst multiple parties or processes to prevent a single point of failure. For example, in financial systems, the person who authorizes payments should not be the same person who processes them, to reduce the risk of fraud.
  - *Psychological acceptability.* The unwillingness of users to interact with security mechanisms should not be underestimated (see also Chapter 9).

Secure software development practices

Finally, various specialist practices can be used to aid the development of secure software. These include:

- *Containers.* These are lightweight, portable software units that encapsulate an application and its dependencies, enabling consistent deployment across different environments. Unlike traditional virtual machines (see Chapter 3), which create new instances of operating systems, containers share the host operating system's kernel while isolating the application processes. This architecture allows for rapid startup times and efficient resource utilization, aiding security.
- *Immutable operating systems.* These are designed with a core underlying principle that the system files and configurations cannot be modified after they

have been installed. This design approach promotes stability and security, since changes to the operating system are made through controlled updates or deployments rather than direct modifications. By preventing users or applications from altering the core system, immutable operating systems reduce the risk of configuration drift, unintended errors and vulnerabilities that arise from system modifications. These often use containers to enhance their functionality and application deployment.

- *Zero-trust architectures*. These follow a *zero-trust* security model that assumes no part of a network is automatically trusted. The main idea behind zero trust is to 'never trust, always verify'. Since we assume that any asset can be compromised, the safest approach is to assume that all assets have been compromised. Unlike traditional security models that rely on perimeter defences (such as firewalls) to protect internal networks, zero trust assumes that threats can come from either inside or outside the network, hence all users, devices and services must continuously prove their identity and confirm appropriate authorization before accessing resources. In practice this means, for example, that it is necessary to verify every access request, encrypt by default and continuously monitor for threats.

KEY POINTS

- Core to software security is identifying and managing vulnerabilities. These can arise in many ways and require continuous management.
- Exploits utilize vulnerabilities to attack computer systems, including through highly prevalent attack vectors such as malware.
- The diversity and proliferation of vulnerabilities means that vulnerability classification systems are important to aid recognition of likely impacts and to support vulnerability mitigation.
- A wide range of secure programming principles and practices exist that can be followed to reduce the likelihood of vulnerabilities arising in the first place.
- Good software development principles that aid security include layering security, keeping systems as simple as possible and minimizing points of trust.
- Defence against software vulnerabilities should be complemented by issues discussed elsewhere in this book, including computer system security, network security, security management and human factors.

EXERCISES

1 Envisage that you are a security engineer for a company, and you have been presented with the following vulnerabilities in a software system: a buffer overflow, missing encryption for sensitive data and weak access controls. Stating any assumptions you make about each of these, prioritize them based on potential impact and suggest an action plan to address them.

2 Create a high-level system hardening plan for a server that will host a critical application. Describe the steps you might take to secure the server, including vulnerability scanning, patch management and configuration changes.

3 A company's infrastructure is frequently attacked by brute force and phishing attacks. Discuss how adopting a zero-trust architecture and implementing defence in depth strategies could mitigate these attacks.

4 Explain how binary hardening techniques could prevent a buffer overflow attack from succeeding.

5 Read the following outlines and classify the type of vulnerability being exploited (for example, broken access controls, code injection, buffer overflow, etc.):

   a. A user sends input with SQL commands in a login form to access unauthorized data.

   b. An attacker provides specially crafted input that overruns the buffer and overwrites the return address in the stack.

   c. A web application allows users to include <script> tags in their comments, leading to malicious JavaScript running in other users' browsers.

   d. A file permission check is performed, but the file is modified right before it is used.

6 Study a real-world security breach (such as the Heartbleed bug). Identify and describe the vulnerability (or vulnerabilities) that were exploited, how the attack was carried out and what mitigation techniques could have prevented it.

7 Develop a patch management policy for a medium-sized organization. Include steps for identifying, prioritizing and applying patches, as well as procedures for handling emergency patches and minimizing downtime during patch deployments.

8 Search online for a common vulnerability code example. Study the code base and explain to a friend, family member or colleague what happens in the code to demonstrate that you have understood what the code does.

9 Find out what the *OWASP Top Ten* is, and relate the latest OWASP Top Ten to the ideas discussed in this chapter.

10 To what extent do you think deployment of a zero-trust architecture might render the use of conventional security technologies such as firewalls superfluous?

FURTHER READING

- Anderson, R (2020) *Security Engineering: A guide to building dependable distributed systems,* 3rd edn, Wiley
- Anley, C, Heasman, J, Litchfield, D and Mehta, N (2007) *The Shellcoder's Handbook: Discovering and exploiting security holes,* 2nd edn, Wiley
- Dowd, M, McDonald, J and Schuh, J (2006) *The Art of Software Security Assessment: Identifying and preventing software vulnerabilities,* Addison-Wesley
- Erickson, J (2008) *Hacking: The art of exploitation,* 2nd edn, No Starch Press
- Harper, A, Harris, S, Eagle, C and Ness, J (2018) *Gray Hat Hacking: The ethical hacker's handbook,* 5th edn, McGraw-Hill Education
- McGraw, G (2006) *Software Security: Building security in,* Addison-Wesley
- Shostack, A (2014) *Threat Modeling: Designing for security,* Wiley
- Stuttard, D and Pinto, M (2011) *The Web Application Hacker's Handbook: Finding and exploiting security flaws,* 2nd edn, Wiley
- Viega, J and McGraw, G (2001) *Building Secure Software: How to avoid security problems the right way,* Addison-Wesley

06 Cyber security management

Enabling and supporting organizational cyber security

This chapter provides an overview of cyber security management. We first outline what cyber security management comprises and why it is important, before discussing the crucial role of standards. We then take a closer look at different aspects of cyber security management, including risk management, the role of people, incident management and maintaining business continuity. We discuss regulatory and ethical aspects, before exploring how to meet responsibilities through audit and compliance. Finally, we present a short case study on managing a serious incident.

LEARNING OBJECTIVES

- How cyber security management supports organizations.
- Approaches to managing cyber security risk.
- Strategies for building cyber security resilience and responding to incidents.
- Compliance with legal and regulatory aspects of cyber security management.
- The role people play in cyber security management.
- Building and maintaining a cyber security management system.

What is cyber security management?

In this section we outline what we mean by cyber security management, and why it is crucial for the successful day-to-day operation of most organizations. This section will also discuss the core principles and concepts that cyber security management addresses.

The importance of cyber security management

Thus far we have been primarily concerned with mechanisms for providing cyber security. These provide a valuable toolkit of resources that an organization could call upon to secure its digital assets and activities. But which cyber security mechanisms should an organization deploy, and how? Perhaps most importantly, how should an organization approach these questions when, inevitably, the budget for supporting cyber security is limited? Such questions need to be tackled systematically, otherwise important issues may be missed or resources to address cyber security may be inefficiently deployed. Cyber security management is the process of systematically addressing the cyber security challenges that an organization faces. In doing so, cyber security management calls on the many different aspects of cyber security addressed throughout this book.

Cyber security management of an organization is the overseeing of four essential, interrelated, activities:

1. *Establishment of security policy*. An *organizational security policy* sets out, at a high level, what cyber security means to the organization in terms of the security principles that will be applied and where overall priorities should lie. A security policy needs to have the support of, and largely to be owned by, the senior management of the organization.
2. *Identification of digital assets*. Effective cyber security management can only be conducted if the organization is fully aware of what needs to be managed. This requires a thorough cataloguing of relevant assets, which include data, the software used to process data, and the hardware and physical environments within which data is processed. This includes identifying who within the organization has ownership of these assets.
3. *Understanding risks*. A vital aspect of cyber security management is to conduct comprehensive risk assessment, identifying the multitude of cyber-related risks that the organization faces concerning its assets, and evaluating those risks so that priorities can be established for addressing them. Such risks do not necessarily concern damage to assets themselves, but can apply more broadly to, for example, reputational loss or other consequences of compliance failure.
4. *Selection and deployment of controls*. Mindful of resource constraints, physical, technical and administrative controls should be selected and deployed to address the primary risks faced by the organization. This involves full consideration of how to make these controls effective, including establishment of any necessary procedures, guidance and staff training.

We will refer to the accumulation of all the processes and controls that an organization deploys to address cyber security management as a *cyber security management system*; however, this remains referred to commonly as an *information security management system*. Note that occasionally the term *cyber security governance* is used to distinguish activities relating to *what* an organization sets out to do concerning cyber security from *how* the organization attempts to achieve these goals. Establishing a cyber security policy would thus fall under cyber security governance, while deciding to deploy a firewall would fall under cyber security management. We choose not to make such a distinction in this chapter since most matters we consider have relevance to both.

Cyber security management principles

Cyber security management is complex and impacts the entire organization, so there is no 'one-size-fits-all' means of approaching it. Instead, we suggest some general principles (see also Chapter 1). In general, cyber security management should be:

- *Tailored*. No two organizations are the same, hence neither is their cyber security management. We will discuss standards for cyber security management that provide guidelines, but an organization's cyber security management needs to be tailored and grounded within the organization's culture and priorities.
- *Embedded by design*. Ideally, cyber security management should be part of the thinking when organizational processes are first being designed, not a later consideration. While not always possible, this is a principle worth aspiring to.
- *Dynamic*. Over time, organizational priorities change, digital assets evolve, and threats emerge and diminish. Cyber security management is thus a process of continuous adaptation and improvement.
- *Balanced*. Absolute security does not exist. Cyber security management involves a balancing act between issues such as reducing risks, controlling costs, managing competing priorities and anticipating future change. There is no perfect point of compromise and trade-offs must be kept constantly under review.
- *Communicated*. Cyber security management decisions needs to be communicated effectively to those impacted. Cyber security management is most impactful when communication portrays relevant cyber security practices as positive and enabling, not as barriers to daily activities.

Cyber security threats, risks and controls

Cyber security management can be thought of as managing controls in order to address risks arising from threats. As discussed in Chapter 1, a threat is something that could harm or disrupt an asset. ISO/IEC 27001 defines a threat as 'the potential cause of an unwanted incident, which can result in harm to a system or organization'.[1] Taylor et al describe a threat as 'something that may happen that might cause some undesirable consequence'. Both these definitions share several important features:

1 Threats can arise from a broad range of situations that all require cyber security management to consider. They could arise physically, virtually or could manifest themselves in a more conceptual way, such as through failure to meet legal obligations.
2 Threats can arise from either accidents or deliberate action.
3 Threats are not always guaranteed to arise. This is why, having identified a threat, the next task of cyber security management is to assess the risk it presents.
4 Threats must be realistic in the sense that they genuinely might arise. There is no point in expending significant cyber security management effort on addressing threats that are highly unlikely to manifest.

The management of risk is such an important part of cyber security management that we devote a later section to this subject. For now, it suffices to note that evaluation of a risk is a combination of an assessment of the likelihood of a threat arising that results in the risk, and an assessment of the possible impact. For example, a potential threat arises from an attacker discovering a password used to protect a database. The risk this presents is determined both by the likelihood of the password being discovered and the potential impact of unauthorized access to the database. Risk management is by no means an exact science and we will later examine different approaches.

Controls are measures put in place to modify (hopefully reduce!) or maintain risk. The precise controls adopted should only be selected after risk has been fully assessed. Controls can be physical, such as locating a key generation server in a locked room disconnected from the internet, technical, such as encrypting a database, or procedural, such as mandating strong password policies. These measures can also be preventative, such as delivering a security awareness campaign, or reactive, such as running an intrusion detection system to detect unauthorized activity on internal networks.

Cyber security management standards

In this section we consider the important role of standards in supporting cyber security management.[2] We focus on two of the most significant, the ISO/IEC 27000 and NIST cyber security frameworks.[3] We also introduce a lighter standard, Cyber Essentials, whose focus is small organizations.

Role of standards in cyber security management

As discussed in Chapter 1, standards play a vital role in supporting cyber security. In some areas such as cryptography (see Chapter 2) and network security (see Chapter 4), standards are fairly prescriptive. However, as we have argued, it is hard to be prescriptive about cyber security management. Cyber security management standards thus tend to focus on:

1. *Good practice.* Cyber security management standards represent the condensed wisdom of a wide community of expert practitioners, containing advice and recommendations, not all of which may be directly applicable to a specific organization.
2. *Matters of compliance.* Some cyber security management standards feature mandatory requirements against which an organization may be measured for compliance, enabling an organization to demonstrate a certain level of competence in its practices.

There are many standards, produced by numerous bodies, containing information relevant to cyber security management. We now discuss the two standards that are most influential worldwide for supporting cyber security management. The ISO/IEC 27000 framework is important because ISO/IEC 27001 can be certified against, creating a global benchmark for cyber security management. The NIST cyber security framework is primarily advisory, but is an influential source of guidance since NIST are highly respected and the standard is freely available.

The ISO/IEC 27000 security framework

The *ISO/IEC 27000 security framework* is a series of standards that support different aspects of cyber security management. ISO/IEC 27001 is the key standard in the series because it is the document against which a cyber security audit can be undertaken in order to measure compliance. ISO/IEC 27001 contains seven main clauses, each capturing a different component of cyber security management compliance:

1. *Organizational context.* This sets out the overall purpose and objectives of an organization's cyber security management. It needs to identify all legal and regulatory aspects, including contractual obligations. Importantly, the precise boundaries and scope of cyber security management need to be identified in order to clarify what the precise target of a compliance audit will be.
2. *Leadership.* This clarifies the direction in place to ensure that cyber security management meets its objectives. It includes the establishment of security policy

and how this will be communicated within the organization, and specification of relevant cyber security roles.

3 *Planning*. This outlines how the organization plans to integrate risk management activities and how the effectiveness of relevant actions will be evaluated. It includes outlining the approach taken to selecting security controls.

4 *Support*. This specifies the resources available for the establishment, implementation, maintenance and ongoing improvement of cyber security management. This includes the necessary documentation, staff training, and relevant internal and external communications.

5 *Operation*. This identifies the processes that will be followed to implement cyber security management. This includes how processes will be documented, how changes to processes will be managed and how any outsourced processes will be controlled.

6 *Performance evaluation*. This clarifies how the organization will evaluate the effectiveness of its cyber security management. This includes clarification of precisely which processes and controls will be monitored, how performance will be measured and how audits will be undertaken.

7 *Improvement*. This defines how cyber security management will be improved, particularly how any matters of non-conformance will be addressed. This includes how causes of non-conformities will be determined, how corrective actions will be reviewed and how any resulting changes will be managed.

While there is a clear logic to the approach adopted by ISO/IEC 27001, demonstrating compliance involves many actions, some quite complex. Fortunately there are many products out there which can help organizations engage with the process.

ISO/IEC 27002 is an extensive reference list that must be consulted as part of an ISO/IEC 27001 certification. It specifies a range of security controls, categorized either as organizational, people, physical or technological. Each control is associated with a number of attributes, including which security services it supports, and whether the control is preventative, detective or corrective. ISO/IEC 27002 includes guidance on the formulation of security policies, from top-level policy that outlines the security principles of the whole organization, down to specific policies addressing activities such as staff recruitment and server configuration.

The NIST cyber security framework

The NIST cyber security framework was designed for US critical infrastructure providers[4] but has subsequently been adopted by many organizations worldwide. Unlike ISO/IEC 27000, the NIST cyber security framework is freely available and does not provide a target against which compliance can be certified.

The NIST cyber security framework consists of three parts:

1 *Framework core*. This outlines general cyber security activities and desired outcomes that apply to any organizational sector. It presents guidelines and practices that can be applied across the different levels of an organization.
2 *Implementation tiers*. These describe the degree to which an organization's risk management practices exhibit the characteristics outlined in the core, ranging in maturity from partial (a rather informal approach) through to adaptive (embedded evaluation and continuous improvement).
3 *Framework profiles*. These enable an organization to tailor the NIST cyber security framework to its specific needs. The organization can create a current profile from a menu of categories, then establish a target profile capturing where it would like its cyber security management to be in the future. This process also supports prioritization and self-assessed measurements of progress towards target profiles.

The NIST framework core is organized in a very different way to ISO/IEC 27001, based around five different cyber security management functions:

1 *Identify*. This covers the activities required to develop an understanding of what the organization's cyber security management needs to address, including asset identification, information flow documentation, compiling inventories of hardware and software, establishing relevant policies and identifying threats.
2 *Protect*. This concerns the development and implementation of appropriate security controls, including access control, data protection, device protection, establishing backups, vulnerability management and user awareness training.
3 *Detect*. This addresses identification of undesirable cyber security events, including intrusion detection, maintenance of security event logs and establishing impact of events.
4 *Respond*. This relates to the aftermath of an undesirable event, including establishment, testing and update of response plans.
5 *Recover*. This deals with organizational resilience and recovery from undesirable events, including communication flows, maintenance of recovery plans and managing the organization's public relations.

Although structured differently, the issues covered by the ISO/IEC 27000 and NIST frameworks are similar, and both advocate a risk-based approach to cyber security management. One significant difference is that the NIST framework offers a means of assessing the progression of maturity towards a desired outcome. The highest (adaptive) implementation tier most closely resembles the requirements of ISO/IEC 27001. The two frameworks are thus quite complementary, since NIST facilitates a means of understanding progress, while ISO/IEC 27001 provides an eventual certification benchmark.

The NIST equivalent of ISO/IEC 27002 is NIST Special Publication 800-53, which provides a catalogue of security controls and advice on selection, organized into 20 separate categories.

Cyber Essentials

Both the ISO/IEC 27000 and NIST frameworks are daunting for smaller organizations to engage with, so the UK National Cyber Security Centre has established a more modest cyber security management standard, *Cyber Essentials*, designed to help such organizations engage in best practice. The scope of Cyber Essentials is a defined part of an organization's internet-connected infrastructure. Cyber Essentials is based around five basic technical controls, namely firewalls, secure configuration, security update management, user access control and malware protection. Organizations can either self-certify against common attacks or have an external auditor evaluate the organization's cyber security management to obtain a Cyber Essentials Plus certification. Schemes such as Cyber Essentials are nowhere close to being as rigorous as either ISO/IEC 27000 or NIST, but by focusing on fundamental controls they can still have a significant impact on organizational cyber security.

Risk management

Perhaps the most fundamental component of cyber security management is how an organization chooses to manage the cyber security risks it faces. In this section we clarify what risk management involves, then focus on how to assess risks and how to approach the treatment of risks.

Managing cyber security risks

All organizations face many potential threats but have limited resources to counter them. The ultimate objective of risk management is to navigate this issue in an informed way. It is essential that an organization adopts a formal approach to risk management.

A widely used model for risk management is that adopted by ISO/IEC 27005 and illustrated in Figure 6.1, whose main phases are:

- *Context establishment*. This has three components. The first is to clearly establish the scope of the assessment, identifying precisely which digital assets the

Figure 6.1 Risk management model

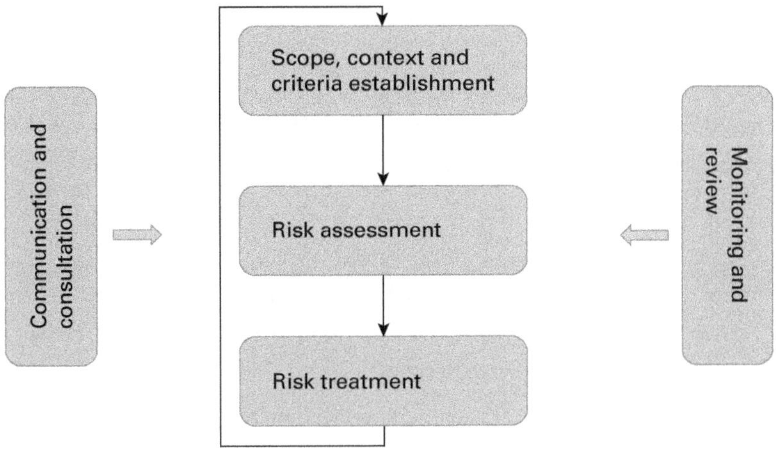

organization is trying to protect. Next, the environment within which the assets reside must be understood, including physical and jurisdictional aspects. Finally, the level of risk the organization is willing to tolerate should be clarified.

- *Risk assessment.*[5] This concerns the identification, quantification and prioritization of risks. Risk assessment involves risk identification,[6] which establishes which risks might occur, risk analysis, which estimates the magnitude of risks, and risk evaluation, which enables estimated risks to be compared with risk criteria in order to determine their significance. Risk assessment includes estimating costs and benefits, understanding legal requirements and determining stakeholder concerns.
- *Risk treatment.* This concerns the response to the assessment of risks. Options include applying security controls to reduce risks, accepting risks, avoiding risks by preventative actions and sharing risk.
- *Monitoring and review.* A risk management process is never complete and needs to be continuously reviewed and updated.
- *Communication and consultation.* Setting risk appetite, understanding impact and identifying risk treatments require engagement with a wide range of stakeholders. All relevant parties must have an opportunity to contribute to the risk management process.

Risk assessment

Since risk assessment lies at the heart of risk management, we expand on its three main components.

The purpose of risk identification is to determine what could happen to cause a security breach, and to gain insights into how, where and why this might happen. There are two well-established ways of performing risk identification:

1. *Event-based.* This considers risk sources by evaluating events and their possible consequences. These are often determined through consultations with senior management and other owners of risk, such as those responsible for specific business processes. This approach enables high-level critical risks to be identified without concentrating on precise assets.
2. *Asset-based.* This more granular approach concentrates on assets, and the threats and vulnerabilities applying to them. If all possible threats to an asset can be identified then, in theory, all risks to that asset can be identified.

There are two main approaches to risk analysis, although these are often combined:

1. *Qualitative.* This uses a descriptive scale of qualifying attributes (such as low, medium or high) to describe the magnitude of potential risk consequences and the likelihood that these might occur. This has the advantage of being relatively easy to apply and straightforward to communicate. The obvious disadvantage, however, is that assigning such attributes is subjective.
2. *Quantitative.* This uses a numerical scale for describing consequences and likelihoods. The effectiveness of a quantitative approach depends on the accuracy and validity of models used to compute the relevant values. Where data exists concerning historical incidents, these can form a basis for such computations.

One important component of both approaches is asset evaluation, which is often conducted by placing monetary values on both the replacement cost of a compromised asset and the business consequences of compromise.

Risk evaluation uses the results of risk analysis to enable decisions about future actions to be made, including establishing priorities for risk treatment based on estimated risk levels.

Risk treatment

On completion of risk assessment, an organization should compile a risk register listing relevant risks and an estimation of their gravity. The next task is to decide what to do about them. There are four general approaches:

1. *Risk modification.* This involves deploying security controls to reduce risk. For example, if a risk is unauthorized access to sensitive data, then risk modification might involve deploying encryption.

2 *Risk acceptance.* This involves taking no action and living with risk. Following the previous example, unauthorized access to non-sensitive data might be deemed of sufficiently low concern that the overhead of deploying encryption is deemed a greater cost than the value of data itself.

3 *Risk sharing.* This involves transferring risk, either internally or to a third party, for example by taking out a cyber insurance policy. Continuing our example, outsourcing data storage to a third-party cloud storage provider is an example of risk sharing, since a reputable provider should have contractual obligations to protect data under its control.

4 *Risk avoidance.* This involves eliminating risk. For example, if an organization stores legacy client data that is no longer of substantive value, the organization might choose to take this data offline in order to eliminate the risk of a remote attacker finding a means of compromising the data via the internet.

People and cyber security

In this section we consider how to engage and manage people in order to support the cyber security of an organization. We explain the importance of focusing on people as part of cyber security management. We then consider how to manage and train people. Next, we discuss the broader role of trust in cyber security management, before arguing why a people-centric view is essential for effective cyber security management.[7]

The need to focus on people

Cyber security management might seem to deal with abstract ideas such as threats, risks and controls, but, ultimately, it is about people. In one sense this is obvious, since cyber security management secures organizations, and those consist of people. The practices of those people thus naturally impact an organization's cyber security.

However, we should never lose track of the fact that organizations also serve people, and that contributing to organizations is a large of part of everyone's everyday lives. Cyber security management practices thus also impact people, such as by limiting actions of people or increasing complexity of tasks. Effective cyber security management thus requires balancing the cyber security needs of an organization with frictions arising from potentially undesirable consequences of security controls.

We need to take particular care when considering the relationship between cyber security management and people since human beings cannot be abstracted in the same way as, say, servers running a specific operating system. People have different personalities, skills, genders, backgrounds, ambitions, feelings, anxieties and risk appetites, amongst many other differences. Cyber security management framed around abstract notions of people, such as through the lens of homogenous concepts such as 'users', ignores this complexity.[8] For example, introducing two-factor authentication to strengthen authentication to a service might improve security for customers who have a mobile phone, but deny access to those who do not.

People are fundamental to managing cyber security, yet they are complex, multi-faceted and often conduct activities in unanticipated ways. Incorporating people into cyber security management involves embracing this diversity and supporting people to be secure rather than simply relying on security controls to prevent bad things from happening. We discuss human aspects in more detail in Chapter 9.

Managing employees

Before we look more broadly at strategies for involving people in cyber security management, we consider two aspects of cyber security management that relate specifically to employees.

The first relates to employment processes. While most cyber security management deals with employees, cyber security management also needs to consider managing people before they start at an organization and after they leave. There may be a need for cyber security management to engage with vetting processes for new employees, particularly for sensitive roles where security clearance might be required. Establishing contracts and terms of employment also sometimes involves cyber security management, since it may be appropriate to include information on non-disclosure agreements, legal responsibilities concerning handling of data, and actions to be taken if cyber security policies and procedures are not adhered to. Cyber security management also needs to engage with departure of employees from an organization, since this may involve revoking of credentials, return of equipment, and managing potential conflicts of interest relating to future work.

One of the biggest cyber security management challenges concerning people is how to communicate desired levels of awareness and good cyber security practice amongst employees. This is no easy task, since people tend to have a (valid) resistance to training activities that appear tangential to their roles. The simplest approach, essentially to focus on prohibited actions and behaviours, may not be the most constructive since it tends to engender a negative cyber security culture, presenting security as a barrier. Much more effective are approaches that encourage a positive cyber security culture,[9] such as focusing on permitted actions and behaviours, communicating how good cyber security practices contribute to organizational objectives, and cultivating an individual responsibility for actions rather than relying on enforcement. However cyber security awareness training is delivered, such as through a mix of acceptable use policies, e-learning and internal media campaigns, it should be selective and oriented towards meaningful engagement, rather than relying on abstract messaging (see also Chapter 9).

Building trust

Underlying many aspects of the relationship between people and cyber security management are notions of trust, which is not an easy concept to define, identify or measure. Broadly speaking, there are two relevant interpretations of trust:

1. *Social trust.* This focuses on the belief that in a world of uncertainty and incomplete information, based on prior experience, an event will unfold in similar ways on separate occasions. For example, an organization may seek to trust that an employee who accidentally clicks on a suspicious link will report the incident in line with policy. In turn, the employee may trust that the organization will respond in a supportive and ethical manner. Failures of trust on either side can be damaging, since an organization that loses trust in its employees may require further security controls that result in a spiral towards a negative cyber security culture, and employees who lose trust in their organization are more likely to lower their sense of responsibility and belonging, and perhaps become more likely to engage in breaches of policy.
2. *Technical trust.* This focuses on a belief that technical components of a system will function as anticipated. For example, a hardware security module is trusted to be impenetrable by any attacker of a system, or a password management system is trusted to enforce selection of passwords of sufficient complexity to render dictionary attacks impractical (see Chapter 3).

Security management involves balancing elements of both social and technical trust. An organization is far more likely to develop a positive cyber security culture if social trust is strong and employees trust the functions and effectiveness of the deployed technical controls. General cyber security management principles upon which to base the development of trust within an organization include:[10]

1. *Openness.* People are more likely to develop trust in cyber security management if they understand what cyber security controls are in place and why these are necessary.
2. *Competence.* A positive cyber security culture is more likely to emerge not just by having cyber security experts with the relevant skills, but also through co-construction of cyber security management with the people on which cyber security management relies.
3. *Integrity and predictability.* Trust is more likely to emerge when people feel confident that cyber security procedures are being followed, and that controls are applied consistently and with accountability, with deviations explained and justified.

4 *Regular communication*. Regular communications concerning matters relating to cyber security management are important. However, care must be taken not to overwhelm, which can lead to fatigue, or only to communicate following incidents, since this can contribute to a negative cyber security culture.

5 *Ethics*. Organizational ethics depend on context, but go beyond basic regulatory requirements. An organization committed to ethical values such as transparency and accountability is more likely to engender trust (we discuss this issue later).

Towards people-centric cyber security

Cyber security management might seem challenging enough without all the apparent complications we have just raised. However, taking a people-centric approach is vital if cyber security management is to be effective. Disastrous consequences await organizations that regard people as a cyber security problem needing to be solved, or ones whose staff regard cyber security management as an obstruction to effective working.

We suggest the following general approaches to engaging in people-centred cyber security management:

1 *People first*. Focus thinking on how people from a diversity of backgrounds will interact and respond to cyber security activities. Recognizing and understanding the different ways in which security controls affect a diversity of people will increase the effectiveness of cyber security management.

2 *Seek inclusion*. Involve as many people as possible in the design of cyber security management. This includes listening to people's cyber security experiences and understanding how they engage with relevant communications.

3 *Document and communicate*. Produce clear and accessible cyber security documentation, communicate this to staff, and establish a process for accommodating changes as they arise. This applies to all forms of messaging, from top-level organizational security policies down to documentation of specific procedures.

4 *Test*. Implement and rigorously test cyber security processes with people to make sure they are working. If necessary run pilots for new controls with small user groups and incorporate feedback into revisions.

5 *Monitor*. Continuously assess the effectiveness of cyber security controls, monitor impact on people and maintain data relating to reviews.

6 *Report*. Keep senior management updated on the effectiveness of cyber security management and its impact on people, advising how it aligns with organizational objectives, including those concerning staff welfare and matters of equality, diversity and inclusion.

In the end, people-centric cyber security is primarily about recognizing that cyber security management is as much a social as a technological process, and that the only way to make it work in practice is to be respectful of the many roles people play in ensuring effective organizational cyber security.

Incident management

No matter how well an organization manages its cyber security, undesirable events will inevitably occur. The key to handling incidents successfully is to be prepared. In this section we focus on cyber security incident management. We begin by considering what incident management involves. We then focus on preparing for incidents, responding to incidents and managing their aftermath.

Cyber security incidents

Informally, a cyber security *incident* is something significant and undesirable that impacts the cyber security of an organization. This could be an attempt to steal intellectual property, a ransomware attack, or a mass phishing attack against the staff. Cyber security incident management not only helps an organization to cope during and after an incident, but also concerns the need to learn from incidents. Note that incidents do not necessarily arise from cyber security management failure. If incidents occur at a rate less than the agreed level of residual risk, and are detected quickly and handled appropriately, cyber security management is probably working well.

A cyber security incident is one or multiple related cyber security events that could harm an organization's assets or compromise its operations. Two aspects of this notion are worthy of further comment:

1. *Incidents v events.* Note the distinction between incidents and events, with an incident possibly arising from multiple events. For example, an event could be detection of an external party scanning the organization's internal network. This is clearly undesirable, but nothing (yet) untoward has necessarily happened as a result of the scan. On the other hand, using the results of this scan to then break into the network and steal data is clearly more significant, and might be regarded as an incident.
2. *Incidents do not necessarily happen.* Something bad does not have to occur in order to be deemed an incident. Indeed, an ideal approach to incident management would be to anticipate all possible incidents in advance and establish plans to manage them so effectively that they never occur! Of course, in reality we can neither anticipate nor prevent every incident, so incident management is about dealing with incidents, whether or not they are anticipated or have eventuated.

There are five stages to incident management:

1 *Planning*. Perhaps the most important stage is preparation for incidents. If appropriate plans are in place then managing an incident should be easier and have better outcomes.
2 *Detection and reporting*. The earlier an incident is detected and reported, the better the response and recovery process should be.
3 *Assessment and decision-making*. When an incident occurs, acquiring reliable information and making the right decisions is critical to a successful outcome.
4 *Response*. Allocating responsibilities and having clear procedures to follow are key to coping with incidents.
5 *Learning*. Incidents provide opportunities for an organization to learn, not just from mistakes but also from successes.

Preparing for incidents

Incident management is about planning for failure. Since failure can arise from, and impact, almost any part of an organization, incident management needs to consider organizational, people, technological and physical aspects of incidents.

The first element of planning is to establish the conditions under which an incident will be declared. This begins with cyber security events which, as discussed earlier, are more granular and not always issues requiring action. Plans need to identify who will monitor cyber security events and how they will respond to them. Most importantly, under what circumstances will cyber security events be escalated and declared a cyber security incident?

The next element of planning is to clarify who will do what as part of the response process. Who will be in overall charge of managing the incident? Who else will have particular roles and responsibilities? This needs to be accompanied by plans for gathering and storing relevant data as the incident unfolds, some of which may need to be reported. Plans should also clarify how communications will be handled, keeping in mind legal obligations and reputation management.

Lastly, plans should set out the process for learning lessons from an incident. Who will oversee this, and how will they ensure that findings are communicated, implemented and reviewed in order to better prepare the organization for future incidents?

Incident management plans need to be regularly tested, whether in response to real incidents or not. Plans can be enacted in full or partially, either through live or simulated exercises. Regularly testing is important since the organizational environment changes over time. Lessons learned from incident management tests should be documented and incorporated into the continuous cycle of building organizational resilience.

Incident response

The first task of incident response is to detect incidents. This requires the collection of data relating to cyber security events, including from public threat feeds, sector-specific information-sharing partnerships and internal data generated from organizational monitoring systems. This type of data typically comes from a mix of proactive processes such as network scans, and reactive sources such as system failures. It is important to develop an understanding of which combinations of data elements are the most reliable indicators of cyber security incidents.

Those responsible for handling the response to an incident are often referred to collectively as an *incident response team* (IRT). The members of an IRT may be internal or external to the organization and are likely to hold a wide range of different specialist skills. Large organizations may have different IRTs responsible for different aspects of incident response. The focus of an IRT is to oversee three core phases of incident response:

1. *Containment*. This is to ensure that a reasonable level of organizational security is provided until sufficient information has been gathered to address vulnerabilities and damage resulting from the incident. Containment is about trying to stop the impact of the ongoing incident from increasing in severity. This phase often involves activities such as data gathering, isolating or shutting down services, and revoking privileges.
2. *Eradication*. This removes any elements relating to the negative aspects of the incident. This might include malware removal, reformatting or physical destruction of affected hardware, and re-authentication of users of an impacted system. Eradication may need to be phased, since it may take time for all relevant information relating to the incident to become known.
3. *Recovery*. This restores the organization to a state resembling the situation before the incident occurred. This might involve restoring from backups, changing passwords and applying system patches. Recovery is only an intermediate stage in progression beyond the incident – the ultimate aim is to improve the organizational cyber security once lessons from the incident have been fully absorbed.

Assessing incidents

There is no single recommended means of learning lessons from cyber security incidents since this process is context specific, but typical activities include changes to security controls, planning procedures, reporting mechanisms and undertaking a revised risk assessment. For serious incidents it may also involve amendments to organizational structure.

While documentation and reporting during an incident should provide valuable input into incident assessment, more informal approaches such as interviews with key staff may help to develop greater insights into what transpired and how to improve resilience. Indeed, investigation often exposes wider issues beyond those of the immediate incident. For example, identification of a misconfiguration relating to the incident might lead to a broader review of settings, which then exposes further misconfiguration issues.

Incident reporting

The issue of reporting cyber security incidents creates some natural tensions. No organization desires publicity about cyber security incidents since this could result in reputational damage. However, there are several reasons why reporting of certain types of incident is generally encouraged and seen as the best approach (particularly when the security of digital assets has actually been compromised):

1. *Reporting may be mandatory*. In some situations, reporting of some types of incident is mandatory. For example, certain categories of organization may be obliged to report security incidents to a relevant national authority. Also, in some jurisdictions, any breach relating to sensitive data must result in impacted data owners being notified.
2. *Enables others to take preventative action*. Reporting and subsequent publicizing of a cyber security incident enables other organizations to take preventative action, assuming that measures for addressing related vulnerabilities have been established.
3. *Contributes to wider threat landscape*. The more cyber security incidents that are reported, the better the related statistics become concerning the wider threat landscape. This bigger picture is regularly captured through a series of security breach reports issued by various national governments and international organizations.[11] These, in turn, improve the effectiveness of risk assessment processes. In this way, everyone benefits from a culture of incident reporting.
4. *Good ethical practice*. Reporting cyber security incidents is the right ethical approach, hence any organization routinely reporting will be seen to be engaging in ethical cyber security management, which should bring reputational benefits.

Organizations should develop a clear strategy for cyber security incident reporting, which establishes who to report incidents to, and under what conditions, as well as how to handle subsequent media queries and client messaging.

Cyber resilience and business continuity

We now consider the need to continuously develop cyber resilience as part of cyber security management. We will explore what cyber resilience means and how it aids business continuity at times of disruption. We also discuss how to nurture cyber resilience through a process of continuous improvement.

Cyber resilience

While cyber security is broadly about deploying processes and controls to prevent bad things from happening, in the last section we noted that undesirable events will still happen and we require strategies for managing them. The concept of *cyber resilience* complements these ideas by capturing a more holistic idea of how an organization might assess its ability to cope with the inevitability of cyber security incidents. Cyber resilience can loosely be defined as 'the ability of an organization to prepare, absorb, recover and adapt to adverse effects caused by cyber attacks, with the ultimate aim of continuously delivering the intended functions or services'.[12] There are two aspects of this definition that merit comment:

1. *Cyber resilience is inclusive but not well-defined.* Deploying cyber security controls and providing incident management, indeed wider cyber security management, are both only part of cyber resilience. However, cyber resilience is a somewhat intangible concept. It is likely that different people will hold different views on precisely what it means for an organization to be cyber resilient.
2. *Cyber resilience captures the unknowable.* While cyber security largely concerns concrete processes for addressing imagined vulnerabilities, the concept of cyber resilience includes aspects of cyber security that relate to the unknowable. For example, those implementing cyber security management may not have visibility of everything that happens in an organization, unanticipated attacks might be launched and the cyber security of an organization might depend on unknown components of a complex supply chain. Cyber resilience thus captures the organization's ability to cope with the unknowable, as well as the known.

Business continuity

The aim of cyber resilience is to enable an organization that has experienced a cyber security incident to continue with its core operations. This *business continuity* capability requires the development of specific plans and processes to enable organizational priorities to be maintained in times of disruption. While business continuity is clearly concerned with availability, other cyber security services are often just as important (i.e. just because an organization needs to keep a core service running during a cyber attack does not mean it should abandon confidentiality of customer data).

Developing a business continuity plan involves a sweeping assessment of the entire organization and its business processes, some of which may not involve digital components. With respect to cyber security, business continuity needs to include consideration of:

1 *Criticality of systems*. Some systems, networks and computing processes are more critical to the core operation of an organization than others. It is thus important to review the organization's digital services as part of a business continuity plan in order to establish a notion of priority. By doing so, critical systems can be identified in advance and focus can be placed both on their protection and, in the event of an incident that impacts them, restoration.
2 *Minimum service levels*. It is important to develop a clear understanding of what represents a minimum level of service in the event of an incident that disrupts the activities of an organization. Identifying day-to-day activities that can be suspended temporarily, for example staffing a user support desk, enables resource to be freed to deal with an unfolding emergency.
3 *Recovery timelines*. An estimate of the various timelines relating to recovery from an incident is an essential part of business continuity planning. These include predictions for how long it will take to recover data backups, restore core systems and undergo repair of critical infrastructure. It also includes the timing objectives both for establishment of a minimum level of service and for how long it is acceptable to operate on such a service level. Developing relevant timelines involves understanding interdependencies since, for example, it may be possible to rapidly restore a system on which a particular service runs, but that service may not be meaningfully restored until data on which it depends has also been recovered.

Business continuity planning deals with consideration of disruptive events. While all such events are problematic, most are not catastrophic. At the extreme end of business continuity, special consideration needs to be paid to disasters, which are exceptional events that are extremely unlikely to occur but would cause extensive disruption should they unfold. These include natural disasters such as fire and flooding, extended power outages, war and terrorism, and pandemics. However a disaster could also arise through failure of core system hardware or, indeed, through a large-scale, sustained cyber attack on an organization. A particular challenge for planning to recover from disasters is that, because they are unlikely to happen, there is normally (fortunately!) limited opportunity to experience them and subsequently refine relevant business continuity processes. This is one reason why many organizations choose to partially offset the risks of disasters through cyber insurance policies.

Aiming for continuous improvement

A common theme throughout our discussion of cyber security management has been the need for ongoing review in order to nurture continuous improvement. This is particularly true for both cyber resilience and business continuity, since both are impacted by all aspects of an organization and its activities. As with other aspects of cyber security management, this requires business continuity plans to be clearly documented, communicated, tested and reviewed. It is also advised that business continuity plans are formally audited on at least an annual basis.

Law, regulation and ethics

We now consider three important factors that guide the practice of cyber security management. We first consider legal obligations, then discuss how more specific regulatory compliance impacts cyber security management. Next, we assess how matters of ethics might impact cyber security management. Finally, we discuss the benefits of building on compliance and ethics to develop positive cyber security cultures.

Legal obligations

There are a wide range of different legal obligations, varying across jurisdictions, that organizations must follow when conducting cyber security.[13] We first consider obligations arising from state or international law, before considering corporate regulation. Organizations must keep in mind all legal and regulatory obligations when designing their cyber security management since failure to do so could result in investigations, fines and, in severe cases, imprisonment of responsible individuals.

There are several ways in which a state might impact cyber security management, including:

1. *Legislation*. States are responsible for producing legislation, which may include laws that impact the practice of cyber security. In many states, legislation is drafted through a process of consultation, so organizations may also wish to contribute to calls for evidence during the drafting of future legislation.
2. *Regulatory bodies*. States are normally responsible for setting up regulatory bodies to govern compliance with relevant regulations. For example, a state might set up a regulatory body to whom organizations are required to report data breaches.
3. *Criminal investigations*. States are responsible for criminal investigations. This might be required if an incident concerning cyber security involves a potential criminal act.

4 *Support services*. States often provide support services of relevance to cyber security, including development of professional bodies, information-sharing networks and development of national cyber security skills. In some states these are run through a national cyber security centre.

With respect to cyber security, it is rare for an organization to only need to focus on legal obligations to a single state. While many organizations are international by nature or conduct business internationally, even those with a primarily national focus may conduct operations and use data that is produced and shared across states, for example through cloud-based services. Further, connectedness to the internet means that threats to an organization based in one state can readily arise from actors based in different states.

This internationalization of cyber security has led to many issues concerning cross-border interactions and the applicability of various state laws to different aspects of organizational activities. These can be relatively straightforward to address with respect to issues concerning people, since where someone lives normally dictates the relevant jurisdiction for matters concerning contracts, payments and individual responsibilities. However, for issues concerning the storage, sharing and manipulation of data, jurisdictional relevance can be far more complex. This has led to arguments for greater cross-border cooperation between states, such as through the development of international data-sharing agreements.

Corporate regulation

Regulations are not always explicitly articulated in law and may also be produced by a regulatory body, for example to provide greater guidance on the law. This is sometimes described as *corporate regulation*, which may involve interacting with a regulator or even through more informal agreements and practices relevant to a specific sector.

One motivation for corporate regulation of particular relevance to cyber security is that laws often struggle to keep up with technological change. Laws typically take time to draft and are intended to be long-lasting, providing a broad foundation. Laws are thus often supplemented by sets of regulations and guidance that are not necessarily legally binding, but provide an interpretation of how to implement the law more precisely to the needs of the day. These are capable of changing far more often and facilitate the application of the law to new technologies and developing practices.

Corporate regulations are just as relevant to cyber security management as state laws. Failure to comply with corporate regulation can lead to any of the previously mentioned sanctions, but could also result in severe sector-specific implications such as expulsion from industry bodies or removal of critical certifications, both of which could potentially put an organization out of business.

The range of regulatory bodies that can be relevant to cyber security management is extensive, and both sector- and state-dependent. For example, in the UK there are separate regulators who deal with matters concerning data breaches, financial governance, customer protection, age verification and child protection, and intellectual property protection. It is thus essential that organizations familiarize themselves with which corporate regulations are likely to impact their activities, and seek relevant advice on how to comply with them.

Ethical issues

A healthy organization should regard compliance with relevant laws and regulation as guiding a minimum standard for cyber security management. Going beyond this baseline involves consideration of ethics, which represents the moral principles that shape behaviour. Of course, morals vary between individuals and organizations, and can sometimes conflict with regulations. Nonetheless, ethics offers a framework for thinking about good cyber security management practice. One way of thinking about cyber security ethics is to consider the following four components:

1. *Respect for people*. Embedding respect for people within an organization can be done in a number of ways, including giving people autonomy for decision making, trusting people, being transparent and enabling people to challenge practices. Such ideals sometimes run contrary to the instincts of those conducting cyber security management, who may be inclined to impose rules, assume people cannot be trusted, conduct covert activities such as staff monitoring and assume others do not understand enough to challenge cyber security practices.
2. *Beneficence*. This is the principle of securing the well-being of people and protecting them from harm. In one sense, cyber security management is all about protecting from harm, but many security practices involve exclusions or restrictions, some of which might cause inadvertent harm. The beneficence principle thus cautions that we should make every effort to understand the consequences of cyber security management decisions and seek to minimize negative impacts. It also encourages a constructive approach to cyber security, for example by avoiding negative consequences for staff who self-report breaches of policy.
3. *Justice*. This concerns fair treatment for all, including avoidance of discrimination against historically marginalized individuals or groups. This could impact decisions regarding deployment of particular security controls. For example, fingerprint-based biometric technologies (see Chapter 3) are often less effective for people from some ethnic backgrounds, anomaly detection tools might be biased against staff working atypical shifts and cyber security training might be ineffective for staff of certain personality types (see Chapter 9).

4 *Respect for law and the public interest.* Although ethics and the law do occasionally conflict, this principle extends our recent discussions on law and regulation to going beyond minimum requirements when deemed in the public interest to do so. For example, it may not be a legal requirement to disclose a vulnerability or reveal a cyber attack vector, but it might be deemed in the public interest to do so since this improves the overall cyber resilience of society.

Cyber security management involves a balancing of ethical values against organizational priorities and regulatory obligations. There are likely to be conflicts and unlikely to be absolutely correct solutions. As with all aspects of cyber security management, it is wise to document relevant discussions, monitor outcomes and regularly review decisions.

Positive cyber security cultures

Much of what we have discussed in this section, indeed chapter, is about how to develop a positive cyber security culture within an organization. By this we mean an organizational attitude towards cyber security that regards it as a necessary and valued facilitator of the organizational objectives, as well as a protector of the individual. There is no recipe for developing a positive cyber security culture, but there are three important components:

1 *Leadership.* Positive cyber security cultures do not emerge by chance. Leadership of the process is important, including the involvement of senior management and demonstrating by example. Where possible, members of the organization should be given ownership of relevant aspects of cyber security.

2 *Communications.* Clarity of communications about cyber security is essential, with a focus on positive behaviours rather than sanctions. Communications should be contextual and enable staff to comprehend the reasons for cyber security controls. Communications should also be two-way, enabling staff to contribute to cyber security management decisions.

3 *Training.* A positive cyber security culture involves the entire organization, not just select roles, and will most likely evolve if training is inclusive, based on positive messaging, and nurtures continuous improvement.

Audit and compliance

In the last section we discussed the need for legal and regulatory compliance. We will consider the means of compliance, particularly the process of conducting audits. We first discuss the concept of internal control and then consider different types of audit that are relevant to cyber security. We then briefly consider two particular types of audit, namely penetration testing and ISO/IEC 27001 compliance audits.

Internal control

The concept of *internal control* originates from the world of business accounting, but has wider relevance to cyber security management. Internal control is a process put in place by an organization's leadership to ensure that organizational objectives are met in terms of operational effectiveness and efficiency, reliability of reporting, and compliance with applicable laws and regulations. It provides a means of directing, monitoring and measuring the ways that resources are deployed, including those directed towards cyber security.

Our definition of internal control is based on that given in a key report by the Committee of Sponsoring Organizations of the Treadway Commission (COSO).[14] The COSO report was originally published in the early 1990s and forms a framework underpinning the influential US Sarbanes–Oxley requirements for financial reporting controls, as well as those of other laws and regulations. The COSO report identifies five components of internal control that each cut across the three target areas, including relevant principles to be applied. These components are:

1 *Control environment*. This sets the tone for internal control by establishing the management view. Relevant principles include the need to demonstrate organizational commitment to integrity and ethical values, provide board-level oversight over the development and performance of internal control, and to hold individuals accountable for their internal control responsibilities.

2 *Risk assessment*. This refers to the identification and analysis of relevant risks and using this as the basis for determining how risks should be managed. Relevant principles include the need to specify objectives with sufficient clarity to enable the identification and assessment of risks, identify and analyse risks to provide a basis for determining how these risks should be managed, and identify and assess changes that could significantly impact the system of internal control.

3 *Control activities*. These are the policies and procedures that help ensure management directives are carried out, including approvals and authorizations, reviews of operating performance and segregation of duties. Relevant principles include the need to select and develop control activities that contribute to reducing risks to acceptable levels, and to deploy control activities through policies that establish what is expected, as well as procedures that put these policies into action.

4 *Information and communication*. As we have discussed previously, pertinent information helps people carry out their responsibilities, while effective communication helps them understand their roles and responsibilities. Relevant principles include the need to obtain and use relevant quality information to support the functioning of internal control, internally communicate relevant information and communicate with external parties regarding matters affecting the functioning of internal control.

5 *Monitoring*. This involves assessing the quality and effectiveness of the internal control system's performance over time. Relevant principles include the need to perform ongoing evaluations to check whether the components of internal control are present and functioning, and evaluate and communicate internal control deficiencies in a timely manner to those parties responsible for taking corrective action, including senior management.

Audits

Much of this chapter has dealt with aspects of cyber security management relevant to supporting internal control. One aspect we have not discussed is monitoring, specifically through the process of audit. In general terms, an *audit* is the provision of independent assurance to stakeholders that the subject matter is free from significant misstatement. Note that while an audit should be independent, many organizations have internal auditing departments that can play this role.

There are several different types of audit that have relevance to cyber security management. These include:

1. *Financial audits*. All organizations need to undertake sweeping financial audits, which are designed to prevent fraud and ensure that financial integrity is maintained. Financial audits involve cyber security in a number of different ways, particularly with respect to assessment of risks and the wider processes governing the information technologies upon which financial data is maintained.
2. *Security audits*. These review the implementation and effectiveness of security controls in different ways. Some security audits might focus around specific business processes, while others might focus on information technology operations. We will shortly discuss in more detail a specific security audit category known as penetration testing. Security audits can be conducted in isolation or may form part of a wider financial audit.
3. *Compliance audits*. Another class of audits relate to compliance with specific standards or regulatory requirements. We will discuss one important example in more detail shortly.

Audits are valuable and often mandatory, but they should not be over-relied upon. Limitations of audits include their often narrow focus, the fact that they are typically conducted by humans and thus subject to error, and that they often engage in sampling rather than auditing everything. Most importantly, audits represent a snapshot in time rather than a continuous process. Audits should thus be seen as just one supporting part of a continuous monitoring process for cyber security management.

Penetration testing

Penetration testing (see also Chapter 5) is a special type of security audit which involves attempting to gain access to a system using the same tools as might be employed by attackers. Penetration testing is very widely used and can be an extremely effective tool to detect cyber security weaknesses.[15]

Today there are widely adopted standardized approaches to penetration testing. These involve deploying a variety of techniques, including network scans which seek configuration errors or unpatched software vulnerabilities, web application penetration tests which focus on detecting vulnerabilities in web-facing systems, setting up bogus wireless networks and social engineering aimed at fooling users into permitting access to critical systems (see Chapter 7).

It is possible to use internal penetration testing teams, but many organizations prefer to hire external experts to conduct this type of work. Indeed, hiring a variety of different external teams over time can be a very healthy approach to having an organization's systems thoroughly tested for vulnerabilities. Since penetration testing can potentially be disruptive, it is wise to deploy it selectively on high-value targets. Naturally, results of penetration tests need to be safeguarded and any serious weaknesses found need to be acted upon, particularly by identifying the root cause of vulnerabilities.

Auditing for ISO/IEC 27001 compliance

For cyber security management, one of the most important compliance audits relates to ISO/IEC 27001. As discussed in a previous section, one of the seven main clauses of ISO/IEC 27001 makes explicit requirements relating to audit. If an organization wishes to be certified as compliant with ISO/IEC 27001, then it is necessary for the cyber security management practices of the organization to be subject to an external audit by an accredited ISO/IEC 27001 certification body.

An ISO/IEC 27001 certification process involves a thorough audit of the entire cyber security management system. As a result, accredited certification bodies need themselves to be audited to verify a high standard of competence. Each country has its own process for approving ISO/IEC 27001 auditors and for conducting the compliance audit process. One approach to conducting a compliance audit is that followed by the British Standards Institution:

1. *Gap analysis.* The existing cyber security management system is examined and compared with the ISO/IEC 27001 requirements, with the goal of discovering any broad areas needing work before the formal assessment is performed.
2. *Formal assessment.* An auditor first checks that all the ISO/IEC 27001 specified procedures and controls have been implemented, allowing the client to rectify any

omissions. This includes both a documentation review and an investigation into whether the specified policies and procedures are being followed. Once any identified gaps have been addressed, the full set of procedures and controls are examined to ensure that they are working effectively.

3 *Issuing certificate.* A three-year certificate of compliance is issued. The auditor will visit regularly during the certificate lifetime to confirm that the organization remains compliant.

Of course, many organizations require other types of compliance audit, each of which has its own audit processes. For example, organizations handling card payments need to be audited against the Payment Card Industry, Data Security Standard (PCI DSS)[16] and smaller organizations based in the UK can choose to be audited for compliance against Cyber Essentials rather than ISO/IEC 27001.

REAL-WORLD EXAMPLE The Maersk Notpetya disaster

We close our discussion of cyber security management by discussing a short case study concerning a major cyber security incident that affected a large multinational organization. We will discuss what happened, why and what lessons concerning cyber security management can be derived from the events that unfolded.[17]

Background

Maersk is one of the world's largest container shipping companies, with close to 100,000 employees worldwide. In 2017, Maersk was a major victim of a piece of malware known as NotPetya. As a result of the attack, Maersk's operations were disrupted for several months. The financial and reputational losses for the company were huge, with some estimates placing the financial losses at well over $300 million.

NotPetya is a member of the Petya family of related malware. The original Petya, first publicly discovered in 2016, is a piece of ransomware (see Chapter 2) that targets Windows systems. If successful, Petya encrypts key parts of the file system on a victim computer's hard drive. It first overwrites the Windows bootloader software that runs when the computer starts up (see Chapter 3), and triggers a restart. When the computer restarts, the maliciously modified bootloader encrypts the master file table of the Windows file system which controls access to all files and folders on the system. Petya then displays a ransom message demanding payment in Bitcoin. While the original Petya ransomware propagated by means of infected email attachments, the much more dangerous NotPetya variant appeared in June 2017 and differs in some significant ways from Petya, including in its method of propagation. Notably, NotPetya is not strictly ransomware since its encryption is not reversible, and is purely destructive, suggesting that the NotPetya author's goal was not financial gain (such malware is often referred to as *wiper* malware).

NotPetya includes a vulnerability exploit known as EternalBlue, which appears to have been originally developed by the US National Security Agency, NSA, and became widely known as a result of hacker activity in April 2017. This exploits a Windows vulnerability for which Microsoft had released a patch in March 2017, one month before the exploit was made public. NotPetya combines password-harvesting tools with EternalBlue, enabling it to propagate rapidly between devices like a worm (see Chapter 5). This means that NotPetya has the capability of spreading very rapidly across corporate networks.

Although Maersk was one of the major victims of NotPetya, it seems it was not the intended target since a substantial body of evidence suggests NotPetya may have been a politically motivated cyber operation deployed by Russia against Ukraine.[18] However, whether or not it was an intended target, there is no doubt that the NotPetya attack was a major disaster for Maersk.

The Maersk attack

The following account of what happened during the Maersk NotPetya disaster is based on information widely reported on the internet, but cannot all be verified. However, even if there are some inaccuracies, the reported events present a compelling case for how a major incident might unfold.

The origin of the Maersk attack appears to lie with a single malware infection during an update of a company computer in the Black Sea port of Odessa, Ukraine. This computer ran a copy of a Ukrainian tax preparation application called M.E.Doc, which had been infected (probably by state actors) with NotPetya. Like most tax software, M.E.Doc is automatically updated frequently to cover changes in tax rules and regulations. From a security perspective, this is perfectly normal – a server communicates with a supplier to check if it has the latest version of the software and, if necessary, downloads an update. Such a routine activity should not normally generate alarm.

Maersk had in fact applied the necessary patches to remove the vulnerability exploited by EternalBlue around three months before the attack. However, as previously noted, NotPetya primarily uses harvested credentials to compromise a system and then uses internal Microsoft command tools to propagate. Two days before the attack, a Maersk domain administrator had logged onto a server compromised with the M.E.Doc update, leaving a cached domain administrator credential on that server. NotPetya obtained this credential, allowing the malware to infect thousands of global devices within a mere seven minutes.

As the infection spread, Maersk systems went down rapidly. At this point, Maersk took the decision to shut down every machine; however, the entire stored content of any device not shut down at the time of the infection was lost. As a result, around 49,000 laptops and computer devices were affected.

Maersk is an enormous global company with a complex network infrastructure. At the time, Maersk operated approximately 1,200 critical business applications, all of which were rendered inaccessible. Although some applications were still running on mainframes or other pieces of Linux-based hardware, hence not affected by NotPetya, the loss of so many Windows machines meant that these had no wider network to connect to. As a result, Maersk's entire network was completely destroyed. At the time of the attack it was believed that all 147 of Maersk's Microsoft Active Directory instances used to manage user accounts and privileges had been lost. This means that phone numbers were lost, since contact lists were synchronized with the inaccessible Microsoft Outlook. As a result, Maersk largely lost the ability to communicate globally.

Response to the Maersk attack

Initially, Maersk had no information about what was going on. A few hours after the attack, the company was still unsure about exactly what had happened. Gradually, through contact with suppliers and partners, it became evident that this incident was a major global issue, and not a targeted attack against Maersk.

By the morning of the next day, some progress had been made. Microsoft had been able to decrypt one device at the cost of 22,000 computing hours, although this was clearly not a solution that would scale, given the large number of devices that had been compromised. Fortunately, things were not quite as bad as initially believed. Due to a power cut in Lagos, the local Maersk office was offline at the time of the attack, so a full, unencrypted copy of Active Directory was still available. This facilitated the start of a slow recovery process.

Around two weeks after the attack, Maersk had restored its basic business technology. While this only enabled a reduced volume of operation, the company was at least up and running. Returning to full operations took another month, partly as a result of the difficulty of acquiring 17,000 new end-user devices. To supplement its small internal digital forensics team, Maersk partnered with the security consultancy Deloitte to help them through the response to the disaster. On the first day of the incident, five of Deloitte's forensic team were on site, but just three days later there were 180. Maersk also relied on its technology partners to help distribute data to local offices. Between days four and nine following the attack, new builds were created for clients and servers, which had to be delivered to almost 600 sites. Further, Active Directory needed to be restored across the global network, which took nine days. Faced with this huge logistical problem, Maersk sought the assistance of Deloitte, IBM and Microsoft to transmit the system build data to their own local offices that were nearest to Maersk's sites, and these builds were then picked up by local Maersk employees.

Transparency was a key feature of the Maersk response, something that won them praise afterwards. It also helped generate enough goodwill to get others to aid with Maersk's recovery efforts. Notably, customers were willing to lend key staff to help with the recovery operation. It is estimated that the recovery process alone cost Maersk around $30 million.

Lessons learned

As with every security incident, especially a security disaster on the scale of the Maersk attack, there are lessons to be learned. We identify several different lessons that apply both to Maersk and more widely:

1. *Cyber security management is relevant to everyone.* Perhaps the core problem that Maersk faced was that the company had not really absorbed how vital cyber security was to its core business operations. It had done the basics and had many cyber security controls in place, but it had not placed cyber security high enough up the organizational priorities. This deficiency arguably applied right across the maritime industry at the time of the attack, which is an industry for whom digitization has crept into place rather than ever being a focus of operations. This same criticism could be applied today to many other organizations around the world.

2. *The need for a systematic, holistic approach to cyber security management.* If Maersk had adopted the broad approach to cyber security management outlined in this chapter then it is much less likely that the incident involving NotPetya would have arisen. The Maersk attack originated from a security failure by just one supplier of software in just one of Maersk's regional offices. A large organization such as Maersk should govern its entire system and related dependencies, otherwise single points of weakness have potential to impact the entire organization. Maersk has subsequently adopted the NIST cyber security framework, implementing a risk-based approach to cyber security. Following best practice outlined earlier in this chapter, its defensive and recovery plans are now built around the most critical business processes.

3. *The need for incident (disaster) management.* It would appear that Maersk was caught completely unprepared for an incident of this magnitude. For example, it would seem evident that Maersk had simply never considered the risk of loss of all copies of Active Directory. Having multiple copies of the database worldwide indicates their awareness of the need to protect against accidental loss, but maintaining offline backup copies (which they did not do) would have offered protection against a concerted malware attack such as NotPetya – it is mere fortune that the Lagos office was temporarily off grid when the attack unfolded. Due to a lack of incident planning, Maersk's recovery from NotPetya was slow and very costly. Maersk has now taken steps to ensure it can recover more quickly from any future incidents of this type. While recovering some capabilities took nine days in 2017, Maersk's current goal is to be able to recover critical services within 24 hours.

4. *The risks presented by interdependencies.* The Maersk attack highlights the many interdependencies that concern cyber security management. Maersk's problem arose within the supply chain of the company, and most modern organizations have increasingly complex supply chains. The fact that Maersk is unlikely to have even been

an intended target also highlights contemporary interdependencies, where threats need to be considered that may not have any obvious relationship to the day-to-day business objectives of an organization.

5 *The benefits of an open approach to reporting.* A positive lesson to be learned from the Maersk incident is that by demonstrating an open approach to disaster response, Maersk won friends who were able to help them address some of their problems. Without the assistance of their partners, it would have taken Maersk much longer to recover.

KEY POINTS

- Cyber security management is ultimately about managing the cyber security-related risks faced by an organization.
- While cyber security management practice cannot be prescribed, its design can be informed by various cyber security management standard frameworks.
- Good cyber security management requires a sound understanding of an organization's structures, operations, business priorities and critical systems.
- People are core to delivering effective cyber security management.
- Cyber security management is a constant process, requiring continuous improvement.
- All aspects of cyber security management involve planning, documentation, communication and regular review.

EXERCISES

1 Some cyber security management standards are informative only, while others can be certified against. Compare the risks and benefits of both approaches to using standards to support cyber security management.

2 Cyber security management is based on an assessment of the risks faced by an organization. Compare different approaches that an organization could take to determining which risks it faces and how serious these different risks are.

3 Write a short essay that refutes the oft-made claim that *people are the weakest link* in an organization's management of its cyber security.

4 Cyber security incident management plans should be informed by lessons learned from past incidents. How should an organization facilitate the learning of such lessons through its cyber security management? You might want to use the case study of the Maersk attack as an example around which to frame part of your answer.
5 Cyber resilience is an abstract concept, but clearly something an organization should strive to establish. Propose your own definition of what it means for an organization to be cyber resilient, explaining how good cyber security management practices might support cyber resilience, but perhaps not be sufficient to guarantee it.
6 Provide some examples of situations concerning organizational cyber security management where ethical issues might conflict with legal and regulatory obligations, and where personal staff ethical issues might conflict with organizational ethical issues.
7 What does it mean for an organizational cyber security culture to be either positive or negative? Explain, by means of examples, how cyber security management practices can both create, and be impacted by, positive and negative organizational cyber security cultures.
8 Many organizations around the world seek certification of compliance against ISO/IEC 27001. Provide a summary of the ISO/IEC 27001 certification process in your home country. You might want to consider issues such as who conducts security audits, who approves auditors, the approximate cost of an audit, how long certification is valid for, what government advice exists concerning obtaining certification, etc.
9 It is important that cyber security management is provided on a continuous basis, not regarded as an isolated activity that is planned once and then implemented. Explain how the different aspects of cyber security management can realistically be conducted in a manner that could be regarded as continuous – you might want to analyse different aspects separately.
10 In this chapter we presented a case study of the NotPetya cyber attack on Maersk. Select a different well-publicized cyber security incident and present your own case study, following our structure of background, incident, response and lessons learned.

FURTHER READING

- BSI (2023) ISO/IEC 27001 Information Security resources, https://www.bsigroup.com/en-GB/iso-27001-information-security/Resources-for-ISO-27001/ (archived at https://perma.cc/B8U3-VXHM)
- Cichonski, P, Millar, T, Grance, T and Scarfone, K (2012) *Computer Security Incident Handling Guide, NIST Special Publication* 800-61 Revision 2
- National Cyber Security Centre (2023) About Cyber Essentials, https://www.ncsc.gov.uk/cyberessentials/overview (archived at https://perma.cc/VXF7-GQUY)
- NIST (2023) Cybersecurity Framework, https://www.nist.gov/cyberframework (archived at https://perma.cc/56E3-PCM9)
- Sutton, D (2022) *Cyber Security: The complete guide to cyber threats and protection*, 2nd edn, BCS, The Chartered Institute for IT
- von Solms, B and von Solms, R (2004) The 10 deadly sins of information security management, *Computers & Security*, 23, pp. 371–76
- Taylor, A, Alexander, D, Finch, A and Sutton, D (2020) *Information Security Management Principles*, 3rd edn, BCS Learning and Development
- Workman, M (2021) *Information Security Management*, 2nd edn, Jones & Bartlett Learning

Notes

1 Taylor, A, Alexander, D, Finch, A and Sutton, D (2020) *Information Security Management Principles*, 3rd edn, BCS Learning and Development

2 For an introduction to cyber security standards, see: Scarfone, K, Benigni, D and Grance, T (2009) Cyber security standards, in *Wiley Handbook of Science and Technology for Homeland Security*, Wiley, https://tsapps.nist.gov/publication/get_pdf.cfm?pub_id=152153 (archived at https://perma.cc/P5D3-FSBH)

3 For a comparison of these two approaches, see for example: Leal, R (2014) NIST Cybersecurity Framework or ISO 27001 – Which is the better choice for your company? https://advisera.com/27001academy/blog/2014/02/24/which-one-to-go-with-cybersecurity-framework-or-iso-27001/ (archived at https://perma.cc/X4Q9-PAEX)

4 For a list of critical sectors defined by the US Cybersecurity and Infrastructure Security Agency, see: https://www.cisa.gov/topics/critical-infrastructure-security-and-resilience/critical-infrastructure-sectors (archived at https://perma.cc/H69M-RWSR)

5 For further information see, for example: ISACA (2010) Performing a security risk assessment, https://www.isaca.org/resources/isaca-journal/past-issues/2010/performing-a-security-risk-assessment (archived at https://perma.cc/ADA7-3Z2R)

6 An overview of risk identification can be found at: SafetyCulture (2023) Why risk identification is important for your business, https://safetyculture.com/topics/risk-identification/ (archived at https://perma.cc/3FUU-9C7D)

7 An interesting article challenging conventional perspectives on the role of people in cyber security is: Sebastian, G and Kolluru, P (2021) Rethinking the weakest link in the cybersecurity chain, *ISACA Journal*, 2021:5, https://www.isaca.org/resources/isaca-journal/issues/2021/volume-5/rethinking-the-weakest-link-in-the-cybersecurity-chain (archived at https://perma.cc/H3SD-8YSX)

8 For a fascinating example of how reality on the ground often challenges abstract views of the role people play in cyber security, see: Coles-Kemp, L and Hansen, R R (2017) Walking the line: The everyday security ties that bind, *Human Aspects of Information Security, Privacy and Trust, Lecture Notes in Computer Science*, 10292, 464–80

9 An informative case study of an organization using an awareness campaign to foster a positive cyber security culture is: Blum, D, Sherry, D and Schaufler, T (2020) Case Study: Transforming Princeton's security culture through awareness, *ISACA Journal*, 2021:1, https://www.isaca.org/resources/isaca-journal/issues/2021/volume-1/case-study-transforming-princetons-security-culture-through-awareness (archived at https://perma.cc/CW2B-R3X7)

10 See: Flowerday, S and von Solms, R (2006) Trust: An element of information security, in Fischer-Hübner, S, Rannenberg, K, Yngström, L and Lindskog, S (eds) *Security and Privacy in Dynamic Environments*, Springer, pp. 87–98

11 For example, the UK Government publishes an annual Cyber Security Breaches Survey: Gov.UK (2023) Cyber Security Breaches Survey, https://www.gov.uk/government/collections/cyber-security-breaches-survey (archived at https://perma.cc/UY4F-GYL7)

12 See: Dupont, B, Shearing, C D, Bernier, M and Leukfeldt, R (2022) The tensions of cyber-resilience: From sensemaking to practice, *SSRN*, http://dx.doi.org/10.2139/ssrn.4224537 (archived at https://perma.cc/MV3E-C8LD)

13 See: Carolina, R (2021) Law and Regulation Knowledge Area, Version 1.0.2, https://www.cybok.org/knowledgebase1_1/ (archived at https://perma.cc/9GAK-CUDC)

14 For access to the latest version of the report and other guidance documents, see: https://www.coso.org/guidance-on-ic (archived at https://perma.cc/67C3-MNCS)

15 For more details, see: National Cyber Security Centre (2023) Penetration Testing, https://www.ncsc.gov.uk/guidance/penetration-testing (archived at https://perma.cc/7KAZ-2QJP)

16 For more information about the governing body, the Payment Card Industry Security Standards Council, see: https://www.pcisecuritystandards.org/ (archived at https://perma.cc/C54X-D8PV)

17 All reported information about the Maersk incident is taken from public domain information. A good starting point is: McQuade, M (2018) The untold story of NotPetya, the most devastating cyber attack in history, Wired, 22 August, https://www.wired.com/story/notpetya-cyberattack-ukraine-russia-code-crashed-the-world/ (archived at https://perma.cc/M4Z7-KQ7R)

18 See, for example: Kovacs, E (2018) U.S., Canada, Australia attribute NotPetya attack to Russia, Security Week, 16 February, https://www.securityweek.com/us-canada-australia-attribute-notpetya-attack-russia/ (archived at https://perma.cc/8Y36-CGTD)

07 Cybercrime

Threats presented by malicious actors

In this chapter we discuss the broad topic of cybercrime, since this is the source of many (though not all) threats to digital environments. We first explore how cybercrime is defined and categorized. We then consider the profiling of cybercriminals and how their activities have evolved over time. We take a specific look at social engineering, since this is a critical component of many cybercrimes, and then discuss how cybercrime relates to cyber war and cyber terrorism. Finally, we reflect on some of the most challenging aspects of cybercrime and how society responds to it.

LEARNING OBJECTIVES

- Defining cybercrime and categorizing cybercriminal activity.
- Profiling and classifying cybercriminals.
- How cybercrime and related business models have evolved.
- Explaining the critical role of social engineering in cybercrime.
- Clarifying the relationship between cybercrime, and cyber war and terrorism.
- Outlining the challenges involved in effectively combating cybercrime.

Introducing cybercrime

In this section we introduce cybercrime. We begin by considering how to define cybercrime and how it differs from more traditional forms of crime. We then consider different perspectives on cybercrime. Finally, we comment on some of the legal aspects of cybercrime.

Defining cybercrime

Cybercrime is a hard concept to define. It is a term frequently encountered in the media. Incidents associated with cybercrime have impacts that range from the personal to the organizational, and sometimes to a global scale. So, while we all have our own concept, and perhaps personal experience, of cybercrime, how should we formally define it? While there is no widely accepted definition of cybercrime, we will now attempt to formulate one.

First, what is a crime? The Oxford English Dictionary defines a crime as 'an action or omission which constitutes an offence and is punishable by law'. This suggests that a definition of cybercrime will need to be equally broad and also have a legal component.

For inspiration, here are some definitions of cybercrime from the related literature:

- 'The occurrence of a harmful behaviour that is somehow related to a computer.'[1]
- 'Computer-mediated activities which are either illegal or considered illicit by certain parties and which can be conducted through global electronic networks.'[2]
- 'Any crime that is facilitated or committed using a computer, network, or hardware device.'[3]
- 'A broad range of different criminal activities where computers and information systems are involved either as a primary tool or as a primary target.'[4]

An important point emerging from these definitions is that digital technology can be both the means and/or the target of cybercrime.

We thus propose a definition that is both a synthesis and an extension of these previous definitions, and is loosely based on one adopted by the United Nations Office on Drugs and Crime. Namely, a *cybercrime* is an act punishable by law, which utilizes digital technology either to:

1. target data, systems, networks, technology or humans, or
2. facilitate the commission of further offences.

Significant features of cybercrime

Having defined cybercrime, it is now worth revisiting the features of the digital environment first identified in Chapter 1 to consider their potential implications for cybercrime and how it relates to traditional (non-cyber) crime:

- *Distance.* In contrast to many traditional crimes, there are no physical or geographical boundaries to cybercrime, which can be conducted from anywhere in the world against targets anywhere else in the world.
- *Anonymity.* Cybercrime benefits from the relative anonymity of digital environments, thus encouraging certain types of criminal behaviour and presenting challenges to law enforcement that do not exist to the same extent for traditional crime.

- *Costs.* Cybercrime is often cheaper and easier to conduct than traditional crime.
- *Scale.* Cybercrime can be conducted at greater speed and scale than traditional crime. Further, cybercriminals can develop, share and enhance automated tools for conducting their activities.
- *Complexity.* The lack of understanding of the digital environment by users creates numerous opportunities for cybercriminals to exploit that are not so readily available in non-digital environments.

Perspectives on cybercrime

Cybercrime can be considered from a range of different perspectives, only some of which will be touched on in this chapter. These perspectives include:

- *Technological.* Cybercriminals rely on a constantly evolving set of technical tools, including malware and exploits of vulnerabilities in operating systems. Consideration of relevant technology is discussed elsewhere in this book, particularly in Chapters 3, 4 and 5.
- *Victims.* An understanding of cybercrime can be developed from the perspective of victims. This can help develop defences, particularly with respect to security behaviour, which is something we discuss further in Chapter 9.
- *Perpetrators.* Perhaps the most informative perspective comes from the study of cybercrime perpetrators, their motivations and the ways they operate. We explore this further in this chapter.
- *Enforcement.* Cybercrime can be considered from the perspective of those seeking to prevent it or respond to it. These include police, national agencies and private companies engaging in cyber threat intelligence. We discuss some of the related challenges of enforcement later in this chapter.

The legal component

Recall that our definition of cybercrime requires it to be 'punishable by law'. This means that a cybercrime is an act that violates explicit moral and social rules that have been legally codified. Of course, such legal codification varies across the world. Throughout this chapter we will refer occasionally to legislation and public bodies from the UK and the European Union in order to provide definitions or to analyse specific cases. These are merely examples and we strongly encourage readers to map such references to the law and legal infrastructure in other regions of interest to them.

As an example of relevant legislation that can be used to specify cybercrimes, consider the UK Computer Misuse Act (1990), which includes identification of the following offences:

- **Unauthorized access to computer material.** This indicates that it is an offence to access a system or information in an unauthorized manner, even if no further action is taken.
- **Unauthorized access with intent to commit or facilitate commission of further offences.** This is included since most unauthorized offences lead to further, more serious offences, such as fraud.
- **Unauthorized acts with intent to impair, or with recklessness as to impairing, operation of computers, etc.** This captures unauthorized modification (breaches of data integrity), including denial-of-service attacks (see Chapter 4) or any other direct or indirect disruptive action.
- **Unauthorized acts causing, or creating risk of, serious damage.** This is intended to capture attacks on critical infrastructure, the environment, the economy and anything impacting overall human welfare.
- **Making, supplying or obtaining articles for use in offences under the previous sections.** This makes it an offence to make, adapt, supply or offer to supply any article (such as a tool, software, etc.) intended to commit any of the aforementioned offences.

Note that the moral and social rules that govern a society tend to evolve over time, often very slowly. This means that an act that is not unlawful at some point in time might later become punishable as the law evolves. The legal aspects of cybercrime are thus particularly challenging because digital technology, and therefore potential cybercriminal activity, tends to evolve much faster than the law.

One common legal response to this is to ensure that descriptions of technology are deliberately high-level and non-specific, so that they are able to capture new types of cybercrime. A representative example of such deliberate abstraction is the use of the term 'article' in the UK Computer Misuse Act to indicate 'any program or data held in electronic form'.

Categorizing cybercrime

As previously observed, the range of criminal activities that could be deemed cybercrimes is very large. In order to obtain a general picture of the cybercrime landscape, in this section we categorize cybercrimes. Note that this categorization is neither definitive nor comprehensive.

Two important classes of cybercrimes

Recalling our previous attempt to define cybercrime, the use of digital technology to both commit and facilitate crime presents a useful, top-level categorization of cybercrime into two important classes:

1. *Cyber-dependent crimes* are crimes that can be committed only through the use of digital technology. In other words, digital technology is both the means of committing the crime and also the target of the crime. Such crimes typically involve disrupting, modifying, copying or misusing data or digital services. Cyber-dependent crimes rely entirely on the relevant digital technology and could not occur without them.
2. *Cyber-enabled crimes* are traditional crimes that are conducted using digital technology, which typically increases their reach and scale. Some of the main traditional crimes that are particularly pernicious when cyber-enabled relate to fraud, intellectual property and personal attacks. In cyber-enabled crime, digital technology provides the means to conduct a crime that could be conducted traditionally, and whose ultimate goal is normally not digital (commonly financial gain).

In general, cyber-enabled crime represents a broader class of crimes. While some of the most serious traditional crimes, such as extortion and sexual abuse, can also be cyber-enabled crimes, we should not underestimate the damage that can be caused by cyber-dependent crimes, especially in a world where we rely more and more on digital technology and services.

In the next sections we identify some of the most common types of cyber-dependent and cyber-enabled crimes.

Cyber-dependent crimes

The following contains a list of terms relating to malicious digital activities that are often associated with cybercrime. Note that conducting these activities is regarded in many legal jurisdictions as being a cyber-dependent crime in itself. However, these activities can often also provide the means to conduct a later cyber-enabled crime:

- *Hacking/cracking*. The concept of hacking tends to be very loosely associated with unauthorized access or use of digital technology, typically by exploiting vulnerabilities or bypassing security controls. Although the initial meaning of hacking was not explicitly malicious, today it tends to be considered a crime on its own. Cracking is a term sometimes used in relation to openly malicious hacking.
- *Deploying malware*. As discussed in Chapter 5, malware is software that can spread between systems with the malicious intention to interfere with operations. Typical examples of malware are viruses, worms, trojans and spyware. Malware can be deployed to overcome almost any of the core cyber security services discussed in Chapter 1, including data confidentiality (through data compromise), data integrity (through data modification) and availability.

- *Deploying ransomware.* As mentioned in Chapter 2, ransomware is a particularly prevalent form of malware that denies access to data by encrypting it. Ransomware attacks themselves are cyber-dependent crimes, but they are typically followed up by a demand for a ransom to release the data, which is a cyber-enabled crime.
- *Denial-of-service (DoS) attacks.* These attacks aim to disrupt the availability of digital services by directing excessive traffic or requests to systems, networks or servers. As discussed in Chapter 4, distributed denial-of-service (DDoS) attacks are particularly serious DoS attacks, where the disruption is coordinated through a botnet of malware-infected devices.

Content crime

Content crime refers to cyber-enabled crimes relating to possession, distribution or production of digital materials and communications that exceed the limits of what is considered legally acceptable within a society. Note that such limits might not always be clear, and are often subjective. Examples of such content include:

- *Indecent or obscene images.* The term obscene typically refers to images of adults (generally, from 18 years old), and more broadly indicates images with the tendency to deprave and corrupt individuals who are exposed to them. The term indecent generally refers to depicted individuals younger than 18 years old. Note that such images do not necessarily refer to photographic content and may also apply to, for example, cartoon materials representing child-like figures engaging in sexual acts.
- *Hate speech.* This is typically used to describe malicious communications generally targeting people with protected characteristics. For example, one definition describes hate speech as 'any form of speech or representation that depicts individuals or groups in a derogatory, intentionally offensive, manner with reference to their race, ethnicity, gender, religion, sexual orientation, or physical or mental disability in such a manner as to promote or provoke hatred'.[5]
- *Trolling.* This is malicious online communication, such as the use of abusive, explicit and hurtful comments on social media, typically targeting a specific individual. Depending on the volume and the nature of the communications, trolling can constitute coordinated harassment, which we discuss later.
- *Misinformation and disinformation.* This is the unintentional spreading of inaccurate information (*misinformation*) and the deliberate distribution of false or misleading information (*disinformation*), which are both particularly commonly conducted using social media.
- *Harmful content.* This is digital content that promotes or glorifies acts that may not be illegal in themselves, but are extremely dangerous, such as attempts of suicide, self-harm or eating disorders.

Interpersonal crime

Broadly speaking, interpersonal cybercrime refers to cyber-enabled crimes relating to unwanted activities and behaviours with the intention to violate a victim's dignity or to shape an environment for the victim that is intimidating, hostile, degrading, humiliating and/or offensive. Many interpersonal crimes also involve the manifestation of content crime. Examples of interpersonal crimes include:

- *Child sexual abuse and exploitation.* This refers to crimes enabled through materials that constitute a representation, by whatever means, of a child engaged in real or simulated explicit sexual activities or representation of the sexual parts of a child for primarily sexual purposes. This includes the online distribution of child sexual abuse and exploitation material (CSAEM), sexual coercion and extortion of minors for the creation of CSAEM, and online solicitation of children for sexual purposes.
- *Grooming.* The United Nations Office on Drugs and Crime defines online grooming as the enticement of children or solicitation of children for sexual purposes. It usually includes methods such as an adult 'befriending' a child with an intention of later sexually abusing them.
- *Image-based sexual abuse.* This refers to sharing sexually explicit media publicly, without the consent of one of the involved individuals (sometimes referred to as revenge pornography). It is usually observed in relation to a breakdown of an intimate relationship and the intention of the offender is to embarrass, intimidate, control, humiliate, defame, cause distress, harm or extort the victim.
- *Cyberbullying and harassment.* The Advisory, Conciliation and Arbitration Service (ACAS) in the UK, defines bullying as 'offensive, intimidating, malicious or insulting behaviour, an abuse or misuse of power through means that undermine, humiliate, denigrate or injure the recipient'. Closely related is harassment, which is defined in the UK Equality Act 2010 as 'unwanted conduct related to a relevant protected characteristic which has the purpose or effect of violating an individual's dignity or creating an intimidating, hostile, degrading, humiliating or offensive environment for that individual'. Cyberbullying can, thus, be defined as the cyber-enabled version of bullying, whereas harassment usually captures both in-person and online harassment.
- *Cyberstalking.* This refers to repeated acts of threatening to harm, harassing, intimidating via messages, or any other digital activities with the purpose of annoying, alarming, threatening or making an individual afraid for their safety. The actions themselves may or may not be illegal in isolation. Overall, cyberstalking can be considered as a type of cyber-enabled harassment, with the majority of reported victims being women.

Fraud

For all the reasons previously identified, including the facilitation of anonymity, digital technology has particularly enabled large volumes of cyber-enabled fraud. Such frauds can manifest themselves in numerous ways, so we highlight just a few as illustrative special cases:

- *Identity fraud.* This involves identity theft, which is the collection of a victim's personal information (such as social security numbers, passport numbers, credit card numbers, bank account details, etc.). Data obtained as a result of identity theft is often subsequently used to impersonate the victim with the purpose of conducting fraud, for example to obtain goods or services by deception. This might include opening bank accounts, obtaining credit cards, loans or state benefits, ordering goods or obtaining documents in the name of the victim.
- *Investment fraud.* This involves tricking victims into investing in financial scams, and is greatly facilitated by the distance and scale advantages of cyber-enabled crime.
- *Intellectual property fraud.* In this case criminals either create counterfeit goods and sell them online, often presenting them as genuine, or illegally provide protected digital content. The illegal streaming of movies or sports games constitutes a common example of the latter type of fraud. Another example is the reposting on social media of other people's digital content without permission or attribution.
- *Catfishing.* This is a particular type of identity fraud that involves the creation of fake social media accounts by using another person's personal information (perhaps including photos and videos) with the intention to engage in fraudulent activities such as romance scams.

Cybercriminals

One means of tackling cybercrime is to better understand the nature of cybercriminals. In this section we consider the process of profiling and classifying cybercriminals.

Cybercriminal profiling

The first attempt to determine the type of person who committed a crime by *profiling*, which involves collecting information from a crime scene, was conducted by the FBI's Behavioral Analysis Unit in the 1960s. The aim of profiling is to distinguish an

Figure 7.1 A model for profiling cybercriminals

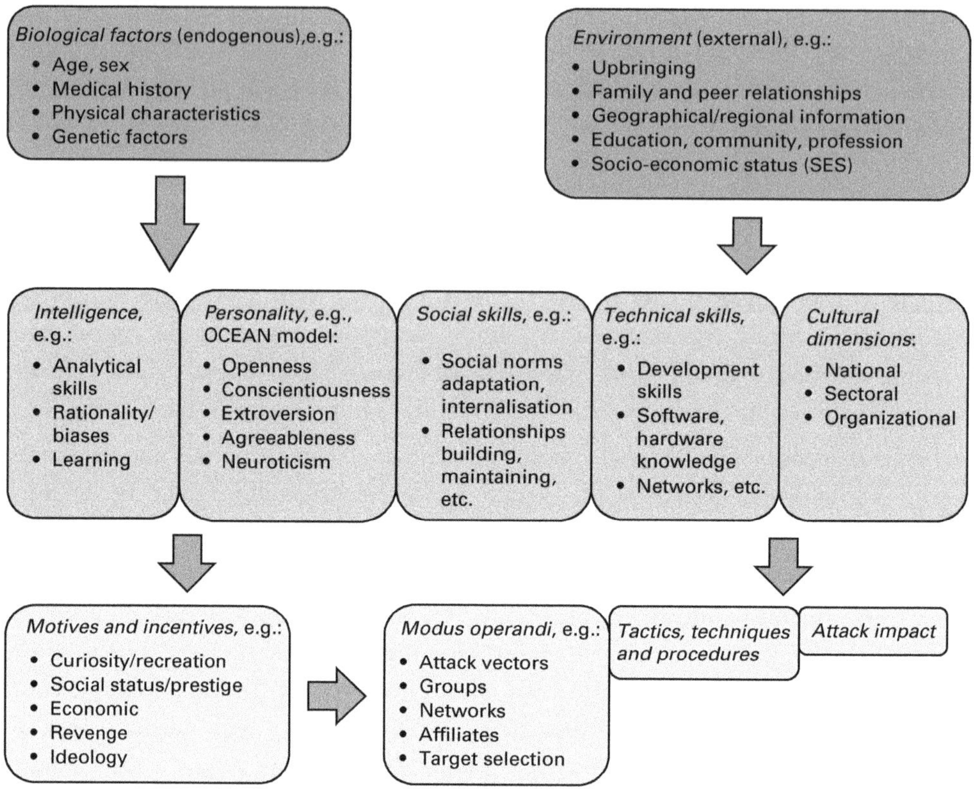

individual from the general population, hence narrow down the search for the perpetrator of a crime. The first criminal profile was created in response to the murder of a woman by stabbing and it predicted that the murderer was an adolescent living nearby, which proved remarkably correct.

Since then, criminal profiling has increased greatly in sophistication. Profiling helps to explain the nature of cybercriminals, as well as their capabilities, motivations and methods. In Figure 7.1 we propose a high-level model for profiling cybercriminals, adapted and expanded from previously proposed models.[6] The model factors are by no means exhaustive, but indicate the main components and the complexity of cybercriminal profiling.

This profiling model identifies a flow that captures the background of a cybercriminal, which then influences their skills and capabilities, and ultimately their motivations and techniques.

We now expand on several aspects of this model:

- Intelligence is generally believed to be a key factor for committing some types of cybercrimes. This relates to motivation in terms of curiosity and sometimes to technical skills.
- Personality was not initially included in cybercriminal profiling, but it is an influential factor. Personality traits such as neuroticism, extroversion and openness to experience, along with low scores of agreeableness, have been associated with propensity for aggressiveness and criminal engagement. We discuss this further in Chapter 9.
- The relevance of social skills depends on individual cases and types of crime. For example, alienation and an inability to form close relationships has been linked to certain cybercriminal activities such as hacking, while social engineering (which we discuss shortly) requires certain specialist social skills.
- The relevance of technical skills was traditionally seen as an important factor in conducting cybercrime, but, for many types of cybercrime, this aspect is fading with the rise of new business models that enable less technically skilled perpetrators to conduct cybercrime. We discuss this in the next section.
- The cultural dimensions of cybercrime are less understood but are undoubtedly influential. Norms and practices within national, organizational or sectoral cultures can impact cybercriminal activity, for example through the acceptance of certain behaviours within one cultural group that are deemed unacceptable by others. The topic of culture is explored further in Chapter 9.
- Motives and incentives are potentially complex, since there often exist multiple motives and incentives for a given cybercrime, and also because incentives can emerge opportunistically.

Classifying cybercriminals

There is no widely accepted classification of cybercriminals, but information extracted from cybercriminal profiling can be used to group cybercriminals in different ways. In Chapter 1 we presented a high-level classification in terms of adversarial capabilities. In Figure 7.2 a more complex classification is proposed based on a combination of motivation (the broad outer segments) and sophistication (increasing from the centre to the perimeter).[7] The cybercriminal classes emerging from this process, in roughly increasing levels of sophistication, are:

- *Novices*. These are beginners, traditionally referred to as *script-kiddies*, who are generally non-malicious, although their motivation can sometimes be less benign.
- *Hacktivists*. These have similar motives to coders but are more likely to be cause- or revenge-driven, while generally having less technical expertise.

Figure 7.2 Hacker motivations and sophistication

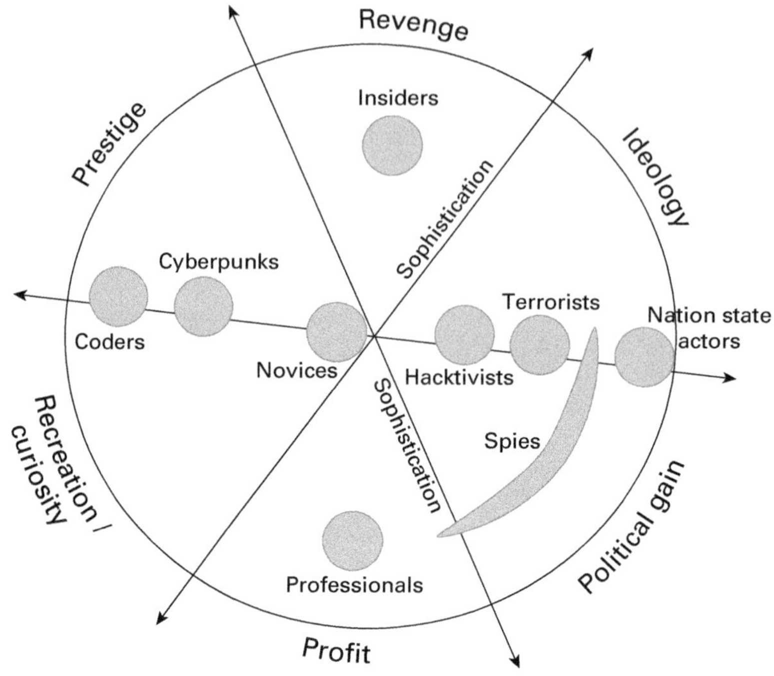

- *Cyberpunks.* These are normally relatively skilled hackers whose motivation varies, but is often simply curiosity and recreation.
- *Insiders.* These tend to be motivated by revenge and profit, and are often seeking reparation for a perceived injustice relating to an organizational relationship. Insiders often have elevated privileges or access to a digital environment.
- *Cyber terrorists.* These actors are normally motivated by ideology or political reasons. They are typically less sophisticated than nation state-sponsored actors.
- *Professional criminals.* These are normally motivated by profit and are often linked to organized crime. This category can include *criminal entrepreneurs*, i.e. actors in the gig economy, which we discuss shortly, who create, distribute and sell services and tools to the market for other cybercriminals to utilize, and *cyber mercenaries*, who offer services to other groups or nation states. This category requires moderate or high technical skills.
- *Cyber spies:* These actors engage with espionage, gathering intelligence or sensitive information. Their motivation can be linked to ideological and political goals, for example, for political agendas (through targeting nation state classified information), for hacktivism causes, or for profiteering through gaining of competitive advantage. Their level of sophistication can vary.

- *Coders.* These are highly skilled actors who might be motivated by recreation, curiosity, prestige and ideology, thus are not necessarily inherently malicious.
- *Nation state (-sponsored) actors.* These are powerful and sophisticated cybercriminals, either employed by or hired by a nation state, and hence typically possess significant resources. Their motivations often blur the boundaries between advancing a state's agenda and financial gain. Such actors are often associated with *advanced persistent threats*, which are sophisticated attacks that are undertaken over prolonged periods.

The associated motivations according to which cybercriminals operate are:

- *Profit.* This aim is simply financial gain.
- *Ideology.* This can be on a political, social, religious or other ideological basis.
- *Revenge.* This aim is to cause harm, either to other individuals or to organizations.
- *Recreation/curiosity.* This aim is enjoyment, experimentation or learning.
- *Prestige.* This aim is to gain recognition and elevate status, perhaps amongst peers.
- *Political gain.* This aim is influencing political outcomes, destabilizing societies or creating tension or confusion. The associated drivers can be ideological or tactical.

Note that a threat actor or cybercriminal type can have more than one motivation.

Cybercrime business models

In this section we consider a number of different cybercrime business models, as well as the use of digital technology to transfer the proceeds of financially related cybercrime.

Evolution of business models

Cybercrime has risen as our use of digital technology has proliferated. Over time, what was once opportunistic criminal activity, or an adoption of digital technology by perpetrators of traditional crime, has morphed into an environment where cybercrime itself is an industry with its own business models.

As an industry, cybercrime is dynamic and fast-paced, involving many different types of actors. Today's cybercrime industry is very much part of the *gig economy*, where cybercrime customers are connected with freelancers and independent contractors for short-term services or asset-sharing, via digital platforms. This enables cybercriminals with specific skills to market their services to those seeking to engage with cybercrime. It also means that traditional boundaries between different actors are increasingly blurred, for example, between the state and private sector contractors. At the same time, the potential pool of cybercriminals has expanded, since almost anyone can engage in cybercrime, not just an elite of highly skilled and tech-savvy individuals.

This evolution has led to the establishment of several cybercrime business models, which we now briefly review.

Cybercrime as a Service

An important milestone in the evolution of cybercrime has been the emergence of *Cybercrime as a Service* (CaaS), which is the provision of technological cybercrime tools such as malware for purchase or rent, or for collaborative usage. The primary criminal advantage of such an approach is that perpetrators of cybercrime no longer need to have the in-house skills to develop and deploy their own cybercrime technology.

CaaS providers adopt different approaches to provision of their services. For example, a CaaS provider might directly sell a tool, or enter into an agreement to share the profits from usage of a tool. Such tools are often not available on the open market for fear of law enforcement posing as buyers. Hence cybercriminals often form networks of affiliates who are considered trusted and can collaborate with CaaS providers. In doing so, entire criminal networks can join forces and mutually benefit from the CaaS provider's services, which often include extensive technical support. This in turn facilitates feedback loops, enhancement of the tools' features and capabilities, opportunities for customization, etc. In some cases as much as 20 per cent of the profits of cybercrime activities is returned to the CaaS developers.

Ransomware as a Service

Arguably the most significant type of CaaS provision is Ransomware as a Service (RaaS). Since so much of our modern lives depends on data, whether business-related or personal, any cybercriminal who takes possession of our data and holds it to ransom is in a very powerful position, thus, ransomware has become prevalent.

Consequently, RaaS has become a very successful business model for conducting cybercrime. In some cases different tiers of RaaS are offered, based on whether a particular tool is feature-rich with a well-established recorded history of successful attacks, or whether it is a new, unproven tool.

The emergence of RaaS has also diversified and specialized the CaaS market. For example, some CaaS providers might simply sell exploits that can be used to break into digital environments. Having purchased and activated such an exploit, a cybercriminal might then turn to a RaaS provider to conduct a ransomware attack. A RaaS provider might also offer support, perhaps via a call centre, to aid victims with the process of ransom payment and (sometimes, but not always) subsequent recovery of data.

Access as a Service

Another special CaaS business model is Access as a Service (AaaS), which deals with the provision of stolen credentials. Since many cybercrimes involve personal credentials, and gathering such data can be time-consuming, AaaS providers sell databases of such credentials to cybercriminals as a business model in itself.

The AaaS business has been evolving alongside our use of digital technology. What was once simply login credentials to specific computer accounts now includes access credentials to the likes of cloud storage, web services, company networks, etc. Different charges will be made for credentials with elevated administrative rights, accounts of senior management or employees in finance departments. Costs of different credentials typically vary from a few to several thousand dollars, and are also impacted by the perceived 'market value' of the targets.

Cryptocurrencies

An important technological development utilized by cybercriminals is that of *cryptocurrencies*, such as Bitcoin, which provide a means of digital payment that is not governed directly by the traditional financial industry and offers a degree of anonymity. This makes it easier to move the proceeds of financial cybercrime around – for example, the transfer of ransomware demand payments.

Prior to the emergence of cryptocurrency, transferring the proceeds of cybercrime was a more complicated endeavour. For example, when a cybercriminal obtained access to a victim's bank account they could not directly transfer funds to their own account since such a transaction was traceable by financial authorities. Instead, they typically used money mules, who were individuals recruited to transfer stolen money between accounts or countries, or withdraw physical money from ATMs and deliver it to the criminals. Such operations, however, posed significant overheads related to hiring and managing potentially non-trustworthy money mules. Moreover, money mules were needed in large numbers so that transactions could be kept to small monetary amounts to avoid raising red flags within the banking systems.

It is important to recognize that use of cryptocurrency itself is not a cybercrime, and neither does cryptocurrency explicitly facilitate cybercrime. Prior to the development of cryptocurrency, some cybercriminals used online services such as Western Union or e-Gold for withdrawing and transferring funds. Cryptocurrencies certainly make it easier to move funds around but, should cryptocurrency ever be outlawed, cybercriminals will undoubtedly find other ingenious methods for moving their money.

Social engineering

In this section, we discuss social engineering and its underlying psychological principles in detail. The reason for this focus is that the human attack vector is consistently being reported as one of the most significant components of succesful cyber attacks, thus how social engineering works and why it is succesful merits examination. For further discussion of human aspects and behaviour, see Chapter 9.

What is social engineering?

Social engineering refers to any act or conduct that influences individuals to act in fashions that may not be in their best interest.[8] In the cybercrime context, social engineering tends to involve the manipulation of individuals into revealing information that is valuable to the cybercriminal by means of deception.

Recall our layering of the digital environment in Chapter 1 (and depicted in Figure 1.1). The reason that social engineering is so important to cybercriminals is that the human layer tends to be the most accessible and easiest to manipulate. The goal of most cybercriminals is to access elements of the data layer, thus social engineering can be considered as the most comon means by which vulnerabilities in the human layer are exploited in order to access the data layer, normally via the technology layer.

Many impactful cyber attacks have been traced back to successful social engineering exploits. There is no shortage of suitable examples since social engineering is such a common component of cybercrime. For example, the infamous 2020 SolarWinds hack resulted in several US government agencies and corporations being compromised. This attack used sophisticated malware, which was spread by means of an orchestrated phishing campaign where attackers pretended to represent legitimate companies in order to capture employees' credentials. Similarly, the well-publicized 2020 Twitter hack was initiated when attackers impersonated colleagues of Twitter staff in order to convince them to reset account credentials, and as a result obtained access to internal systems and, ultimately, hacked the accounts of Barack Obama, Elon Musk, Bill Gates and Apple.

The social engineering attack cycle

The stages of a social engineering attack can be captured as part of the Social Engineering Attack Cycle, which we illustrate in Figure 7.3.

Figure 7.3 The Social Engineering Attack Cycle[9]

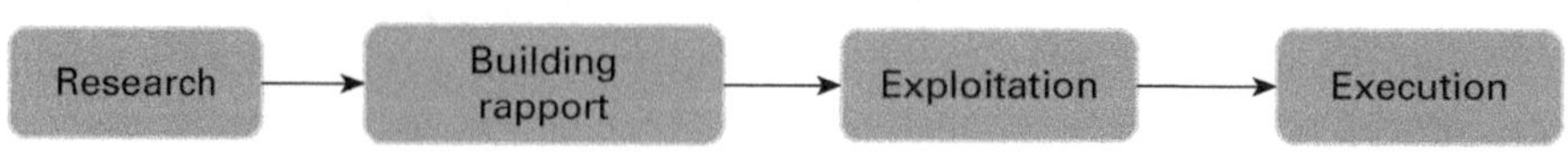

1 *Research*. A social engineering attack typically starts by obtaining some information, usually via open source intelligence, that will help an attacker to trick a victim.

2 *Building rapport*. During this stage, the social engineer uses the prior intelligence to build rapport with the victim and develop a level of trust that will motivate the victim to take the desired action. This establishes a pretext for action, which might include a background story or false representations that will convince, reassure and ultimately influence the victim.

3 *Exploitation*. The social engineer then takes advantage of the established trust to direct the victim into taking the desired action. This process commonly involves *elicitation*, which is the extraction of information during a communication in a deceptive fashion.

4 *Execution*. Ultimately, the social engineer terminates the interaction with the victim and utilizes the results of the action, which is often obtained information. For example, the social engineer might install malware or use elicted credentials to gain unauthorized access.

Note that the social engineering attack cycle is often carried out entirely online but, in sophisticated attacks, may also involve in-person interaction (particularly during the building of rapport).

Phishing

Perhaps the most prevalent and familiar social engineering technique is *phishing*, which is the use of digital messages appearing to originate from reputable, legitimate or known sources, with the intention to trick victims into taking an action. We will use phishing to illustrate the stages of the social engineering attack cycle.

1 *Research*. This stage varies across different forms of phishing. Some phishing attacks have almost no research phase and simply involve mass targeting of victims in the hope that some will respond. More specialist forms of phishing involve a degree of research. *Spear phishing* is phishing that is targeted at specific individuals or groups and thus requires research relating to these victims. *Whaling* targets high-profile individuals, such as senior executives of organizations, and typically requires extensive research.

2 *Building rapport*. Typical mass phishing attacks are conducted by email and attempt to build rapport simply by claiming to come from a recognized authority. Historically, such attacks involved (ludicrous) hardship stories that attempted to seek sympathy from potential victims. Spear phishing and whaling require careful use of the prior research information to convince victims of the validity of the presented pretext. In *vishing* attacks, rapport is built by means of a telephone interaction.

3 *Exploitation.* In most phishing attacks, exploitation involves persuading the victim to click on a malicious link and/or reveal login credentials or other sensitive information.

4 *Execution.* The results of a successful phishing attack depend on what the victim has been persuaded to do. Since this often involves revealing of credentials, the results can be almost anything, and are potentially severe, as we saw in the previous examples.

Psychological principles behind social engineering

There is a misconception that only certain people are susceptible to social engineering. This is not true; indeed almost anyone can fall for the likes of a well-orchestrated spear phishing attack. We now present some of the psychological principles behind social engineering, which indicate why humans are particularly susceptible to this type of attack:[10]

1 *Influence.* This concerns human susceptibility to persuasion and is often used in conjunction with nudging techniques, which we discuss in Chapter 9. Influence is often enacted via the use of justification. It has been experimentally demonstrated that whenever a request is made to someone, if it is accompanied by a reason then the chances of compliance are higher. Hence building rapport in social engineering by using justification, such as that the IT admin team need a password in order to upgrade a system, can be very effective.

2 *Reciprocation.* This principle refers to the desire of individuals to return favours, invitations, gifts, etc., whenever they have the opportunity. A social engineer can thus exploit this principle by presenting a contextual scenario where the victim is involved in an exchange, for example by inserting a USB stick into a device under the pretext of helping a social engineer who has offered them something. Indeed, experiments indicate that often a victim will return an objectively higher favour than the one received.

3 *Commitment and consistency.* This concerns the desire of individuals to be consistent with their own previous actions and with things they have committed to, even more so if the commitment has been announced publicly. Hence a spear phishing target who has consistently made donations to a cause is more likely to respond positively to a social engineer's pretext request for a similar donation.

4 *Social proof.* Most people do not like to deviate from apparent norms in order to avoid mental discomfort. This means that people tend to follow others if they are uncertain what to do. Social proof constitutes an important component in the formation of a security culture. A social engineer could, for example, manipulate a victim to conduct an action by persuading them that colleagues have already taken the same action.

5 *Liking*. Individuals are more likely to respond favourably to someone they like, where liking can be through observed similarities (of any kind), receipt of flattery, mutual cooperation and attractiveness. This creates myriad opportunities for a well-researched social engineer to exploit, for example, through compliments, mutual friends or claimed affiliation with a target's past employers or supported sports clubs.

6 *Authority*. People tend to indicate obedience or compliance with authority, whether manifested through claimed affiliation or portrayed through appearance, titles, contacts, confidence or writing style. Many social engineers portray authority either directly or sometimes indirectly, such as by pretending to hold delegated authority from someone else.

7 *Scarcity*. This refers to the perception that something that is scarce and of limited availability is more valuable. Hence a social engineer can create a pretext representing scarcity, such as by presenting a 'special offer'. Scarcity can also be applied to time, by pressuring individuals due to time limitations. Ransomware groups who have successfully encrypted a victim's data often portray visually vivid clock countdowns on the screen and present their victims with a limited-time opportunity to pay the ransom.

Cyber war and terrorism

In this section we briefly consider the notions of cyber war and cyber terrorism. These are both closely related to cybercrime, particularly since their boundaries are often blurred and subjective. For example, in some societies ideological viewpoints might render some cybercriminal activities as cyber terrorism, while many cyber-criminals offer their services to nation states or organized groups conducting acts associated with terrorism. Additionally, the tactics, techniques and procedures involved in cyber attacks are often similar, whether conducted with the aim of committing crimes, national security manoeuvres or acts of terrorism.

Cyber war

The terms *cyber war* as a state of conflict, and *cyber warfare* as the methods used to conduct war-related activities, have been used for years, in many cases interchangeably, but with significant debates regarding the appropriateness of such terminology.

Some people embrace these terms, based on the increasing featuring of digital technology within conflicts, both as a means and target of warfare, for example through the use of cyber attacks to damage another state's information networks and digital assets. In this sense, cyber warfare has been considered as an extension of a nation state's capabilities to pose serious threats to another nation state.

On the other hand, others advocate that cyber war has not happened and may never take place, since cyber attacks are simply new versions of traditional activities of warfare.[11] For example, Stuxnet, which disrupted Iran's ability to enrich weapon-grade uranium, might not be an example of cyber warfare, but should rather be labelled as an example of traditional sabotage.

Perhaps the best compromise, which to an extent supports both positions, is that adopted by agencies such as the European Defence Agency, the UK Ministry of Defence and the US Department of Defense, all of which consider cyberspace as a fifth domain of warfare, of equal importance and criticality to land, sea, air and space. The interconnections of the other four domains with cyberspace and their dependency on it indicate that operations in the physical domain are increasingly reliant on cyberspace. This acknowledges that theatres of war are increasingly dependent on cyberspace, at least to some degree. Note that one consequence of this, which is less problematic in physical warfare, is that attribution of attacks can often prove to be difficult.

Similarly to cybercrime, we can also classify cyber warfare into cyber-enabled and cyber-dependent. Indicative examples of cyber-enabled warfare, where traditional forms of warfare are strengthened by cyber-related components, are the use of digital propaganda, misinformation, disruption of digital logistics and supply chains, and cyber intelligence gathering. Examples of cyber-dependent warfare are very similar to cybercrime and include the use of denial-of-service attacks and malware against targets of war.

Note that while cyber warfare might often be similar to cybercrime in terms of the ways in which it is conducted and its intended consequences, when such activities are conducted by military agencies rather than civilian organizations, acts of cyberwarfare might not technically be cybercrimes.

Cyber terrorism

There is no universally accepted definition of cyber terrorism, and the notion of terrorism itself is highly contested and subjective. We will avoid any formal definition and loosely associate this concept with activities that utilize cyberspace to spread propaganda, radicalize potential supporters, raise funds and communicate and coordinate plans, with the intention to disrupt or destroy critical national infrastructure, and to instil fear and panic amongst a population. Such activities are typically performed in pursuit of political, ideological, racial, religious, social or economic objectives.

Similarly to cyber warfare, there is a debate as to whether cyber terrorism is a concept in its own right, or whether it is a natural extension to methods deployed to conduct traditional acts of terror. Indeed, such acts are often deemed crimes rather than explicitly being labelled terrorism. For example, the UK Computer Misuse Act of 1990 links cyber-related activities with serious offences without mentioning terrorism. In particular, in Section 3ZA it refers to 'unauthorized acts causing, or creating risk of, serious damage', which includes injuries, risk to human life, human welfare, the economy, the environment and national security. When terrorism is referred to explicitly, it is notable that physical harm and damage are not necessary for the characterization of an act as terrorism. For example, the UK Terrorism Act of 2000 indicates that actions that seriously interfere with or seriously disrupt an electronic system are also deemed acts of terrorism.

Challenges for countering cybercrime

In this final section, we consider some of the main challenges relating to the countering of cybercrime. We first consider reasons why cybercrime is so challenging to deal with. We then consider why it is so difficult to even assess the extent of cybercrime.

Challenges of dealing with cybercrime

At the start of this chapter we briefly commented on some of the features of the digital environment that make cybercrime different to traditional crime. We now take a deeper look at some of the particular challenges these features raise for dealing with cybercrime:

- *Opportunism.* The ease with which cybercrime can be conducted provides an opportunistic capability for cybercrime to rapidly exploit evolving circumstances. A good example is provided by the Covid-19 pandemic. The surrounding events saw an almost instant adaptation of cybercriminals to exploit various aspects of the new landscape. For example, cybercriminals introduced malware to exploit Covid-tracking apps, recruited money mules amongst people facing sudden financial uncertainty, and introduced phishing attacks based around the new propensity of people for increased home delivery services. Similar reactions and adaptations are observed during geopolitical conflicts, such as the expansion and diversification of cybercriminal groups to incorporate war-related activities on the outbreak of the Russia-Ukraine war.
- *Evolution of tools and technologies.* Digital tools and technologies evolve at a fast rate, with new tools often being substantially more powerful than their predecessors. Sometimes technologies rapidly emerge that present game-changing opportunities, such as the sudden emergence of cryptocurrencies and new artificial intelligence tools.

- *Interconnectivity*. The ever-progressing interconnectivity and adoption of the likes of Internet-of-Things (IoT) devices provides increasingly fertile ground for malware to spread and propagate at unprecedented scales. At the same time, the protection of this environment is an increasingly complex task, providing additional vulnerabilities for cybercriminals to exploit. Appropriate security behaviour and security hygiene practices at individual, business and nation state levels struggle to keep up, leaving opportunities for cybercriminals to exploit.
- *Automation*. Tools used in cybercriminal activities are being increasingly automated. Traditional small-scale crimes, such as credit card fraud, have now massively expanded due to the benefits of scale provided by digital environments. Attacks such as phishing, which may have very low success rates, are likely to become highly productive when deployed at enormous scale.
- *Confidentiality and anonymity*. The very tools that support cyber security, such as encryption (see Chapter 2) and privacy-enhancing tools supporting anonymity (see Chapter 8), provide potential challenges to law enforcement when used by perpetrators of cybercrime. Indeed, the ability to obtain a degree of anonymity online also encourages certain types of criminal behaviour. However, both confidentiality and anonymity are important for law-abiding citizens and law enforcement itself. We first commented on this type of dilemma in Chapter 2 with respect to encryption.
- *Jurisdiction*. This refers to the provision of states with the power and authority to define and preserve the duties and rights of people within their territory, enforce laws and punish violations of laws. As far as cybercrime is concerned, however, given the lack of traditional geographical boundaries in cyberspace, the matter of jurisdiction is often far from straightforward. For example, it is often hard to determine where a cybercrime originated, in which countries data related to the crime was transferred or stored, and which entities within cyberspace facilitated the cybercrime and might bear some responsibility. Even when such issues can be resolved, many cybercrimes potentially involve multiple jurisdictions, which adds complications. In some cases this might involve extradition of individuals from one country where the individual is physically, to another that has a significant link with the crime, creating international political tensions.
- *International cooperation*. Related to jurisdiction, the international nature of cybercrime can make it challenging to come to common understandings of what cybercrime is and how to respond to it. International attempts have been made to establish a common front against cybercrime. For example, the Budapest Convention on Cybercrime was initiated by the Council of Europe and has been signed by over 70 countries with the objective of international cooperation amongst law enforcement agencies, the harmonization of legislation and the enhancement of prosecution processes for cyber-related offences. The United

Nations has also introduced working groups and committees on countering the use of digital technologies for criminal purposes.

- *Evidence and investigation*. In order for evidence to be presentable and accepted in court, there are typically strict requirements regarding how this evidence is collected, stored, analysed and transferred. In the case of cybercrime, this requires extremely careful handling of digital evidence, since it is so easy to alter, copy and manipulate digital data. There have been many cases where indicted individuals were not prosecuted, despite overwhelming circumstantial evidence, due to doubts about the handling of digital evidence.
- *Interdisciplinarity*. As this book hopefully illustrates, the study of cyber security and cybercrime is inherently interdisciplinary. This means that countering cybercrime requires the shared expertise of people with many different backgrounds, including technical, behavioural, social and legal. Bringing together the appropriate expertise to counter cybercrime is arguably more challenging than for some traditional crimes, which lack the technical component and occur in better understood and established environments than cyberspace.

Assessing the extent of cybercrime

In order to be able to effectively counter cybercrime, it is important to understand the cybercrime landscape. This partially involves developing a clear understanding of what degree of cybercriminal activity is occurring and how this is evolving. There are two significant barriers to achieving this effectively:

1. *Underreporting of cybercrime*. A major challenge in understanding the degree of cybercrime is the extent of underreporting of cybercrime. Organizations are often reluctant to report a security breach arising from cybercrime since their priority is restoration of their business operations (see Chapter 6) and such reporting might result in reputational damage. Victims, too, are often reluctant to report cybercrime. For example, cyberbullying is often associated with anxiety and psychological costs and many victims do not know whether or how to report such offences. Underreporting of cybercrime hinders a more accurate understanding of the nature and the frequency of such crimes and is just one of several reasons why regulations such as the General Data Protection Regulation (GDPR) in the European Union make reporting of some types of cybercrime mandatory.
2. *Measuring cybercrime*. Even when reported, the challenges of measuring cybercrime are substantial. The most common means to obtain data on cybercrime is through law enforcement agency reports. However, reliability and consistency of the provided data is questionable, since there is no universally accepted classification of cybercrime, cybercrime is underreported (as previously noted),

and such reports are influenced not just by cybercrime volumes but also by the effort put into enforcement, which can vary extensively. Large-scale organizational surveys and individual victimization surveys provide some useful measurements, but the design and collection of this data relies on population samples that may not always be representative.

KEY POINTS

- Cybercrime has characteristics distinct from traditional crime and includes a wide range of diverse offences.
- Cybercriminals have a range of different backgrounds, varying in their capabilities and motivations.
- Cybercrime takes place within a rapidly changing environment, evolving in its use of technologies, techniques and business models.
- Social engineering is an important component of cybercrime and is an effective attack vector due to inherent human psychological and behavioural characteristics.
- Cyber war and cyber terrorism relate closely to cybercrime and share many of its characteristics.
- Combating cybercrime faces many significant challenges, arising from both the nature of the digital environment and the difficulties in assessing the extent of cybercrime.

EXERCISES

1 In 2016, the Commonwealth of Independent States Agreement defined cybercrime as 'a criminal act of which the target is computer information'. Provide a critique of this definition, indicating the extent to which you believe this to be a suitable description of the nature of cybercrime.

2 Identify a notable cybercriminal attack that has been widely reported in the media. Use the terminology and frameworks within this chapter to analyse this attack. Was this attack cyber-enabled or cyber-dependent? How was the attack conducted? By whom was it conducted and why? What role did social engineering play in the attack? What challenges make combating an attack like this difficult to enact?

3 Identify which cybercrime-related laws have been passed in your country and describe, generally, what they cover.

4 Write a short essay that either supports or refutes the following statement: *It is much easier to commit and evade prosecution for a cybercrime than a traditional crime.*

5 We provided a classification of cybercriminals in terms of their levels of sophistication. Now revisit this list and justify, with respect to your everyday activities in cyberspace, how to order this list from the perspective of the danger these different cybercriminals present to your daily life.

6 Do you think the emergence of Cybercrime as a Service (CaaS) makes it easier or harder for law enforcement to combat cybercrime?

7 Test out the psychological principles we identified that underpin social engineering. We do not suggest that you attempt to social engineer people (!) but you could, for example, test out how effective principles such as reciprocation or liking are in aspects of your daily life. Note down any anecdotal observations and reflect on how they might work within a broader social engineering context.

8 Search the media for reporting on conflicts that involve cyber activity. As well as identifying how digital technology has been used in these reports, pay attention to the terminology deployed in the reporting. To what extent have terms such as cybercrime, cyber war, cyber terrorism and cyber weapon been used? Do you think these terms have been used constructively and appropriately?

9 Find an example of a cybercrime report (these are often available online). Critically examine how the data was collected, analysed and reported. Elaborate on the potential limitations of the approach.

10 For each of the other chapters in this book (excluding Chapter 1), explain how the content discussed in that chapter is of potential relevance to understanding and combating cybercrime.

FURTHER READING

- Cialdini, R (2001) *Principles of Persuasion*, Arizona State University, eBrand Media Publication
- Lickiewicz, J (2011) Cyber Crime psychology-proposal of an offender psychological profile, *Problems of Forensic Sciences*, 2 (3), 239–52
- Nykodym, N, Taylor, R and Vilela, J (2005) Criminal profiling and insider cyber crime, *Computer Law & Security Review*, 21 (5), pp. 408–14

- Seebruck, R (2015) A typology of hackers: Classifying cyber malfeasance using a weighted arc circumplex model, *Digital Investigation*, 14, pp. 36–45
- The UK Computer Misuse Act 1990, Legal Document, https://www.legislation.gov.uk/ukpga/1990/18/contents (archived at https://perma.cc/6ZQS-YHJ5)
- Yar, M (2005) The novelty of 'cybercrime': An assessment in light of routine activity theory, *European Journal of Criminology*, 2 (4), pp. 407–27

Notes

1 See: Wall, D (2007) *Cybercrime: The transformation of crime in the information age*, Polity Press

2 See: Thomas, D and Loader, B (eds) (2000) *Cybercrime: Law enforcement, security and surveillance in the information age*, Psychology Press

3 See: Gordon, S and Ford, R (2006) On the definition and classification of cybercrime, *Journal in Computer Virology*, 2,13–20

4 See: European Union (2012) The Cyber-security Strategy of the European Union: An Open, Safe and Secure Cyberspace, Brussels, https://www.edps.europa.eu/data-protection/our-work/publications/opinions/cyber-security-strategy-european-union-open-safe-and_en (archived at https://perma.cc/ZU84-D3VL). It was met with calls for its urgent implementation by defence officials, see: Council Doc 7847/13

5 For details on various definitions of cybercrimes see: Yar, M (2016) Online Crime. In *Oxford Research Encyclopedia of Criminology*, https://oxfordre.com/criminology (archived at https://perma.cc/S7XM-TLXA)

6 There is a lack of profiling models for cybercriminals. The model we present is an adapted and expanded version of Lickiewicz's mode. See: Lickiewicz, J (2011) Cyber crime psychology – proposal of an offender psychological profile, *Problems of Forensic Sciences*, 2 (3), 239–52

7 The circumplex is adapted from Rogers (2006) and Seebruck (2015): Rogers, M K (2006) A two-dimensional circumplex approach to the development of a hacker taxonomy, *Digital Investigation*, 3 (2), 97–102, https://www.sciencedirect.com/science/article/pii/S1742287606000260 (archived at https://perma.cc/G5XT-PTCD); Seebruck, R (2015) A typology of hackers: Classifying cyber malfeasance using a weighted arc circumplex model, *Digital Investigation*, 14, 36–45

8 A well-presented description and decomposition of social engineering can be found in Hadnagy (2010, 2018): Hadnagy, C (2010) *Social Engineering: The art of human hacking*, John Wiley & Sons; Hadnagy, C (2018) *Social Engineering: The science of human hacking*, John Wiley & Sons

9 The social engineering attack cycle was created by Kevin Mitnick: Mitnick, K D and Simon, W L (2003) *The Art of Deception: Controlling the human element of security*, John Wiley & Sons.

10 Psychological principles can be found in Cialdini (2001, 2016). Notably, the formation of the principles is largely based on experimental studies, i.e. the principles are not merely theoretical, but consistently observable: Cialdini, R, (2001) *Principles of Persuasion*, Arizona State University, eBrand Media Publication; Cialdini, R (2016) *Pre-suasion: A revolutionary way to influence and persuade*, Simon and Schuster

11 The details of this view can be found in: Rid, T (2012) Cyber war will not take place, *Journal of Strategic Studies*, 35 (1), 5–32

08 Privacy

Addressing the risks presented by data collection

In this chapter, we investigate the complex concept of privacy, looking at the challenges that it presents and some of the mechanisms that can be used to address it. We begin by attempting to define privacy, and discuss how privacy relates to other concepts, including security. We will look at some of the principles that underpin privacy and discuss privacy paradoxes. We then consider how privacy can be supported through regulations, standards and policies. We also discuss how to engineer privacy into digital systems. Next, we discuss a range of privacy-enhancing technologies, each supporting privacy in quite different ways. Finally, we consider how privacy might impact, and be impacted by, emerging technology.

LEARNING OBJECTIVES

- The challenges involved in defining privacy.
- Principles and paradoxes concerning privacy.
- How regulations, standards and policies support privacy.
- The engineering of privacy into digital systems.
- How different privacy-enhancing technologies can be used to support privacy.
- The potential future impact of emerging technology on privacy.

What is privacy?

In this section we attempt to define privacy which, for several reasons that we will discuss, is not particularly straightforward to do. We will also consider various closely linked concepts and reflect on how privacy might relate to them.

Motivation for privacy

Privacy is easier to motivate than define. You probably harbour your own intuitive notion of what privacy might mean to you, as well as the extent to which you desire it in various aspects of your life. Undoubtedly these relate to the extent that others are aware of things that you do, places that you go, things that you say, etc.

In its broadest possible interpretation, privacy relates to the right to be 'left alone'. The Oxford English Dictionary describes it as 'the state or condition of being alone, undisturbed, or free from public attention, as a matter of choice or right; seclusion; freedom from interference or intrusion'.[1] However, privacy, even loosely defined like this, is multifarious and complex. This is because privacy has different interpretations (what does being 'left alone' really mean?), is subjective and depends on the context in which it arises. We later discuss these issues in more detail.

Privacy has always been something that people care about. Traditionally, privacy is associated with an individual's personal and physical space. We often associate our personal homes with privacy, and we seek physical seclusion when we want to hold a 'private' conversation.

However, in today's digital environments, privacy is a much more complex issue. However you choose to define privacy, it is increasingly hard to provide in the digital world. Almost all our digital activities leave data trails that threaten to erode our privacy, allowing others to potentially track our activities and predict our future behaviours. Such *information privacy* is the focus of this chapter, and we will generally assume this is the case when using the general term privacy in the subsequent discussion.

Of course, the generation of data trails can be both good and bad, and neither will we all agree, all of the time, which perspective is true. Take the example of a fitness tracker that gathers data about an individual's movements and activities and then shares them with the service provider. This can be good – it helps to inform fitness regimes, leading to better health. This can be bad – the service provider learns a great deal about the personal lives of its customers, leading to risks of data exposure and the potential selling of this data to third parties (including health insurance companies). Some of us might be prepared to sacrifice the privacy loss in order to reap associated benefits, while others might take the opposing view. Some of us might hold passionate opinions, one way or the other, while others might not appear to care. Somehow, all of these differing attitudes towards the fitness tracker will need to be accommodated.

This example illustrates three aspects of privacy that we will explore throughout this chapter:

1 *Transparency*. Providing privacy requires an understanding of what data is being collected and what is being done with it. In some contexts, such as when discussing privacy policies, the term privacy is mainly associated with the provision of this type of information.

2 *Choice*. To an extent, privacy concerns choices. In an ideal world, users of a digital service might be presented with choices about how data is collected and used. At the very least, they should be given enough information to decide whether to use a digital service or not.

3 *Mechanisms*. Providing privacy requires mechanisms. These include privacy regulations, standards and policies. They also require underlying technologies that can be used to enable privacy. We discuss a range of privacy mechanisms later in this chapter.

Monitoring and surveillance

Perhaps the main reason for an increased interest in privacy today is the potential consequences of the powerful data collection capabilities that have been enabled by the spread of digital technology. Two data collection activities that merit special mention are:

- *Monitoring*. This is normally used to refer to data gathering that is specific in its application, overtly happening (in some cases completely transparently) and exists mainly for performance, security and compliance reasons. Monitoring focuses on observing specific activities or conditions in a well-scoped context and usually with the consent of key stakeholders.
- *Surveillance*. This is normally used to refer to data gathering that is broad in its application, covert (generally without consent) and exists mainly for control, tracking and security reasons.

Note that both monitoring and surveillance can be conducted for both benign and more nefarious reasons. For example, in Chapter 6 we observed that monitoring forms a major part of sound cyber security management. As our earlier fitness tracking scenario illustrated, monitoring also plays an important role in desirable services such as healthcare. However, monitoring is also often buried into the small print of privacy policies of digital services such as search engines, enabling the provider to do extensive analysis of data supplied by its customers and then use it for purposes that are often unclear.

Similarly, surveillance forms a major component of national security practices. Some would argue that a degree of surveillance, for example the use of wiretaps, is necessary for national security. Surveillance technologies such as CCTV cameras are routinely used in support of public safety. Yet the extent of data collection possibilities today mean that an authoritarian regime can, in theory, learn a great deal about its population through mass surveillance of digital activity.

Both monitoring and surveillance raise significant privacy concerns due to the increasing ability for both monitoring and surveillance to be conducted at scale by a range of different parties, and for them to potentially arise as part of a 'mission creep' from an initial apparently reasonable data collection activity. As an example of the latter, some people expressed concerns that Covid-tracking application software, initially designed with the intent of controlling the spread of disease, might later be used for other purposes.

Identity

Privacy, as discussed in this chapter, relates to data, but not all types of data. Privacy primarily relates to *personal data*, which is data that can be linked to a human identity. This idea of identity is important to understand, since it has strong ties to all privacy-related concepts in this chapter.

Identity is the set of properties that make an individual (human) distinct, such as their name, appearance, behaviours, beliefs, personality, etc. Our sense of identity also encompasses how we perceive ourselves and how others perceive us. Identity can be associated with various domains, each highlighting different notions relating to how an individual is defined or recognized. These include:

- *Biographical.* This notion of identity refers to the factual, documented aspects of a person's life history. It includes formal, recorded details about the individual, such as their name, date of birth, nationality and other official information.
- *Psychological.* This refers to an individual's cognitive properties, including their beliefs, feelings, emotions, values and personality.
- *Physiological.* This concerns the physical, biological and genetic characteristics that distinguish one individual from another. This can include unique traits such as fingerprints, DNA, facial features and other measurable bodily attributes (including those forming the bases for biometrics, as discussed in Chapter 3).
- *Digital.* This notion of identity captures how an individual is represented and recognized online. This is a collection of data points and attributes that allow systems and other people to identify, verify and track an individual's actions in the digital world.

Privacy relates to all of these different notions of identity, although this chapter is largely motivated by the increasing role and importance that digital identity plays in notions of privacy.

In digital environments, the term *personally identifiable information* (PII) is often used to describe any information that can be used to identify a particular individual (either on its own or alongside other personal data). Personal data, particularly PII, has become a much sought-after commodity. Advertisers use online platforms such as social media, websites and other internet-enabled services to buy the ability to send personalized advertisements to targeted audiences. Cyber criminals also use the personal data of victims to target individuals (see Chapter 7). While this book is generally about the protection of all data, this chapter is particularly concerned with the protection of personal data (and especially PII) which, from a privacy perspective, represents the most sensitive data in a digital environment.

Defining privacy

Having argued that privacy is very hard to define, we will now make an attempt. It will not be perfect (because no definition of privacy is) but it should give us something to work with.

Privacy can be defined as the right to prevent personal data from being disclosed without an individual's explicit and informed consent. We need to expand on several aspects of this definition of privacy:

- *Right*. The use of the word 'right' indicates that privacy is a legal and enforceable concept. In the next section we comment further on the extent to which different societies might regard privacy as a right. When we later look at regulations, we will see that there are in fact many separate 'rights' associated with this general idea. While privacy is a right, in many cases it is more of a privilege requiring resources, knowledge and skill to achieve. Indeed, in digital environments establishing privacy can be very challenging.
- *Personal data*. By this we mean data that is obviously personal such as name, date of birth, passport number, address, digital identities, etc., as well as insights about an individual such as personal characteristics, beliefs, preferences, activities, communications, etc.
- *Disclosure*. By this we mean both revealed by accident, perhaps through inadvertent carelessness, as well as through malicious intervention, such as by means of a cyber attack.
- *Consent*. This refers to an individual's agreement for a specific action to occur, including an ability to revoke such consent without penalty. As we later discuss, consent is a key requirement in many privacy regulations. Individuals must be provided with clear, comprehensible information about what they are consenting to, including the purpose of data collection and how their data will be used. Ideally, consent should be freely given, specific, unambiguous and revocable. Revoking consent should be easy to achieve, involving a clear process and communications about the consequences (for example, loss of access to a service).

Note that this definition captures all three aspects of privacy that we discussed in the opening section:

1. Transparency is required so that an individual knows what actions they have a right to prevent from occuring.

2 Choice is facilitated through the individual's right to make decisions about data disclosure.
3 Mechanisms are inferred since otherwise such choices could not be enacted upon.

Related concepts

We now briefly address the relationship between privacy and three important related concepts:

- *Security*. Ultimately, privacy is about facilitating control of personal data, while security is about protection of personal data from threats. There are some settings where this difference is relevant. For example, following a data breach, privacy is likely to be associated with the need to notify affected individuals about potential exposure of personal data, while security is likely to be associated with identification of the breach's cause, containing the incident and preventing future occurrences. However, the very fact that we have a whole chapter in a cyber security book dedicated to privacy indicates that these two concepts are intertwined and quite difficult to separate. Every chapter of this book touches on issues that potentially relate to privacy.
- *Anonymity*. Privacy clearly relates to anonymity, which (as was discussed in Chapter 1) refers to the state of not knowing an identity. There are situations where anonymity might be a privacy requirement, such as when designing a voting scheme that suppresses the identity of voters. However, there are also situations where privacy does not require anonymity. For example, an organizational website might display images and names of employees but suppress personal data such as contact numbers, role descriptions and salaries. Mechanisms for providing anonymity are thus best thought of as tools, amongst many, that can be used to support privacy in certain contexts. We will discuss examples of anonymity tools later in this chapter.
- *Confidentiality*. Similarly, the provision of confidentiality (see Chapter 1) is best regarded as part of the mechanism armoury that we can call on to support privacy, particularly through the use of encryption (see Chapter 2 and later in this chapter). Not all privacy requirements need the provision of confidentiality (for example, our previous anonymous voting scheme might not require votes to be kept confidential) but confidentiality plays a big role in the provision of privacy in many other settings.

Privacy principles and paradoxes

In this section we reflect on various principles that underpin privacy, as well as some significant privacy paradoxes.

Societal principles driving privacy

The desire for privacy is driven by some fundamental principles that underpin societies. It is worth noting that these apply to some societies much more than others (see, for example, the discussion on national culture in Chapter 9). This, in turn, means that some societies demand privacy much more than others, or place different emphasis on how sensitive certain aspects of personal data are.

Broad principles that influence a desire for privacy include those relating to:

- *Autonomy and freedom.* Privacy supports individuals to exercise autonomy and make independent decisions without concerns about external interference or judgment.
- *Respect for individuals.* Enabling privacy demonstrates a fundamental respect for individuals' dignity, personal boundaries and freedoms.
- *Building positive relationships.* Ethical handling of personal data builds trust between individuals and institutions, fostering positive relationships based on honesty.
- *Personal identity.* Privacy enables individuals to shape and maintain their personal identity. This is particularly important for children and adolescents who are impressionable. Privacy supports the creation of spaces for reflection, introspection, growth and self-expression away from wider scrutiny.
- *Security and safety.* Protecting privacy safeguards individuals from potential harm, such as through identity theft, stalking or other forms of intrusion (see also Chapter 7).

These are grand principles that appear, at first glance, highly desirable. However, we will see that the ambiguity, subjectivity and context-dependence of privacy, which we highlighted at the start of this chapter, mean that the desire to uphold these principles is not always as clearcut as it might at first seem.

Data minimization

Privacy concerns the disclosure of data, so one approach to providing privacy is to minimize the amount of data that *could* be disclosed. The principle of *data minimization* is to only collect, process and store the minimum amount of personal data necessary to achieve a specific purpose. Data minimization is essentially a strategy for avoiding the creation of unnecessary risks to privacy. A data minimization strategy typically includes processes for strictly:

- *Limiting data retention.* Once data is no longer required then it should be destroyed. This reduces the risks of data being disclosed at a future time. This is a particularly sensible practice because unnecessarily retained data often presents a risk to the data holder (with respect to privacy regulations that we discuss later) without maintaining any apparent benefits.

- *Controlling data usage*. Data should only be used for the purpose explicitly stated at the time of collection. As well as supporting privacy, this is simply good practice since it forces organizations to reflect upon what data they are collecting and why.

The principle of data minimization includes an implicit assumption that data that is no longer needed can, and will, be safely destroyed. This is not quite as straightforward as it sounds, since destroying data is a science in itself. More formally, *data sanitization* is the process of permanently and securely removing or altering data to prevent later unauthorized access or recovery. Data sanitization involves making data irrecoverable in such a way that even an advanced data forensic tool cannot retrieve it.

Common methods of conducting data sanitization include:

- *Pseudonymization*. Although not strictly data destruction, pseudonymization involves transforming data into a non-identifiable form by replacing sensitive information with fictitious data. This makes it, in principle, impossible to link the masked data back to an individual.
- *Data overwriting*. Removing a file through standard system commands does not fully wipe the data from hardware storage. The data remains in storage until it is completely overwritten, making it recoverable with digital forensics. Data overwriting involves overwriting the deleted file with random data multiple times, making it much harder to recover.
- *Cryptographic erasure*. As we discussed in Chapter 2, encryption renders data unintelligible to anyone who does not possess the corresponding decryption key. Hence, if data is encrypted and then the decryption key destroyed, data will effectively become sanitized. Of course, this requires the decryption key itself to have been appropriately sanitized. Interestingly, this type of data sanitization is precisely what ransomware attackers threaten their victims with (see Chapter 2).
- *Physical destruction*. The ultimate means of enforcing data sanitization is to physically destroy the hardware on which data is stored. This is arguably the only true means of data sanitization.

Personal privacy paradoxes

Interestingly, there are often contradictions that arise concerning what people say about privacy and what they actually do about it. These discrepancies have become particularly accentuated in digital environments. Note that such discrepancies can apply in either direction. For example:

- A privacy-aware individual might openly express concerns about privacy of personal data. However, they might then freely share surprisingly personal data online on, for example, a social media platform. Similarly, they might hesitate to supply personal data to a digital service until they realize that they can obtain free or discounted access by doing so, in which case they proceed.
- An individual might claim they have no concerns about privacy, arguing that they are not doing anything untoward (they have 'nothing to hide'). However, they might subsequently get upset by targeted advertisements appearing during their web searches. Further, if an attacker pointed a gun at them and then demanded personal information, would this relaxed attitude to privacy still hold in a context where the person seeking the information is clearly not well-intentioned?

Fundamentally, these personal privacy 'paradoxes' (perhaps 'inconsistencies' or 'compromises' are better words) arise from the three complexities of privacy that we outlined at the start of the chapter:

1. *Privacy has different interpretations.* We often focus on different aspects of privacy, or different threats associated with privacy, in a given situation. Our example privacy-aware individual is probably focusing on broad societal principles or commercial exploitation of data when they express their general privacy concerns, yet focus solely on what their friends might think about personal information when they upload their social media posts and not how the provider might subsequently use their data.
2. *Privacy is subjective.* Different people have different views about the extent to which they need privacy, or *think* they need privacy. Feelings of privacy are also inherently subjective because, to an extent, they are emotional. How someone feels about privacy one day might be different the next day. The individual who was upset about the web advertisements one day might just ignore them the next day. We discuss broader issues concerning human security behaviour in Chapter 9.
3. *Privacy is context-dependent.* How we react to privacy-related issues is very context-dependent and sometimes involves conflicts of interest. Our privacy-aware individual seemed much less concerned about privacy when offered a free digital service. This apparent inconsistency is accentuated within the context of digital environments, where people tend to be less privacy conscious. Our example individual who claimed to have no privacy concerns would probably be the first to hesitate if a stranger turned up at their door and requested their date of birth, which is data they may have already freely submitted to multiple web services.

These inconsistencies also arise from several factors that are more specific to digital environments:

- *Lack of privacy awareness*. Individuals need to be sufficiently knowledgeable about privacy to possess the skills and resources to manage and protect their own personal data on digital platforms. Many users do not fully understand how data can be collected, used, shared or stored. This includes technical concepts like tracking cookies, data sharing with third parties and the implications of data breaches.
- *Complexity of privacy policies*. Privacy policies (which we discuss later) are often long, difficult to understand and filled with legal jargon. This makes it challenging for users to make informed choices about their data. They thus often accept privacy policies without really appreciating what personal data uses they are accepting.
- *Rapidly evolving technology*. Technologies and their features are constantly changing, making it difficult for users to keep up with the latest risks that emerging technologies present to their personal data.

Navigating principles and paradoxes

We have seen that privacy is motivated by grand societal principles but that forces of technology and the vagaries of individual attitudes and behaviour make privacy complex to rationalize about and provide. How can these contradictory forces and attitudes all be navigated to the broader satisfaction of society?

While we have used the term 'privacy' somewhat loosely in much of this discussion, it is worth recalling our earlier definition of privacy as a *right* to prevent personal data from being disclosed without an individual's explicit and informed consent. This suggests that privacy needs to be supported by frameworks of data governance that provide oversight of data management practices, while still providing degrees of flexibility. This is what we look at next.

Privacy regulations, standards and policies

In this section we discuss some of the regulations and standards that guide privacy practices. We also take a brief look at privacy policies.

Privacy regulations

Today, various regulations aspire to enable the right of individuals to privacy within digital environments. Data privacy regulations aim to provide a baseline of privacy guarantees for individuals. Examples of such regulations include the:

- General Data Protection Regulation (Europe Union and UK)
- Consumer Privacy Act (California)
- Personal Information Protection and Electronic Documents Act (Canada)
- General Data Protection Law (Brazil)
- Personal Information Protection Law (China)
- Data Protection Act (Kenya)

These regulations, among many others, impose a range of obligations on organizations that collect, process or store personal data to do so securely and respectfully. Such regulations also exist, in part, to use legal obligations to help prevent data breaches.

The *General Data Protection Regulation* (GDPR) is one of the most influential privacy regulations. While it applies directly to member states of the European Union and the UK, it has served as an inspiration for similar legislation throughout the world. The GDPR refers more broadly to 'data protection' to designate the specific legal obligations established by Article 25 of the GDPR.[2] Data protection applies to any sufficiently large organization that processes the personal data (PII) of residents of associated GDPR countries, regardless of location. The GDPR also emphasizes explicit consent, transparency, data subject rights and the need for breach notifications. Non-compliance can result in significant fines.

In the GDPR, individuals are referred to as *data subjects*. Organizations that handle personal data are split into two categories:

1. *Data controllers*. These are the legal entities that decide why and how personal data will be processed. Typically, data controllers are also the entities that collect personal data.
2. *Data processors*. These are the legal entities that apply some transformation to personal data on behalf of data controllers, generally to provide services to data subjects. For example, data processors can be third parties that provide specialist services that data controllers need to perform their own services. Data processors do not have control over personal data beyond what data controllers specify within data processing agreements.

Core privacy-related rights within the UK version of the GDPR, include the following:[3]

- The right to be informed (about the collection and use of personal data).
- The right of access (to receive copies of personal data that is held).
- The right to rectification (to correct inaccurate personal data).
- The right to erasure (the deletion of personal data).
- The right to restrict processing (to request suppression of personal data).
- The right to data portability (the ability to reuse data across other services).
- The right to object (in certain circumstances).
- Various rights related to automated decision-making, including profiling.

In order to conform with regulations such as the GDPR, organizations need to develop a clear understanding of how they engage with personal data. A *privacy impact assessment* (PIA) is a formal process that enables an organization to identify, assess and mitigate privacy risks associated with the collection, storage, processing and sharing of personal data. A PIA helps to ensure that privacy principles, legal obligations and regulations (such as GDPR) are adhered to throughout the lifecycle of data processing activities. A range of PIA templates are available to use, one of which is provided by the UK Information Commissioner's Office.[4]

Of course, privacy regulations cast a wide net in an attempt to address a wide range of scenarios, whether maliciously intended or not. This means that terms such as 'reasonable' are often used in regulations, rather than absolutes. For example, organizations might be tasked with making 'reasonable' efforts to protect personal data from attackers. Such directions are requirements, not specifications. This leaves room both for interpretation and for deciding what needs to be done to conform. As a result, there are potential discrepancies involved in deciding what constitutes compliance.

The main advantage of the emergence of privacy regulations such as the GDPR is that organizations and software developers must now treat privacy rights as requirements that must be met. In practice, however, there are limitations in the extent to which such rights can be manifested in a world where data collection has such power and potential for influence.

Privacy standards

As well as regulations, a variety of standards exist to support privacy. These standards typically provide frameworks and guidelines for embedding privacy into organizational and technical processes, ensuring better data protection practices. Key ISO standards include:

- *ISO/IEC 27561: Privacy Operationalization Model and Method for Engineering (POMME).*[5] This provides a structured approach to operationalizing privacy within engineering processes. It focuses on how to embed privacy requirements systematically into the engineering lifecycle, ensuring compliance with privacy laws and frameworks. The POMME model helps organizations translate privacy principles into operational requirements and actionable tasks in technical development projects. It shares much with the *OASIS Privacy Management Reference Model.*[6]
- *ISO/IEC 27701: Security Techniques – Extension to ISO/IEC 27001 and 27002 for Privacy Information Management.*[7] This is an extension of the information security management standards ISO/IEC 27001 and 27002 (see Chapter 6), designed to manage privacy and personal data. It establishes a privacy information management system, helping organizations meet data protection requirements such as those in the GDPR. It also provides guidance on managing and controlling privacy risks within a broader information security management system.
- *ISO/IEC 29100: Privacy Framework.*[8] This framework defines a common vocabulary and outlines principles for privacy protection in various digital environments. It specifies 11 privacy principles, such as consent, accountability and data minimization, which are foundational for protecting personal data. This standard offers guidance on how organizations can design systems with privacy by design in mind, which is something we discuss in the next section.
- *ISO/IEC 29101: Privacy Architecture Framework.*[9] This complements ISO/IEC 29100 by providing a high-level architectural framework for implementing privacy in digital systems. It outlines technical and procedural measures to manage personal data throughout its lifecycle, helping organizations align system architecture with privacy requirements. The standard is useful for designing systems that support data protection principles and operational requirements for privacy.
- *ISO/IEC 29134: Guidelines for Privacy Impact Assessment.*[10] This standard provides guidelines for conducting a PIA. It offers a systematic methodology for evaluating how personal data is handled and how to assess the potential privacy risks to individuals. These guidelines help organizations ensure compliance with privacy regulations and promote privacy by design.

Note that each of these standards addresses privacy from a different angle, including principles (29100), architecture (29101), operationalization (27561), management systems (27701) and risk assessment (29134).

Privacy policies

In Chapter 1 we outlined the importance of security policies to establishing how security will be enacted within a specific environment. This also applies to privacy, where an organizational *privacy policy* should outline how an organization collects, uses and safeguards personal data. Sadly, privacy policies have developed a fairly negative reputation, primarily arising from the poor practice of requiring users to accept complex and lengthy privacy policy statements prior to being able to access digital services. In addition, the effectiveness of privacy policies is often detracted as a result of:

- *Lack of transparency.* Many digital services involve the hidden sharing or selling of data to third-party entities, which is often undisclosed or poorly communicated to users within a privacy policy. This has led to a degree of mistrust in the honesty of privacy policies.
- *Consent fatigue.* Users are frequently met with requests to consent to different privacy terms and conditions that might vary significantly across regions, making it challenging to make sense of what they are being asked to agree to. As a result, many users choose to agree automatically to such terms, without fully reading them.
- *Limitations on control.* Even when individuals understand and want to exercise control of their personal data, as authorized within a privacy policy, they may find it difficult to put this into practice. The ability to access, delete or modify data held by organizations is often buried behind opaque processes or a lack of facilitating tools. This, in turn, further erodes the trust users have in such policies.

None of this should diminish the importance of the role of effective privacy policies in informing users of privacy practices and enabling users to exercise their regulatory rights. This is an aspect of privacy governance where things simply need to improve.

Privacy engineering

In this section we discuss how to embed privacy into digital systems.

Key privacy engineering steps

Privacy engineering is the discipline of designing and implementing systems that incorporate privacy protections directly into products and services. It focuses on ensuring that privacy concepts such as data minimization, user consent, security and transparency are integrated into the entire lifecycle of a system, from the initial design phase to its deployment and operation.

Specifically, the aim of privacy engineering is to proactively safeguard personal data, ensuring compliance with legal regulation and addressing privacy risks while balancing usability, functionality and innovation. This involves using techniques such as data anonymization, encryption and PIAs to minimize the exposure and misuse of sensitive information.

To determine whether systems built using privacy engineering in mind are compliant with regulations (such as the GDPR), organizations can follow structured approaches. Key steps that might form part of privacy engineering include:

- conducting a PIA to assess how existing systems handle personal data and identify key privacy risks;
- building systems that support privacy from the outset (we further discuss this shortly);
- conducting regular audits to identify changes in digital systems (see Chapter 6);
- implementing user rights management;
- ensuring lawful basis for data processing;
- documenting implemented privacy features to be able to provide evidence in case of external audits;
- performing third-party risk management to ensure that data is only shared with partners who have adequate privacy measures in place, and documenting these relationships (see Chapter 6);
- implementing incident response and breach notification (see Chapter 6);
- implementing privacy education, training and awareness programmes (see Chapter 9).

Privacy engineering can take a principles-led approach using regulation as a set of requirements that must be met (and adopting an ad hoc set of methods to reach those requirements) or can adopt a privacy framework that is more aligned with software engineering and management processes. We now review relevant examples of each.

Privacy by design

Privacy by design[11] is a set of seven key principles that integrate privacy and data protection into the design and operation of products, systems and services from the outset, rather than as an afterthought. It emphasizes that privacy should be a fundamental consideration in any new technology or business process, rather than something to be retrofitted later. Privacy by design was later adopted as part of the GDPR.

The seven principles are:

1 *Proactive not reactive; preventive not remedial.* Stakeholders should aim to anticipate and prevent privacy issues before they occur, rather than reacting to them after the fact.

2 *Privacy as the default setting.* Personal data should be automatically protected without individuals asking.

3 *Privacy embedded into design.* Privacy should be integrated into the design and architecture of digital systems, business practices and networked infrastructure.

4 *Full functionality: positive-sum, not zero-sum.* A zero-sum game suggests that there are winners and losers in the design and implementation of privacy features. By shifting the perspective of privacy as a feature, rather than a burden, the idea is that risk owners and individuals can have a win-win situation.

5 *End-to-end security; full lifecycle protection.* Personal data should be protected throughout its entire lifecycle, from the moment it is collected to when it is securely destroyed.

6 *Visibility and transparency: keep it open.* Organizations should operate with transparency, making it clear to individuals how their data is being used, and ensuring that the processing of personal data is open to verification by stakeholders.

7 *Respect for user privacy: keep it user-centric.* Privacy by design emphasizes that systems and processes should be user-centric, providing strong privacy defaults, appropriate notice and empowering users with control over their data.

NIST privacy framework

The NIST privacy framework[12] provides a structured approach to building privacy protections into operations, helping organizations align their practices with legal, ethical and business objectives. Similarly to the broader NIST cyber security framework discussed in Chapter 6, the NIST privacy framework is built around three key components:

1 *Core.* A set of privacy protection activities and outcomes organized into five functions: Identify, Govern, Control, Communicate and Protect. These help organizations understand their privacy risks, develop governance structures and communicate with stakeholders.

2 *Profiles.* These align the core functions with their specific privacy goals and risks.

3 *Implementation tiers.* These describe an organization's approach to privacy risk management, ranging from partial (Tier 1) to adaptive (Tier 4), helping organizations determine their maturity in managing privacy risks.

MITRE privacy framework

The MITRE privacy framework[13] is a structured approach to help organizations manage privacy risks. Key elements include applying design principles to ensure privacy is considered in the development of computer systems and processes. This approach emphasizes both the technical and governance aspects of privacy protection. It serves as a practical guide for integrating privacy considerations into the entire system lifecycle.

PANOPTIC

MITRE PANOPTIC (Pattern and Action Nomenclature Of Privacy Threats In Context)[14] is a privacy threat modelling framework developed to help organizations systematically understand and address privacy risks. This framework focuses on external threat actors as well as considering the actions, inactions and system behaviours that can lead to privacy risks. The model includes both benign and malicious intents and recognizes that privacy threats can arise from within the system itself. This approach supports a broader, more comprehensive assessment of privacy risks.

Unlike traditional cyber security frameworks that focus mostly on malicious threats, PANOPTIC includes threats with benign intent – actions that might compromise privacy without malicious intent, such as unintentional data over-collection or insufficient user notifications. Malicious intent includes explicit privacy attacks, like unauthorized access or misuse of personal data. PANOPTIC acknowledges that threats can originate from both internal systems (like poor configuration or data retention policies) and external actors (such as hackers or third parties). This dual focus encourages organizations to look inward at system vulnerabilities as well as defend against external attacks.

LINDDUN

LINDDUN[15] is a privacy threat modelling framework to help identify and mitigate privacy risks in software systems design and development. The framework aims to be a structured, systematic approach to assess privacy threats and suggest mitigation strategies. LINDDUN aims to be compatible with other security threat models, including STRIDE and DREAD (see Chapter 5). It includes seven categories of privacy threat, namely:

1. *Linking*. The unauthorized correlation of data that can identify individuals.
2. *Identifying*. Exposing personal identities through available data.
3. *Non-repudiation*. Inability to deny past actions due to tracking or logging.

4 *Detecting*. Unauthorized discovery or inference of actions or identities.
5 *Data disclosure*. Excessive or inappropriate exposure of data.
6 *Unawareness*. Users being uninformed about how their data is used.
7 *Non-compliance*. Failure to adhere to privacy laws or best practices.

Privacy-enhancing technologies

Having established a regulatory need for privacy, we now review just some of the wide range of technological mechanisms that can be used to enable different aspects of privacy. These are often generally referred to as *privacy-enhancing technologies* (PETs). It is important to recognize that most PETS are designed to tackle certain specific aspects of data minimization, and that no PET provides a general mechanism for facilitating privacy. Many PETs, but not all, are special cryptographic tools (see Chapter 2). It is also worth observing that most of the technologies we have discussed in other chapters of this book can be used to support privacy. For example, secure hardware devices, as discussed in Chapter 3, create safe places where personal data can be kept private. Thus PETs might reasonably be regarded as a specialist addition to the toolkit of technologies facilitating privacy, and certainly not the only tools for doing so.

Privacy and encryption

The first technology that many people think of when seeking to provide privacy is encryption, which we discussed in Chapter 2. This is because encryption provides confidentiality, which plays a major role in the implementation of privacy.

It is worth observing that use of encryption is insufficient to guarantee certain aspects of privacy. For example, a suspect in a criminal investigation might reasonably choose to communicate using a secure messaging scheme that offers *end-to-end encryption*, which means that data is encrypted on the sender's device and can only be decrypted on the receiver's device, but nowhere in between. Investigators are thus unable to view the contents of messages that the suspect sends. However, it might be possible for investigators to make deductions about correspondence from associated *metadata*, which is data related to the communication other than the content, such as date and time of correspondence, recipient address, etc. In this way privacy might be seen as not being fully provided, despite the use of encryption.

As another example, the communication channel between a contactless bank card and a reader is *not* traditionally encrypted. This is because the data exchanged on such a channel is not regarded as security-sensitive enough to merit confidentiality protection. However, because this data is static (it largely consists of the bank card number), this creates a privacy concern because the static data can be used to track a card user across multiple reader connections. Privacy requirements arising from the GDPR mean that future plans are to encrypt this channel. If a straightforward form of encryption is used then the same ciphertext will be generated each time the same card number is encrypted. This will provide confidentiality of the data, but not privacy, since this same ciphertext could still be used to track a card user across multiple reader connections. For this reason, the encryption technique used will need to include random input in order to achieve the privacy objective.

While all forms of encryption can be used to support privacy, there are also some special forms of encryption that have been designed to support specific privacy objectives. An example is *homomorphic encryption*, which is a form of encryption that enables computations to be performed on ciphertexts that have an equivalent impact on the underlying plaintext. Using homomorphic encryption, for example, the addition of two ciphertexts will result in the ciphertext that is the encryption of the addition of the two plaintexts, a property that does not hold for standard encryption mechanisms. The motivation for homomorphic encryption arises from privacy requirements of cloud storage environments. Without homomorphic encryption, a data owner who has placed encrypted data into cloud storage would only be able to perform a computation on that data (for example, compute an average data value) either by downloading it and decrypting locally, or by providing the storage provider with the decryption key that enables them to perform the computation on behalf of the data owner. The former strategy is inefficient, while the latter strategy raises potential privacy concerns.

Data manipulation for privacy

An alternative approach to encryption is to manipulate data in different ways in order to reduce, or eliminate, the privacy-related information that can be deduced from it. Two examples of this type of approach are:

- *Data anonymization*. The idea behind this approach is to remove or alter any data that explicitly links to an individual. For example, a medical database being offered to a research project might go through a data anonymization process where sensitive fields such as names and addresses are either removed or replaced with pseudonyms. Of course, care must be taken not to leave sufficient information in the database that enables identities to be inferred. As an extreme example, a workplace with only one female employee that uses data anonymization to suppress names on a database but not genders, has clearly failed to protect the privacy of all of their employees. Pseudonyms are sometimes used to provide a degree of anonymity in communication protocols. An example is telecommunications, where a pseudonym is used to mask the real identity of a caller (represented by the identity associated with the SIM card being used).

- *Differential privacy*. In order to address data inference problems of the type previously discussed, differential privacy provides techniques for adding controlled noise to data sets that enable statistical analysis to still be conducted while masking individual data points that could lead to breaches of privacy requirements. This approach to supporting privacy is adopted by some machine learning applications.

Onion routing

Onion routing addresses the lack of anonymity on the internet. The idea behind *onion routing* is to utilize a network of special *routers* (referred to as nodes) that each act as intermediaries between the originator and the destination of an internet connection. Each node applies a separate layer of encryption to each leg of the internet connection, resulting in each router only knowing the identity of the previous and subsequent onion router, but not the entire connection path from sender to receiver. The best-known example is *Tor*, which provides a special web browser and uses paths consisting of three onion routers to mask the identity of a user making a web request from the web server that receives it.

Onion routing provides a degree of anonymity since no single component of the resulting network is aware of both the originator and destination. However, it does not necessarily provide anonymity if a third party is able to gain control of a significant number of the onion routers, nor does it prevent metadata associated with end points from being analysed and connections inferred.

Naturally, making use of multiple layers of communication affects performance significantly, but Tor has proven popular and provides a reasonable degree of anonymity to internet users who seek additional levels of privacy.

Zero-knowledge proofs

A *zero-knowledge proof* is a cryptographic tool that enables one party to prove the truth of a statement (such as knowledge of a value) to another without revealing any unnecessary information relating to that statement. The need for zero-knowledge proofs is very much motivated by data minimization. Consider, for example, a user accessing a digital service where they have to demonstrate that they are over 13 years of age (for example, for a social media account). The traditional approach is for a service provider to request the date of birth of the applicant. But this does not conform with the principle of data minimization, since the service provider does not *need* to know the applicant's date of birth – all they need is evidence that they are at least 13. Use of a zero-knowledge proof in this context enables cryptographic evidence to be generated that attests the proof of such a statement without further data leakage. Other examples of uses of zero-knowledge proofs to support privacy include:

- *Entity authentication*. To prove knowledge of an authentication credential such as a password without revealing it.

- *Compliance.* To prove that compliance conditions have been met without revealing sensitive underlying business processes.
- *Voting.* To prove that a vote in an electronic voting scheme is well-formed and has been cast by a legitimate voter, without revealing the identity of the voter or the nature of the vote.

Multiparty computation

One source of threats to privacy arises from the fact that data is typically gathered and stored in centralized locations. The goal of *multiparty computation* (MPC) is to avoid data ending up in such centralized locations by enabling multiple parties to jointly compute a function while keeping their inputs private. The classical motivation for MPC is known as the *millionaires' problem*, which concerns a fictitious group of millionaires who wish to know who has the most money without openly revealing their wealth to the others. The most obvious solution, and one which resonates with most real situations analogous to the millionaires' problem, is for each millionaire to submit their wealth to a trusted third party who establishes the highest value and then informs the millionaires. Seen from a privacy perspective, this solution is not ideal since it does not support data minimization (a third party learns a great deal of unnecessary information) and creates a privacy risk (the third party could suffer a data breach and leak the wealth of each millionaire). The use of MPC enables situations like this to be resolved through a series of communications between the various parties (in this case millionaires) that enables the result to be computed without any single party learning any of the other input values.

Uses of MPC (beyond pointless wealth speculation!) include:

- *Auctions.* Some forms of auction involve sealed bids, where the details of an individual bid should be kept private. Use of MPC enables such an auction to take place while preserving individual bid privacy, even from an auctioneer.
- *Key management.* As we observed in Chapter 2, key management is critical to supporting use of cryptography. Use of MPC enables cryptographic keys to be distributed into components across multiple locations, reducing the risk of a key compromise while enabling cryptographic computations to still be performed using a distributed key.
- *Federated learning.* This is a broad class of machine learning approaches in which models are trained across multiple devices without sharing individual pieces of data. The use of MPC enables training on sensitive data (like healthcare records) without exposing personal data.

Private database operations

A significant amount of data ends up stored in central databases. However, interactions with such databases often present privacy challenges. Several PETs have been developed to tackle specific aspects of database privacy. These include:

- *Private information retrieval* (PIR). The privacy problem that PIR addresses is that a user querying a database inherently leaks private information. For example, a user querying a medical database might reveal, through the nature of their queries, private information about a health condition that they are suffering from. The goal of PIR is to facilitate such queries without the database learning what data was accessed. Potential uses of PIR also include facilitating private web browsing.
- *Private set intersection* (PSI). This concerns privacy arising from the interaction between two databases. For example, the owners of two database services might be interested in learning what users they have in common. The crude solution of sharing the two databases is clearly unacceptable from a privacy perspective. The goal of PSI is to enable two database holders to deduce items of common data without revealing any data that the other does not hold.

Privacy-focused blockchains

Blockchains (see Chapter 2) can be used to support privacy. While cryptocurrencies based on blockchains, such as Bitcoin, only offer limited anonymity, more privacy-preserving digital transactions are enabled using a range of techniques such as ring signatures (a special anonymous form of digital signature) and mixing services that obscure the identities of participants by blending their transactions with others (making it harder to trace individual activity). Privacy-focused blockchains such as Monero or Zcash implement this natively, offering privacy through built-in features that anonymize transactions and user data.

Deploying PETs

In this section we have reviewed several PETs that supplement the range of technologies that we have discussed throughout this book that could be used to support privacy. While some of these technologies are well accepted, others are relatively immature. Notably, many PETs such as MPC and homomorphic encryption create significant overheads, particularly with respect to computational efficiency. We can expect to see more standardization and more use of PETs in the future, but for now much of this technology remains in development.

The future of privacy

We end this chapter with some reflections on what the future of privacy might look like in the light of emerging technology. These are areas where we expect to see developments that impact privacy (positively and negatively), but we certainly cannot predict with accuracy exactly how events will unfold.

- *Data proliferation and ubiquity.* One thing we can be confident about is that more devices will become interconnected, more data will be generated, and hence the need for privacy will only get greater. This is likely to be particularly accentuated by the rise of technologies such as smart homes, wearables, autonomous vehicles, extended reality environments and biomedical sensing. Managing this vast data landscape will be a major privacy challenge moving forward.
- *Artificial intelligence.* Both machine learning and other artificial intelligence technologies rely on massive datasets for training and operation, using data relating to human behavioural patterns, locations and personal preferences. While these technologies offer significant benefits, they also pose many privacy risks, including those arising from data inferences and inadvertent discrimination. We will have to work very hard to preserve privacy in a digital world hungry for data to feed such technologies.
- *Mechanisms for consent.* Current consent mechanisms (including privacy policies) are generally fairly ineffective. Future privacy efforts will need to develop more user-friendly consent mechanisms and empower individuals to have meaningful control over their personal data, especially given the likely increased future threats to privacy.
- *Regulatory lag.* As new technologies emerge, privacy laws often fall behind. Furthermore, even existing regulations struggle to keep up with the dynamic landscape of data processing, algorithmic decision-making and global data flows. This is also a problem for security regulation, but it is particularly poignant for privacy regulation.
- *Ethical data handling.* As we have discussed, the forces pushing data collection and analytics flow somewhat against those of privacy. Society in general will need to establish ethical norms for what types of data gathering and use are acceptable, especially as organizations may become increasingly reliant on data analytics. What will all this mean for privacy?
- *Disruptive technologies.* It is likely that advancements will be made in a variety of game-changing technologies, whose impacts are potentially dramatic for society at large, and particularly for privacy. These include *brain-computer interfaces* that enable direct communication between the brain and external digital devices, and

biohacking, which uses technology to optimize an individual's physical and mental performance. Such technologies start to blur the boundaries of what a human is, and therefore raise enormous privacy questions.

The future of privacy will certainly not be dull!

KEY POINTS

- Privacy is a hard concept to define and rationalize. This is partially because privacy has different facets, and is subjective since attitudes to privacy tend to be context dependent.
- Various principles underpin privacy; however, privacy is subject to various paradoxes arising from opposing forces and personal inconsistencies.
- Several important regulations have been introduced to support privacy rights. These are generally broad in scope and allow for compliance ambiguity. A number of standards also support privacy in different ways.
- A wide range of privacy-enhancing technologies have been designed to support the provision of particular aspects of privacy. These supplement core security technologies in providing mechanisms to enable privacy.
- While society has progressed a great deal in terms of recognizing and responding to the need for privacy, many challenges still remain, especially in the light of emerging technology.

EXERCISES

1 Privacy is a hard concept to define. Conduct a survey of different definitions of privacy taken from a range of sources. Which ones do you prefer, and why?

2 Reflect on your own personal attitudes towards privacy:

a. To what extent would you say, in general, that you care about privacy?

b. How consistent do you feel you are when making decisions about privacy?

c. Provide examples of any situations where you have compromised privacy in order to gain utility.

3 Find an example of a recent high-profile data breach:

a. What happened, what data was compromised and who was affected?

   b. What were the consequences for the organization and the individuals involved?
   c. Suggest measures that could have been implemented to prevent the breach, including both technical and organizational practices.
4. Compare privacy regulations from two different geographical regions. Create a comparison table that addresses the following:
   a. How do the laws define personal data and privacy?
   b. What are the rules around consent for data collection in each region?
   c. What rights do consumers have under each framework?
5. Privacy policies have a fairly bad press:
   a. Find an example of a privacy policy that you feel is ineffective, explaining why.
   b. Find an example of a privacy policy that you feel is effective, explaining why.
   c. Tools exist purporting to automatically generate privacy policies using generative artificial intelligence. What are the various possible risks and benefits of such an approach?
6. Consider the following scenario: A company uses artificial intelligence (AI) to analyse customer behaviour, collecting vast amounts of data without explicit user consent. The AI system can predict personal preferences and suggest purchases, but customers are unaware of the extent of the data collection. The company does not intend to sell this data to third parties, but intends to use it to improve services for their customers:
   a. Explain the extent to which you believe this practice is ethical.
   b. Create two statements: one defending the company's right to use data for innovation and the other arguing for stricter privacy protections. Each side must provide supporting arguments based on privacy laws and ethical considerations.
7. You are tasked with developing a new wearable fitness tracker that collects location, health and activity data:
   a. Identify potential privacy risks associated with the device (state any assumptions you make).
   b. Propose technical solutions to mitigate these risks.
   c. Suggest how privacy by design principles might be applied to ensure that privacy is embedded throughout the product lifecycle, from design to deployment.

8 Select two privacy-enhancing technologies and compare them based on:
   a. What aspect of privacy they protect.
   b. Potential weaknesses or limitations in their privacy protection.
   c. The types of users or industries that might benefit most from using them.
   d. Their current maturity as a technology.

9 Governments might attempt to justify surveillance as necessary for public security and safety. However, surveillance can infringe on individual privacy.
   a. To what extent do you believe that national security and individual privacy can coexist? What compromises might be required?
   b. To what extent do you believe that governments should be transparent about the extent of their surveillance activities?
   c. To what extent do you believe surveillance technologies should be regulated to ensure they do not violate privacy rights?

10 At the close of this chapter we suggested some possible future developments with respect to privacy. What are your own personal views about likely future developments in threats to privacy and mechanisms for supporting privacy?

FURTHER READING

- Bhajaria, N (2022) *Data Privacy: A runbook for engineers*, Simon and Schuster
- Christen, P, Ranbaduge, T and Schnell, R (2020) *Linking Sensitive Data: Methods and techniques for practical privacy-preserving information sharing*, Springer
- Kang, R, Brown, S and Kiesler, S (2013) Why do people seek anonymity on the internet?: informing policy and design. In *CHI 13: Proceedings of the SIGCHI Conference on Human Factors in Computing Systems*, pp. 2657–66
- Richards, N (2022) *Why Privacy Matters*, Oxford University Press
- Meiklejohn, S, Pomarole, M, Jordan, G, Levchenko, K, McCoy, D, Voelker, G M and Savage, S (2013) A fistful of bitcoins: Characterizing payments among men with no names. In *IMC '13: Proceedings of the 2013 Conference on Internet Measurement*, pp. 127–40
- Solove, D J (2011) Why privacy matters even if you have 'nothing to hide', *Chronicle of Higher Education*, 15

- Torra, V (2017) *Data Privacy: Foundations, new developments and the big data challenge*, (Vol 28) Springer International Publishing
- Troncoso, C (2021) Privacy & Online Rights Knowledge Area, Version1.0.2, https://www.cybok.org/media/downloads/Privacy_Online_Rights_v1.0.2.pdf (archived at https://perma.cc/5L9L-R5R3)

Notes

1 Oxford English Dictionary, 'Privacy', www.oed.com/search/dictionary/?scope=Entries&q=privacy (archived at https://perma.cc/894A-CX7U)

2 European Data Protection Supervisor (2018) Preliminary opinion on privacy by design, www.edps.europa.eu/sites/default/files/publication/18-05-31_preliminary_opinion_on_privacy_by_design_en_0.pdf (archived at https://perma.cc/22ZE-PFTG)

3 Information Commissioner's Office (n.d.) A guide to individual rights, https://ico.org.uk/for-organisations/uk-gdpr-guidance-and-resources/individual-rights/individual-rights/ (archived at https://perma.cc/8V4T-6Y6W)

4 Information Commissioner's Office (n.d.) How do we do a DPIA? https://ico.org.uk/for-organisations/uk-gdpr-guidance-and-resources/accountability-and-governance/data-protection-impact-assessments-dpias/how-do-we-do-a-dpia/ (archived at https://perma.cc/2Y4Z-ZVNV)

5 ISO/IEC 27561, www.iso.org/standard/80394.html (archived at https://perma.cc/L8NX-5A9Y)

6 OASIS Privacy Management Reference Model, https://docs.oasis-open.org/pmrm/PMRM/v1.0/cs02/PMRM-v1.0-cs02.html (archived at https://perma.cc/54E7-N57Z)

7 ISO/IEC 27701, www.iso.org/standard/71670.html (archived at https://perma.cc/27K3-5RS2)

8 ISO/IEC 29100, www.iso.org/standard/85938.html (archived at https://perma.cc/B4UH-567A)

9 ISO/IEC 29101, www.iso.org/standard/75293.html (archived at https://perma.cc/QEQ2-M8N5)

10 ISO/IEC 29134, www.iso.org/standard/86012.html (archived at https://perma.cc/647L-UMBC)

11 Cavoukian, A (2011) Privacy by design: The 7 foundational principles – implementation and mapping of fair information practices, https://privacy.ucsc.edu/resources/privacy-by-design---foundational-principles.pdf (archived at https://perma.cc/4DZC-9FCF)

12 NIST (2020) Privacy Framework, https://www.nist.gov/privacy-framework/privacy-framework (archived at https://perma.cc/X38W-L74A)

13 MITRE (2019) MITRE's privacy engineering tools and their use in a privacy assessment framework, www.mitre.org/news-insights/publication/mitres-privacy-engineering-tools-and-their-use-privacy-assessment (archived at https://perma.cc/M2RT-K59V)

14 PANOPTIC™ Privacy Threat Model, https://ptmworkshop.gitlab.io/#/panoptic (archived at https://perma.cc/LQM9-3KLP)

15 LINDDUN, https://linddun.org/go/ (archived at https://perma.cc/7R78-6K5Y)

09 Human aspects

The role of personality, behaviour and culture in cyber security

This chapter discusses some of the human and behavioural aspects of cyber security. We begin by recapping why humans and their behaviour are so integral to cyber security. Next, we review human behaviour and personality, and the role of collective human security behaviour in the shaping of security culture. We then discuss how systems supporting cyber security can be designed to best accommodate human needs. Finally, we reflect on some of the challenges and approaches involved in changing human behaviour to better support cyber security objectives.

LEARNING OBJECTIVES

- The range of different human and behavioural aspects of cyber security.
- How human behaviour and personality impact cyber security.
- The components and influences that shape a security culture.
- How security processes can be designed to best engage humans.
- Approaches, frameworks and processes for encouraging security behaviour change.

Humans and cyber security

In this section we recap why humans are an inseparable part of cyber security. We then consider various human roles and reflect on the fallacies behind the adage that 'humans are the weakest link' in cyber security.

Why humans matter for cyber security

From the previous chapters of this book, it should already be clear that humans play an important role in cyber security. In the main, cyber security is something that serves human endeavour, hence it would be very surprising if humans were not part of it! This was something we formally recognized in Chapter 1, where we identified the human layer as being one of the three fundamental layers of a digital environment.

In previous chapters we have seen the importance of humans to cyber security. In Chapter 1 we discussed the cyber security ecosystem, noting that this consisted of consumers, producers and enforcers. This ecosystem consists of both individuals and organizations, but even the latter are essentially groups of humans who are coordinating activities towards specific goals relating to cyber security. In later chapters we have focused on different aspects of cyber security, with humans regularly featuring in key roles. For example, we have seen humans as:

- *Data owners*. This is the default role of humans throughout this book, with every chapter discussing cyber security technologies and processes designed to protect the data that every human who engages with a digital environment relies upon.
- *Managers of cyber security*. This is a role we focused on in Chapter 6, particularly from the perspective of organizations who seek to defend their digital environments from security incidents.
- *Exploiters*. In Chapter 7 we discussed the different ways that cybercriminals seek to exploit digital environments for a variety of different types of gain.

In any given context, humans often fall into different functional classes. For example, the security manager of a commercial organization might regard humans of relevance to the organization's cyber security as being:

- *Insiders*. Staff working for the organization.
- *Customers*. External clients of the organization.
- *Outsiders*. Any other people that the organization does not legitimately engage with who might pose threats to the organization.

Even within a classification of this type, humans might fall into significantly different groups with specific needs. For example, amongst the customer base there might be:

- individuals with limited experience of using digital technology
- individuals with disabilities
- different age groups such as children, adolescents and the elderly

Most importantly, however, regardless of human role or specific classification, there is one fact that is of extreme importance to cyber security and is often overlooked. Every human is different. This suggests that an ideal approach to cyber security is to consider the needs of every individual separately, which seems impractical. Fortunately, however, it is possible to identify common human characteristics, shared traits and behavioural patterns that enable us to take a more manageable approach to considering the needs of individuals. We explore these issues in more depth within this chapter by considering different aspects of human characteristics and behaviours, and why they matter to cyber security.

Are humans the weakest link?

There is an oft-repeated notion amongst some people (most commonly cyber security practitioners responsible for end-user cyber security) that humans constitute the 'weakest link'.

In one sense this is true and well-evidenced. Most cyber security incidents involve humans in some way. In Chapter 7 we devoted a section to discussing social engineering, which is broadly the manipulation of humans to facilitate cybercrime, and we discussed why humans are particularly vulnerable to social engineering, hence create a significant point of vulnerability in any digital environment. Humans are also prone to making mistakes.

However, there are several reasons why describing humans as the weakest link in cyber security is unhelpful and, in some cases, simply wrong. These include:

- *End-user focus.* The concept of humans as the weakest link most commonly implies that the humans concerned are end users. However, all humans can make mistakes or be subject to social engineering, whether they are cyber security consumers, managers or even enforcers. For example, the Maersk NotPetya disaster discussed in Chapter 6 would appear to have arisen as a result of mistakes made by Maersk employees in a range of different roles within the organization.
- *Misplaced responsibility.* Assigning blame to humans is often a lazy means of misdirecting responsibility onto a component of a digital environment that is deemed erratic and beyond the control of designers of cyber security processes. An organization might design a strong password management system but then 'careless users' write down their passwords and leave this information lying on their desks. But is this really the sole fault of those employees or might the authentication process be unsuitable, or poorly explained and communicated? There is an argument which can be made, at least sometimes, that any cyber security process that fails due to an inappropriate human action arises through poor process design or implementation. We will revisit this issue later in this chapter.
- *Failure to recognize the underlying reasons for human behaviour.* Continuing the previous point, one reason that humans end up playing a role in cyber security incidents is through a failure of designers of cyber security processes to recognize

that humans are not homogeneous. There is no one-size-fits-all approach that works for *all* humans, and any cyber security process that does not take this into account runs the risk of failing. There are many legitimate reasons why a human might write down their password (perhaps they have poorer than average memory or lack the digital skills to store them securely) or fall for a social engineering attack (perhaps they lack confidence or are particularly respectful of apparent authority). Security approaches have only recently begun to incorporate psychological and behavioural principles of human conduct, including the limitations of human cognition, stamina and attention, and how humans behave when only having access to partial information and limited time.

Humans make errors, forget things, take sub-optimal decisions, are inconsistent and react in different ways to different situations. Humans get tired, confused, take short-cuts and misplace trust. In this chapter we will argue that these are simply part of being human, not deficiencies. Thus, when considering cyber security from the perspective of the human layer in a digital environment, we need to recognize that humans are *humans*, not computers, and take the many different impacts of this into account.

Human behaviour

The first aspect of being human that we will discuss in more detail is human behaviour. Different humans behave in different ways, whether they are end users of a digital system, cyber security software designers or cyber criminals. Recognizing different aspects of human behaviour is important for the design of cyber security. Later in this chapter we will also discuss the considerable challenges involved in trying to change human behaviour.

What is human (security) behaviour?

Human behaviour can be loosely defined as the aggregate of human responses to a specific situation. This rather abstract concept needs to take into account a range of perspectives that include:

- *Rationality*. Human behaviour can be considered as a rational attempt to attain or maximize objectives while, simultaneously, seeking to avoid or minimize undesirable outcomes. While regarding human behaviour as an attempt to pursue goals rationally can be helpful, the extent to which humans behave rationally varies enormously.
- *Individuality*. Humans behave in different ways for many reasons. These arise from different components of individuality, including personality (something we later discuss in more detail), perception, attention, memory and past experience.

- *Situational and environmental factors.* Human behaviour in a particular setting is impacted by a range of local factors such as social norms, culture, resource availability, time pressure and group dynamics.

In this book we are particularly interested in human behaviour with respect to security. We can thus define human *security behaviour* as an individual's acts, responses and conduct in relation to security. Making sense of security behaviour relies on overlapping knowledge from a wide range of different general fields of study, including economics, psychology and sociology, as well as specialist disciplines such as the study of human-computer interaction. Our goal in this chapter is to introduce some of the most important ideas emerging from these studies. We direct the reader to further resources for a deeper understanding.

The dual-system model

One important concept relating to human behaviour (and hence security behaviour) arises from studies in an area known as behavioural economics. The *dual-system model* proposes that humans possess two different modes of thinking, both of which influence how a human makes decisions and behaves in a given situation. These modes can be characterized as follows:

1. *System 1* is the mode that captures instinctive functions. This is behaviour that can be characterized as fast, automatic, and requiring limited or no conscious effort. The recognition of familiar objects and responses to familiar situations fall into System 1. To an extent, System 1 concerns functions that are either natural or have been learnt and developed over time.
2. *System 2* is the mode that captures cognitive, non-instinctive functions. It can be characterized as slow and complex, requiring concentration, focus and effort. Human functions involving calculations, problem solving, reasoning and other demanding mental activities fall into System 2.

For different humans, different actions might fall into System 1 and System 2. For example, learner drivers call on System 2 when they first learn to drive a car, while an experienced driver will more heavily call on System 1 and conduct many aspects of driving almost automatically. Within a cyber security setting, a user will need System 2 when they first create and type a new password, but might soon find that entry of a regularly used password has become an action associated with System 1.

Importantly, human behaviour arises as a result of both System 1 and System 2 activity. This has some important implications for security behaviour. For example, individuals need to be encouraged to utilize System 2 in relation to critical thinking, learning and training processes, whereas security design should aim to accommodate System 1 decisions in order to minimize human effort.

Heuristics and cognitive biases

Two key interrelated notions associated with human behaviour are:

- *Heuristics*. These are 'rules of thumb', acting as mental shortcuts and practical approaches to simplifying complex tasks. Heuristics are usually fast, not necessarily accurate, but generally save time and effort.
- *Cognitive biases*. These are human thinking patterns that exhibit systematic deviation from fully rational behaviour.

In the following discussion we will not concern ourselves too much with separating heuristics from cognitive biases, since they are very closely related concepts.

We now review some of the most well-known heuristics and cognitive biases that are of relevance to security behaviour:

- *Optimism*. This is the observed tendency of humans to overestimate the probability of future occurrence of a positive event, while conversely underestimating the probability associated with negative events. This partially arises because forming accurate notions of probability is a complex Type 2 activity. For example, a home computer user might not install anti-virus software due to an overly optimistic 'it will not happen to me' optimism bias with respect to the likelihood of malware attacks.
- *Overconfidence*. This arises from a human tendency to have confidence that their own abilities and performance are superior to what objective observations and previous evidence suggests. This particularly applies to areas of perceived expertise. For example, a cyber security manager might make mistaken assertions about the security processes they have designed because they believe themselves to possess more expertise than they do. On completing your reading of this book, beware of overconfidence!
- *Control*. This relates to the human tendency to be overly optimistic about their level of influence on situations. In other words, humans tend to believe they have more control over potential outcomes than they really do. For example, as readers (and writers!) of this book, we probably all believe that we are capable of successfully identifying a phishing attack (see Chapter 7) sent in an email and hence are 'in control' of phishing management. But are any of us really capable of identifying a well-researched and crafted spear phishing attack?
- *Availability*. This concerns the human tendency to make choices based on the information that is immediately available to us, rather than analysing all relevant information. This can be both a heuristic (since it represents a fast option) and a bias (since it might result in flawed decisions). For example, a media story reporting on a security incident associated with an encryption technology might result in some people perceiving the risk of this technology as inflated in comparison to other risks.

- *Confirmation.* This is the notion that humans pay attention to information selectively, in a fashion that confirms their existing beliefs, while discounting contradicting information. The confirmation bias is reinforced via social media, where, aided by selective algorithms, information is filtered and absorbed in a way that reinforces existing views and attitudes. This then hinders objective decision-making. In a security context, the confirmation bias might result, for example, in a security manager failing to learn the lessons from reported phishing attacks, under the belief that the existing security training program is adequate. They might selectively focus on 'convenient data' such as high training completion rates, ignoring or dismissing subsequent incidents as anomalies.
- *Anchoring.* This is the phenomenon of humans being influenced in their decisions by an initial piece of information, even if irrelevant. In a security context, the cause of a security breach in a company might be speculated as a firewall misconfiguration. This might set an 'anchor' if it is the first hypothesis provided. Subsequent investigations and perceptions might then be influenced in the direction of firewall-related issues, even if the breach is ultimately shown to have been caused by an insider.
- *Herding.* This refers to the human tendency to follow the crowd. This often plays a role in the development of cultures. For example, in terms of security culture (which we later discuss in more detail), everyday practice that devalues security can quickly spread to new employees.
- *Affect.* This refers to the human tendency to favour choices associated with positive emotions, conversely avoiding choices associated with negative emotions. For example, it has been observed that victims of various types of cybercrime are sometimes reluctant to engage in further digital activities.
- *Default.* This captures the human tendency not to deviate from a current situation, perhaps due to inertia or avoidance of costs associated with change. A cyber security example of this is maintaining default security settings such as manufacturers' default passwords on new devices.
- *False consensus.* This is the phenomenon by which people overestimate the acceptance of their own beliefs, views and behaviours, assuming that these are more widely accepted than they are. Most fundamentally, cyber security professionals and practitioners (and readers of this book) are likely to overestimate the perceived importance of cyber security amongst the general human population. This has clear implications for any organization trying to implement cyber security controls.

Note that these behavioural phenomena are not inherently problematic. For example, the widespread adoption of well-respected cyber security technologies and practices is a positive example of herding. What is important is to regard heuristics and biases not as problems with human behaviour that need to be overcome, but as aspects of human behaviour that need to be taken into account when considering security at the human layer of a digital environment.

Presentational phenomena

As well as being influenced by heuristics and cognitive biases, human behaviour is known to be subject to several phenomena that relate to the way in which a situation is presented. Amongst the most relevant presentational phenomena to security behaviour are:

- *Framing effects*. The way in which choices are presented (framed) heavily influences how humans subsequently behave. In general, positive frames are perceived as attractive to humans, while negative frames are disliked. For example, rolling out a new multifactor authentication technology across an organization is more likely to be successful if it is framed in terms of making the working digital environment safer and easier to use, rather than in terms of responding to increased numbers of employee security incidents and the need to optimize shareholder profit.
- *Loss aversion*. This relates to the human tendency to focus more on perceived losses than gains. In other words, something presented as a loss will have more influence than something presented as a gain. Put simply, most humans dislike losing £100 more than they enjoy winning £100! In a cyber security context, this phenomenon can lead to some organizations over-spending on cyber security controls against threats that are less likely to manifest. Note that loss aversion does not apply just to financial notions, but to any concept with a reference point. For example, senior management of an organization whose sector publishes ranked annual lists of organizational cyber security performance are likely to be more upset by a fall of two positions compared to the previous year than pleased by a rise of two positions.
- *Order effects*. This refers to a human focus on the order in which options are presented. For example, decision-makers are known to prefer the first and last of a number of presented options. This could be exploited by a clever social engineer who presents a sequence of options to a victim, thus giving the victim apparent freedom of choice while relying on an ordering effect to increase the chances of manipulating the victim into taking a desired action.

Personality and risk perception

In the previous section we discussed traits and phenomena that apply to humans at large. However, as pointed out at the start of this chapter, every human is unique and engages with those aspects of human behaviour in their own way. In this section we discuss human personality and how it might impact cyber security.

Modelling personality

While every human is indeed different, there are too many humans to take each individual personality into account when considering how an individual might behave. Instead, a number of models have been developed to categorize human personality.

Just one of the leading personality models is the OCEAN model (see Figure 9.1), which categorizes personality into five domains:[2]

1. *Openness to experience.* This relates to interests and interpersonal relationships, including a liking for abstract ideas, creativity and appreciation of nature and art.
2. *Conscientiousness.* This relates to being organized, efficient, systematic, precise and hard-working, including a tendency to stay focused, carry out plans, complete tasks, be tidy and organize schedules.
3. *Extroversion.* This relates to being sensation-seeking, sociable, assertive and dominant, including inclination for experiencing positive emotions, socializing, leading and captivating others.
4. *Agreeableness.* This relates to being cooperative, kind, sincere, sympathetic, altruistic and trusting, including an interest in other people's wellbeing, and an inclination to respect and conform to authority.
5. *Neuroticism.* This relates to moodiness, shyness, anxiety and jealousy, including feelings of being threatened, worried, holding doubts and having a tendency to become annoyed, irritated or angry.

Figure 9.1 The OCEAN personality traits and facets model[1]

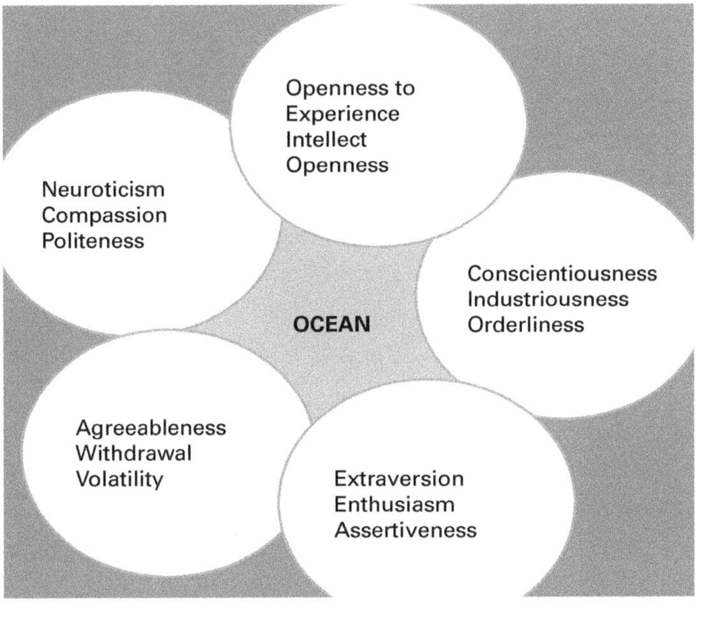

As well as being informative in a general sense about how different human personalities are structured, various tests can be used to position an individual's personality within classifications such as the OCEAN model. These can help to better anticipate how an individual will behave in specific circumstances.

Other personality classifications have been used to try to make sense of particular human behaviours. For example, the *dark triad* consists of three personality traits that are correlated with offensive and malicious activities such as cybercrime-related behaviours. These are:

1. *Machiavellianism*. This is characterized by interpersonal manipulation and deception as a means of achieving personal goals. Individuals with this trait tend to be cynical with a strong self-interest.
2. *Narcissism*. This is characterized by arrogance, entitlement, grandiosity and superiority. Individuals with this trait strive for self-enhancement, are overconfident and exhibit an easiness to start interpersonal relationships.
3. *Psychopathy*. This is characterized by lack of remorse and empathy for others, impulsivity, antagonism and a thrill-seeking attitude. Individuals with this personality are antisocial and uncaring, with a low sense of responsibility.[3]

Risk perception and attitude

Of particular relevance to human security behaviour is human *risk perception*, which is an individual's judgement and evaluation of a hazard. This leads to an individual's *risk attitude*, which is their intention to act on a risky situation. Risk attitude is strongly influenced by personality type, with some personality types being more willing to take risks than others.

We should note, however, that beyond personality, risk perception and attitude are influenced by inherent human inclinations such as loss aversion and framing effects. Additionally, an individual's, indeed an organization's, risk attitude is also impacted by the extent to which levels of risks are defined and understood. To expand on this, consider the following three scenarios:

1. **Risk.** Suppose an organization has information assets worth £1 million and knows that the risk of a particular security incident that comprises these assets is precisely 5 per cent. This means that the expected loss to the organization is 0.05 x £1,000,000 = £50,000.
2. **Ambiguity.** Suppose now, more realistically, that the precise risk of the same incident is not known, but rather is between 1 and 9 per cent. The average probability thus remains 5 per cent and the expected loss remains £50,000, but now with ambiguity.

3 **Uncertainty.** Suppose now that the specifics of the same incident are completely unknown. In this case the expected loss cannot be computed at all. In cyber security, this scenario could represent what is often called a *zero-day attack*, which is a new attack that has not been seen before and has no existing defence mechanisms.

The first two scenarios can be used to characterize risk attitudes. If a human decision-maker (either as an individual or an organization) is willing to invest more than the expected loss of £50,000 in security controls then we describe them as *risk averse*. On the other hand, if they are only willing to invest less than £50,000 then we describe them as *risk seeking*. If they are willing to invest precisely £50,000 then we describe them as *risk neutral*. With regard to uncertainty, humans are shown to have an inherent aversion to this condition, with consistent preferences for more known situations, even if those involve measurably higher expected losses.

The point we wish to convey here is that studies repeatedly show that humans exhibit increased risk aversion as scenarios move from risk precision towards uncertainty. In other words, as the probability of threats manifesting themselves becomes less specific, humans show an increased preference for trying to avoid them.[4] This has significant implications for how we should treat the three scenarios, whether at a personal, organizational or societal level. It shows that the level of investment in security controls, whether in terms of time, money, attention or other resources, is likely to be influenced by the way associated security risks are perceived.

Security culture

In this section we examine the notion of security culture, which relates to the collective values, beliefs and attitudes that impact the security behaviour of members of an organization. However, this relationship is two-way, since security behaviour also ultimately shapes security culture. We define security culture and consider its components, and then identify different cultural components and layers that impact how a security culture manifests itself.

Defining security culture

In Chapter 6 we introduced the idea of a 'cyber security culture' in an organizational security context, without really defining it. We now consider several definitions from the wider literature of the more general notion of a *security culture*, although we will mainly be considering this from a cyber security perspective:

- 'The ideas, customs and social behaviours of a group that influence its security.'[5]

- 'The totality of human attributes such as behaviours, attitudes and values that contribute to the protection of all kinds of information in a given organization.'[6]
- 'The behaviour of humans in an organizational context to protect information processed by the organization through compliance with the information security policy and an understanding of how to implement requirements in a cautious and attentive manner as embedded through regular communication, awareness, training and education initiatives.'[7]

What emerges from these definitions is a sense that cyber security and the collective behaviour of humans within an organization are inseparable and bound together in complex ways. This relationship can be constructive, through the emergence of what we described in Chapter 6 as a *positive* security culture where security beliefs, attitudes and interactions result in security being valued, promoted and integrated into the activities of an organization. However, it can also be destructive, where the opposite impacts are observed in a *negative* security culture.

Components of security culture

In Chapter 6 we identified a number of cyber security management principles that are associated with the development of a positive security culture. We now take a slight step back and identify some of the different components of security culture, whether positive or negative.[8] These are:

- *Attitudes*. These are the perspectives that individuals adopt towards security. Contributors towards attitude include the interest held by individuals in security and the extent to which they are involved in security decisions and processes.
- *Behaviours*. This is the way that individuals behave with respect to security.
- *Cognition*. This refers to the security knowledge and understanding of individuals, including how they utilize this knowledge.
- *Communication*. This refers to the style, channels, framing and detail of security-related information conveyed to individuals within an organization.
- *Compliance*. This is the adherence of individuals to established security policies, procedures and guidelines.
- *Norms*. These are the security-related values and beliefs held by an individual, but often influenced by others around them within the organization.
- *Responsibilities*. This refers to the degree of an individual's involvement with security. Contributors to responsibilities include the degree of proactivity, agency, and whether and how individuals within an organization assist one another.

Note that every organization has an existing security culture, whether strongly formed or loosely defined, and whether positive or negative. Further, security culture is constantly evolving. The challenge for management and governance of an organization is to try to evolve or maintain a positive security culture. We discussed elements of this in Chapter 6 and will explore aspects concerning security behavioural change later in this chapter.

Cultural layers

As we have seen, a security culture emerges from the collective relationship that individuals within an organization have with respect to security. This, in turn, is determined partially by the personalities and behaviours of those individuals. However, security culture is also impacted by other influential cultures (not explicitly associated with security) that individuals within an organization are associated with. These include:

- *National culture*. This relates to the shared values, beliefs and ways of life of individuals associated with a nation state. For any organization, particularly a multinational one, an individual might be influenced by multiple national cultures (for example, their home nation, the nation they reside in and the nation associated with the organization, might all be different). National cultures vary considerably with respect to several factors, including:
  - *Acceptance of power*. For example, respect towards authorities such as decision-makers and enforcers of rules.
  - *Aversion towards uncertainty*. For example, adherence to rules and levels of pragmatism.
  - *Degree of collectivism*. For example, whether individuals prioritize their own needs ahead of those of the wider community.
  - *Competition and achievement*. For example, whether competitive values such as accomplishments and assertiveness are prioritized over nurturing values such as modesty and collaboration.
  - *Openness to change*. For example, whether adaptability and embracing future challenges is prioritized over adherence to traditions and social obligations.[9]

National cultures clearly have the potential to impact security culture, particularly with respect to issues such as the following of security policies, supporting colleagues with security issues and the embracing of new security controls.

- *Organizational culture*. The wider organizational culture has an impact on security culture. Indeed, some researchers categorize security culture as a facet of organizational culture. However, an organization could have a generally positive organizational culture but a negative security culture, and perhaps vice-versa. Much of what we discussed in Chapter 6 regarding the facets of positive security culture apply more broadly to organizational culture. Relevant features of organizational culture that are likely to influence security culture include:

- *Evaluation*. How individuals within the organization are evaluated and how feedback is provided.
- *Leadership*. The leadership structures and styles of the organization.
- *Decision-making*. The means by which decisions within the organization are made.
- *Tolerance for disagreement*. The extent to which open disagreement within the organization is permitted and resolved.[10]

- *Peer cultures*. Even within an organization, different subcultures might emerge amongst particular units of the organization, whether formal (such as departments) or informal (amongst friendship groups or immediate colleagues). These have the potential to impact security culture, both positively and negatively.
- *Sector cultures*. Many individuals within an organization will hold close relationships with individuals in similar roles in other organizations across relevant sectors. For example, Chief Information Security Officers (CISOs) of different organizations regularly communicate with one another and meet at common forums, thus forming a community of senior security practitioners with common responsibilities and challenges, which to an extent creates its own culture. The value of this sector culture has potential to influence the security culture of individuals' associated organizations.

The influence of these different cultures on security culture is hard to disentangle. What is important is to be aware of their potential influence and to seek to harness positive elements and suppress negative ones when seeking to develop a positive security culture.

Usable security

One important aspect of how humans engage with security is the extent to which security is designed in a human-friendly manner. In this section we briefly introduce the concept of usable security and discuss its merits and constraints.

Features of usable security

Broadly speaking, *usable security* is the design of security processes and technologies that accommodate human users' needs and behaviours. It is perhaps worth beginning a consideration of usable security by reflecting on an example of security that is not particularly usable.

Suppose an organization is suffering from a concerted series of phishing attacks. Each time a new phishing attack occurs, the organization immediately sends its entire staff a stern warning in technical language about phishing and penalties for data leakage offences (accompanied by numerous exclamation marks!!) and an intranet link to the organization's security and acceptable digital use policies (which they are required to click on within 24 hours and is subject to monitoring). Users find themselves receiving repeated unpleasant communications and feel increasingly frustrated, anxious and confused about how to respond. Some users start deleting communications from the security team before even reading the messages. This is clearly *not* usable security!

We now use this example to reflect on what potentially desirable features of usable security might be. These include processes and technologies that are:

- *Intuitive*. Ideally, security should involve doing the 'obvious thing' and should not leave users having to engage in tasks that do not make sense to them. In our example, repeatedly being mandated to read policies in response to an incident that did not directly involve them is not intuitive.
- *Comprehensible*. Any notion of usable security should involve users understanding their role in security and any actions that they are required to take. In our example, receiving an overly technical message in response to an incident does not satisfy this criterion.
- *Easy to use*. Security should be easy to use, ideally transparent. In our example the response process demanded of users is not particularly easy to engage with.
- *Accessible*. Usable security should be accessible to all members of an organization. In our example, the 24-hour limit on taking responsive action is clearly not suitable for all members of staff, since some might be away from work, while others may undertake roles where they are not checking their internal messages every day. Another aspect of accessibility is ensuring that security is designed to accommodate people with varying levels of capability and resource. For example, usable security should include consideration of the needs of those with visual impairments.
- *Acceptable*. Security measures should, ideally, be acceptable to those who engage with them. In our example, the communications with staff are not in acceptable language, and the subsequent required response to read policies is arguably heavy handed.

- *Effective*. A security process should work and, ideally, be seen to work. In our example, the control was ineffective because some users ceased to engage with it. (It is also questionable whether any control measure against phishing should involve asking users to click on a link!)

A similar perspective on usable security is provided by the International Organization for Standardization (ISO) 9241-11:2018, which defines usability across three components, namely:

1. *Efficiency*. A security process needs to allow a user to perform their tasks without hindering or distracting them, and without introducing additional time and effort.
2. *Effectiveness*. A security process should be completed with accuracy.
3. *Satisfaction*. Users need to accept and be comfortable with a security process.

An alternative means of thinking about usable security is the design of processes that minimize human error or other deviation from desired behaviour. This means that usable security processes should exhibit features such as:

- *Learnability*. If users are required to engage with new security processes then these should be easy to learn.
- *Memorability*. Security processes should be easy for a human user to remember.
- *Engaging*. Security processes should be packaged in a way that is attractive to a wide range of users.

EXAMPLE

Moving from passwords to face recognition

We now consider a case study of a simple usable security process.

Suppose an organization currently uses a complex password policy according to which passwords need to consist of at least eight characters, including capitals, numbers and special characters, and need to be changed monthly. In terms of usability, there are several problems with this security process, not the least being that complex passwords are not easy to remember and, having done so, a user needs to go through a new process every month. On the other hand, passwords are in general a very familiar and relatively easy security technique to engage with.

To aid usability, the organization decides to replace this security process with the use of biometrics (see Chapter 3). After an internal review they decide to adopt face recognition technology. We now revisit the features discussed in the previous section to see why this might be considered a good usable security solution:

- *Intuitive.* Staring at a screen (which contains an embedded camera) is an entirely intuitive process to conduct.
- *Comprehensible.* Users easily understand that their face is unique and hence can serve as a suitable means of identifying them.
- *Easy to use.* Apart from making sure that the lighting is adequate and that they are positioning themselves in front of the camera, this is a very straightforward process to undertake.
- *Accessible.* This is a very accessible technology unless users need to wear face coverings, perhaps for cultural or medical reasons. Such exceptions need to be considered carefully and, if necessary, alternative means of authentication offered.
- *Acceptable.* Within most cultures, humans broadly accept the use of cameras to identify them. Facial recognition is arguably more acceptable than some other biometrics such as fingerprints, which are sometimes associated with criminality.
- *Effective.* Modern facial recognition technology generally works well.
- *Learnability.* Users quickly learn how to use facial recognition, following a relatively painless initialization process.
- *Memorability.* In this ideal case there is nothing that the user needs to remember.
- *Engaging.* There is very little interaction required and some users might even find it quite 'fun' that they gain access to the organization's system without apparently doing anything.

Limitations of usable security

The word 'ideally' has featured several times within our discussion of usable security. This is because usable security is in some sense an 'ideal' notion. There are, in fact, many legitimate reasons why it might not always be possible for security processes that are strongly usable to be deployed. These reasons include the following:

- *Heterogeneity of users.* A one-size-fits-all concept of usability is hard to achieve when, as we have discussed throughout this chapter, human users are all different. While effective usability should 'ideally' be irrespective of an individual user's characteristics, in practice this is not the case. Put simply, what is usable for one human might not be usable for another. For example, as we have seen, users will be different in the extent to which they are:
    - informed about a particular security process

  - capable of learning and adopting a security process
  - open to trusting a security process
  - willing to follow a security process
- *Contextual aspects*. Usable security is not an absolute concept and needs to be framed within the context of the environment in which it is being considered. For example, security that is deemed usable within the context of a specific organization may not be usable within the context of serving the general public.
- *Trade-offs*. Usability and security sometimes involve uncomfortable trade-offs. After all, humans do not interact with digital systems with security as their primary objective. Rather, security tends to be an additional aspect of engaging with digital technology that sometimes, necessarily, involves a degree of attention, time and effort. Making security usable is aspirational, but not always feasible. For example, there are very good reasons why a user whose work computer has been compromised might have to reset their credentials, undertake a new security initialization process or perhaps undertake some special training. This will be inconvenient and require effort, but from a security perspective might be necessary. Of course, making these tasks as usable as possible is the trade-off that we should seek to achieve.

Changing security behaviour

In previous sections, we explored some of the underlying mechanisms behind security behaviours. We also discussed the design of security processes and technologies in ways that support human users. However, there will always be occasions where it is necessary to try to modify human security behaviour. We begin by explaining why this is the case. We then discuss traditional approaches to security education, training and awareness. Next, we investigate the more sophisticated process of security behaviour change, identifying key components, approaches and frameworks. Finally, we propose a general process for conducting security behaviour change.

Need for changing security behaviour

For much of this chapter we have discussed human personality and behaviour with regard to cyber security. While these are influential in how an individual perceives and responds to security, humans are not automatons and can learn to modify behaviour. There are many reasons why it might be desirable to change human security behaviour, including:

- *Heterogeneity*. As we have seen, humans have a wide variety of different personalities and behavioural profiles. It is arguably impossible to design security that works perfectly for every individual. This means that, inevitably, some degree of security behaviour change may be required to adapt the security behaviour of some individuals.

- *Evolving technology*. The technology deployed within digital environments is constantly evolving, often bringing new challenges with respect to security. For example, the rise to ubiquity of personal devices, particularly mobile phones, initially presented new challenges to organizations with respect to managing personal devices in the workplace. This required policies and security processes for accommodating BYOD (bring your own device), which in turn often required a degree of security behaviour change from device owners.
- *Evolving threats*. The threat environment is also dynamic, meaning that users sometimes need to change security behaviour in relation to new evolving threats. For example, phishing attacks might once have been fairly easy to identify due to certain characteristic presentational weaknesses (poor spelling and grammar, inappropriate use of capitalization, etc.). With the rise of generative artificial intelligence and an increase in sophisticated spear phishing attacks, many users now need to modify their security behaviour in order to address the risks of such attacks.
- *Negative security culture*. As we have previously discussed, there are many factors behind the possible development of a negative security culture within an organization. Countering this in order to develop a positive security culture is likely to require both individual and collective security behaviour changes within the organization.

Security education, training and awareness

The traditional approach to instigating security behaviour change is through a lens of *security education, training and awareness*. The three components of this can be informally defined as:

- *Security education*. The general process of equipping users with foundational knowledge relating to security.
- *Security training*. Practical interventions, such as campaigns, courses and other knowledge transfer activities, designed to equip users with specific skills.
- *Security awareness*. The conscious understanding of the need for security processes and how to respond to them.

Security education and training and are thus a means for achieving security awareness amongst the individuals within an organization. Traditionally, security education, training and awareness is regarded as one of the primary means of protecting an organization from security incidents, as well as being a primary mechanism for enhancing a security culture. Indeed, we made reference to the use of security education, training and awareness for those reasons throughout Chapter 6.

Note that there is nothing inherently wrong with the concept of security education, training and awareness and, indeed, this still forms the basis around which most organizations seek to equip their users with cyber security knowledge and skills. However, the traditional approaches associated with security education, training and awareness are often subject to criticisms, including:

- *Passivity*. Security education and training is often somewhat passive, with users primarily consuming information that they might soon forget.
- *Homogeneity*. Security education and training is often designed in a 'one-size-fits-all' manner, assuming a homogeneous audience. However, as we have seen throughout this chapter, humans are far from homogeneous, which impacts on the ability of some individuals to engage with such a programme. Individual humans will vary in, for example, their willingness to undertake security education and training, their trust in what they are being told, their openness to receiving security information, and their capability of retaining and acting on security information.
- *Lack of ambition*. The state of security 'awareness' is somewhat unambitious. Users are often not equipped with enough security expertise to handle complex security situations. Awareness can be considered as a first step, but is often insufficient to instil long-lasting, desirable security behaviour.

As a result, many traditional approaches to security education, training and awareness do not achieve their intended goals. For example, users who have been through such programmes might have, at the time of training, been aware of how to respond to a security situation. However, this does not guarantee that they deemed this information important, nor that they will behave in the desired fashion at the time of a real incident. What really matters is what humans *do*, not what they have been allegedly *taught*.

Our intention is not to belittle the concepts behind security education, training and awareness, but rather to advocate for an evolution of traditional approaches into security behaviour change practices that are more impactful.

Introducing security behaviour change

Security behaviour change can be generally defined as the modification of human security behaviour through some type of planned action (or series of actions). Such actions are normally termed *interventions*, and tend to be direct and customized, rather than the indirect and general approaches used in traditional cyber security education, training and awareness programmes. Naturally, our focus will be on desirable security behaviour, which is oriented towards security behaviour that reduces the risk of security incidents arising. This can also be thought of as improving *security hygiene*, which is a general term sometimes used in reference to an individual's security behaviour.

At a high level, for an individual to change their security behaviour there are three key components that need to be considered:

1. *Capability*. This refers to the knowledge, skills and abilities that an individual possesses in order to change their security behaviour. For example, if staff are expected to report suspicious email, then capability would include the ability to identify inappropriate communications and knowledge about where and how to report it.
2. *Opportunity*. This refers to the context individuals find themselves in, including socio-economic circumstances, security norms within a work environment and the availability of time to engage with security processes. This component attempts to capture how easy a particular security behaviour is to conduct, particularly whether there are associated transaction costs (relating, for example, to time, effort or attention) for individuals. For example, a staff member struggling to get through their work is less likely to engage with a complex email reporting process such as one that requires completion of a detailed online form.
3. *Motives and incentives*. This refers to an individual's desire and will to change security behaviour. Motive refers to internal drives, such as a sense of duty, whereas incentives relate to external factors, such as rewards. Suppose, for example, that an employee does not currently care about security within an organizational setting. Changing their security behaviour needs careful consideration of how to persuade them to modify their current stance. It may be easiest to commence with incentives while seeking to ultimately develop motives that might cultivate good security habits. For example, email reporting behaviour can be encouraged through a 'top reporter of the month' recognition (a positive approach) or through sanctions for not doing so (a negative approach).

Security behaviour change can be considered as a more targeted approach to security education, training and awareness, with a focus on observable and measurable individual and collective security behaviours. In the remainder of this chapter, we provide a high-level introduction of some theoretical notions and ideas that might be used to inform the design and implementation of a security behaviour change programme.

Approaches to security behaviour change

The general area of human behaviour change has been well studied in a wide range of different contexts. We now briefly introduce some of the key approaches:

- *Fear appeals*. These can be defined as 'persuasive messages designed to scare people by describing the terrible things that will happen to them if they do not do what the message recommends'.[11] Fear appeals have traditionally been prevalent in security messaging since security tends to be concerned with attempts to stop 'bad things' from happening, hence focusing on negative consequences is a natural (albeit not always effective) approach to changing security behaviour. *Protection Motivation Theory* is a model that has been used to design and analyse the effectiveness of fear appeals. This model captures the messaging, how a human user might perceive and then react to it, then whether the message is accepted and behaviour is changed, or whether the message is rejected and the existing behaviour continues. Fear appeals are often ineffective in changing security behaviour. To overcome this limitation, some people have suggested that personalization of the consequences of not changing behaviour might be more effective.[12]
- *Nudges and boosts*. Human behaviour can be influenced by the way options are presented to individuals. A *nudge* is a behavioural intervention intended to change an individual's behaviour without removing their freedom of choice. Nudges subtly guide individuals towards making a desirable choice rather than an undesirable one. For example, users setting up a password might be presented with a green, amber or red nudge as a response to a proposed password, with green being most desirable. *Boosts* are 'educational nudges' with the purpose of overcoming behavioural biases by promoting learning. Boosts encourage reflection, rather than influencing an immediate choice. An example of boost is the UK National Cyber Security Centre's 'three random words' password guidance, which is designed to educate end users and security policy setters on the security and usability benefits of forming passwords from three memorable dictionary words rather than the current widespread use of complex character mixes.
- *Incentives and disincentives*. This relates to the use of 'carrots' or 'sticks' to encourage security behaviour change. *Incentives* relate to rewards or praise for modifying behaviour, while *disincentives* relate to punishments or blame for not modifying behaviour. Research indicates that, generally, incentives are found to be more effective at motivating individuals to take positive actions, whereas disincentives are more effective at discouraging negative actions. However, excessive use of disincentives is also associated with the development of negative security cultures. For example, the once-widespread use of internal phishing campaigns to shame employees who fell for them is now rightly being regarded as an outdated and ineffective means of changing security behaviour. Note that some

types of incentive only work in certain circumstances. For example, it has been shown that financial rewards for changing security behaviour are sometimes only effective during the period of reward provision, with undesirable security behaviours returning when the intervention stops.[13] This is just one reason why behaviour change should be regarded as a continuous process, possibly involving regular repetition and reinforcement.

Frameworks for influencing security behaviour

Frameworks for influencing security behaviour can be useful tools for the design of a security behaviour change programme. In this section we briefly consider one such framework, known by its acronym MINDSPACE:[14]

- *Messenger*. This relates to *who* communicates a message. In a security setting, a message might be received differently if it comes from the CISO of the organization, the Head of Human Resources, a direct line manager or an IT technician. How a recipient acts on receipt of a message is known to depend on the extent to which the messenger is trusted and respected.
- *Incentives*. This concerns much of what we have previously discussed in this chapter. For example, the use of positive incentives or negative disincentives, the human tendency to avoid losses, etc. The way that a security message is presented strongly influences how a recipient will respond to it.
- *Norms*. As previously observed, humans tend to follow the crowd and are influenced by what others do. This is strongly related to our previous discussions about security culture. Encouraging desirable actions within groups can help to initiate similar positive security behaviour elsewhere.
- *Defaults*. Another observation that we observed earlier was the tendency of individuals to maintain status quo behaviours, since deviation tends to involve transactional costs. Changing security behaviour from a default is particularly challenging, and messaging requires careful design and implementation.
- *Salience*. Human attention is drawn by anything novel and of apparent relevance to them. This can be utilized in effective security behaviour change interventions. For example, motivating security practices by mapping them to current events or the impact of personal activities can be effective.
- *Priming and anchoring*. Exposure to subconscious cues influences (primes) human responses to other stimuli, and people tend to rely disproportionately more on the first piece of information they receive (the anchor). For example, employees might be primed by a sequence of legitimate emails from the organization's IT department, which then increases their susceptibility to a subsequent phishing email that mimics the legitimate ones.

- *Affect*. Emotional associations impact the way that humans receive and act on messages. For example, the use of a degree of humour might be positively received by security message recipients. Consider, for example, the degree to which you have previously paid attention to airline safety videos that took a humorous approach to basic cabin safety issues.
- *Commitment*. Humans tend, or at least try, to be consistent with their own public declarations and commitments. Committing to a security practice in front of peers increases the chances that the individual will adhere to this practice. On the other hand, a social engineer might lure a victim into committing to help by presenting themselves as being in a difficult situation. Consistent with their commitment, the victim will comply with the attacker's future requests.
- *Ego*. Humans tend to act in ways that make them feel good about themselves, something long recognized by the advertising industry. Thus, security training programs that target an employee's self-perception as competent and responsible have an increased chance of success.

Implementing security behaviour change

We close this section by suggesting a process for initiating, designing, implementing and evaluating a security behaviour change intervention. This is depicted in Figure 9.2 and consists of the following six steps:

1 **Problem.** The first step is to identify the observable behaviour that needs to change, considering the involved actors and the proposed, desirable behaviour. The approach needs to be clear with regard to attempting to changing a specific human security behaviour (for example, using applications not authorized within an organization). This step includes the identification of the target population (the individuals who need to change behaviour) and the expected goals/behaviour.

2 **Context and environment.** In the second step we investigate how the behaviour manifests within the given environment. This requires an understanding of the wider context and the target population. Security culture is a contextual factor that influences the appropriateness and acceptance of any intervention.

3 **Design and creation.** The third step includes deciding on which approaches and models to use, informed by the context. During this step, frameworks such as MINDSPACE might be helpful. This step should consider issues such as usability, feedback mechanisms, friction minimization or avoidance, timings, ethics and message communication.

4 **Application and implementation.** In the fourth step, the intervention is carried out in line with the previous decisions. This will include the capture of any measurements allowing comparison of behaviour pre- and post-intervention.

Figure 9.2 A process for initiating, designing, implementing and evaluating a behaviour change intervention

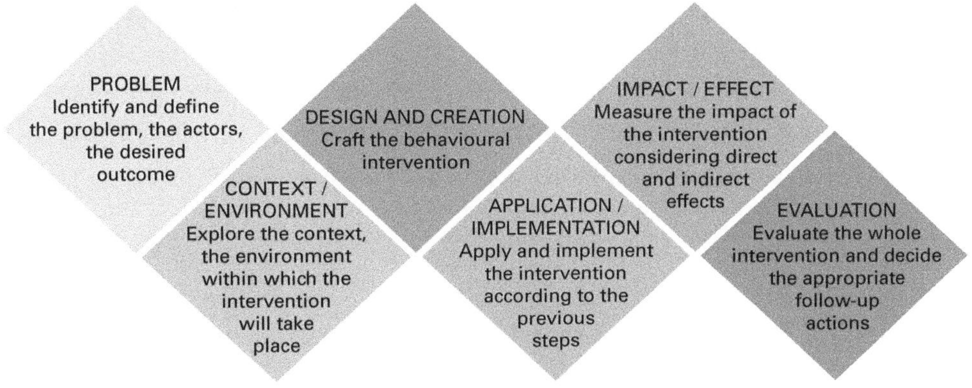

5 **Impact and effect.** In the fifth step, impact and direct and indirect effects are collected. Quantitative metrics and intervention acceptance and rejection rates can be used along with qualitative data relating to targeted individuals' understanding and experiences.

6 **Evaluation.** In the final, sixth step, we evaluate and decide on follow-up corrective actions. We determine the level of success and failure in influencing security behaviour. The fifth step's results are then mapped against an identified threshold of acceptable behaviour to determine satisfactory outcomes. We can then decide either to update, continue or end the intervention.

KEY POINTS

- To understand how humans behave with respect to security, we need to consider broad human traits, cultural dimensions and individual aspects of personality.
- Human security behaviour depends not only on human nature, but also on factors such as incentives and motives, knowledge, skills, and the environment and context within which a security behaviour is anticipated.
- Security culture is a dynamic, complex construct that needs to be nourished if it is to develop into one that has generally positive traits.
- The design and deployment of technology needs to take into account the many aspects and variations in human behaviour.
- Changing security behaviour is complex and goes far beyond the goals of traditional cyber security education, training and awareness.

EXERCISES

1. Provide an evidenced argument in support of the following claim: *humans are not the weakest link in cyber security.*
2. Elaborate on how different aspects of personality and risk attitude might change the way an individual user might respond when they receive a phishing email.
3. Provide an alternative security example to the ones given in this chapter for each of the identified behavioural heuristics and cognitive biases.
4. Consider the phenomena related to *presentation* in this chapter and explain how this might impact the convincing of employees in an organization to follow a security policy. Then select a specific policy and suggest how you might present it effectively to employees.
5. Multinational organizations have to deploy cyber security to branches across different countries and continents. Identify three aspects of security culture that you would consider particularly challenging given national diversity of employees and explain how they might influence security behaviour.
6. Suppose that employees within your company do not appear to currently care about security. Identify and elaborate on which components of security culture you would focus on in order to make people engage more with security and thus grow a positive security culture.
7. Identify an example of a 'bad design' which currently makes security unusable. Suggest how to make this design more usable.
8. The principle of security-by-design concerns the design of security from the outset of a project rather than being later retrofitted. Explain how the various human aspects of security might be particularly problematic if the principle of security-by-design is not followed. Conversely, suggest how these human aspects should be incorporated into a security-by-design process.
9. Security behaviour change might need to be done at scale, yet every human is different. Explain how security behaviour change can be instigated at scale, keeping in mind the variations in human personality and behaviour.
10. Identify a security behaviour that needs to change in an organization. Describe the steps that you would follow to implement an effective intervention.

FURTHER READING

Carpenter, P (2019) *Transformational Security Awareness: What neuroscientists, storytellers, and marketers can teach us about driving secure behaviors,* John Wiley & Sons

Dolan, P, Hallsworth, M, Halpern, D, King, D, Metcalfe, R and Vlaev, I (2012) Influencing behaviour: The mindspace way, *Journal of Economic Psychology,* 33 (1), 264–77

Hofstede, G (2011) Dimensionalizing cultures: The Hofstede model in context, *Online Readings in Psychology and Culture,* 2 (1)

Kahneman, D (2011) *Thinking, Fast and Slow,* Farrar, Straus and Giroux

Meyer, E (2014) *The Culture Map: Breaking through the invisible boundaries of global business,* Public Affairs

Sasse, M A, Hielscher, J, Friedauer, J and Buckmann, A (2022) Rebooting IT security awareness – how organisations can encourage and sustain secure behaviours. In *European Symposium on Research in Computer Security,* Springer International Publishing, pp. 248–65

Service, O, Hallsworth, M, Halpern, D, Algate, F, Gallagher, R, Nguyen, S, Ruda, S and Sanders, M (2014) EAST: Four simple ways to apply behavioral insights, The Behavioural Insights Team, www.bi.team/wp-content/uploads/2015/07/BIT-Publication-EAST_FA_WEB.pdf (archived at https://perma.cc/CCV3-BT6Y)

Thaler, R H and Sunstein, C R (2008) *Nudge: Improving decisions about health, wealth, and happiness,* Penguin Books

Notes

1 Costa, P T and McCrae, R R (1992) The five-factor model of personality and its relevance to personality disorders, *Journal of Personality Disorders*, 6 (4), 343–59, https://doi.org/10.1521/pedi.1992.6.4.343 (archived at https://perma.cc/PY23-3TPR)

2 There are other models such as the HEXACO model (Honesty–Humility, Emotionality, eXtraversion, Agreeableness, Conscientiousness, Openness). See: Ashton, M C and Lee, K (2008) The HEXACO model of personality structure and the importance of the H factor, *Social and Personality Psychology Compass*, 2 (5), 1952–62.
The OCEAN model is also called Big-5, or the Five-Factor Model (FFM) model and has been further broken down into additional traits, called personality facets, namely: Assertiveness and Enthusiasm (Extraversion), Compassion and Politeness (Agreeableness), Industriousness and Orderliness (Conscientiousness), Withdrawal and Volatility (Neuroticism), and Intellect and Openness (Openness to Experience). See: DeYoung, C G, Quilty, L C and Peterson, J B (2007) Between facets and domains: 10 aspects of the Big Five, *Journal of Personality and Social Psychology*, 93 (5), 880

3 There are proposals to expand the dark triad into a dark tetrad, with a number of personality variables competing for entering the tetrad. Namely, *status-driven risk-taking* is a candidate variable, indicating a willingness to take physical risks for the purposes of achieving power and wealth. Another candidate is *sadism*, described as pleasure or gratification resulting from inflicting humiliation, pain or suffering to others. The symptom phenotypes of borderline personality disorder are manifested with intense, unstable and not easily regulated emotions, impulsivity, feelings of emptiness, fear of abandonment, paranoid ideations and difficulty in establishing stable relationships. Researchers suggest that the common underlying attribute is callousness (Furnham et al, 2013), i.e. the lack of compassion, emotional frigidness and an overall apathy. Furnham, A, Richards, S C and Paulhus, D L (2013) The Dark Triad of personality: A 10 year review, *Social and Personality Psychology Compass*, 7 (3), 199–216

4 For more details on risk perceptions and attitudes of security professionals, in comparison to student samples, see: Mersinas, K, Hartig, B, Martin, K M and Seltzer, A (2016) Are information security professionals expected value maximizers? An experiment and survey-based test, *Journal of Cybersecurity*, 2 (1), 57–70

5 See: Carpenter, P and Roer, K (2022) *The Security Culture Playbook: An executive guide to reducing risk and developing your human defense layer*, John Wiley & Sons

6 Dhillon, G and Dhillon, G (1997) The context of information system security, *Managing Information System Security*, 8–28

7 See: Da Veiga, A, Astakhova, L V, Botha, A and Herselman, M (2020) Defining organisational information security culture – perspectives from academia and industry, *Computers & Security*, 92, 101713

8 See: Carpenter and Roer (2022) as per note 5

9 This is a simplified version of the cultural dimensions. For more details see the six cultural dimensions of Hofstede (2011) and the eight cultural dimensions of Meyer (2014); for an overall discussion of the cultural dimensions as measurable observations and their use in research refer to Minkov (2011). Hofstede, G (2011) Dimensionalizing cultures: The Hofstede model in context, *Online Readings in Psychology and Culture*, 2 (1); Meyer, E (2014) *The Culture Map: Breaking through the invisible boundaries of global business*, Public Affairs; Minkov, M (2011) *Cultural Differences in a Globalizing World*, Emerald Group Publishing

10 These are dimensions from Meyer (2014), as per previous note. Some of Meyer's dimensions overlap with Hofstede's. For statistical research that associates security behaviours of a substantial sample within the EU with cultural dimensions of Meyer and Hofstede, see: de Bruin, M and Mersinas, K (2024) Individual and contextual variables of cyber security behaviour – An empirical analysis of national culture, industry, organisation, and individual variables of (in) secure human behaviour, arXiv preprint, arXiv:2405.16215

11 See: Witte, K (1992) Putting the fear back into fear appeals: The extended parallel process model, *Communications Monographs*, 59 (4), 329–49

12 This suggestion refers to cyber security specifically. Several practitioners take the approach of personalizing and presenting cyber risks as a 'story' to appeal to employees and senior management. For a more detailed discussion on the limitations of fear appeals and other means of behavioural interventions, see: Mersinas, K and Bada, M (2023, July) Behavior change approaches for cyber security and the need for ethics. In *The International Conference on Cybersecurity, Situational Awareness and Social Media,* pp. 107–29, Springer Nature Singapore

13 In a study with a small sample of employees, financial rewards were provided resulting in an increased use of stronger passwords. However, once the rewards provision stopped, employees gradually returned to their pre-intervention behaviours. The explanation is that extrinsic incentivization has limited-duration effects. See: Goel, S, Williams, K, Huang, J and Warkentin, M (2020) Understanding the role of incentives in security behavior. In *Proceedings of the 53rd Hawaii International Conference on System Sciences*, 3, 4241–46

14 For details on the MINDSPACE framework, see: Dolan, P, Hallsworth, M, Halpern, D, King, D, Metcalfe, R and Vlaev, I (2012) Influencing behaviour: The mindspace way, *Journal of Economic Psychology*, 33 (1), 264–77

Conclusion

We have now completed our overview of cyber security. We would like to end with four closing observations.

Fundamentals, technology and society

This book has dealt with cyber security fundamentals, before looking at both technological and societal aspects of cyber security. Perhaps you did not anticipate just how all-encompassing cyber security seems to be. You might have been particularly surprised to discover the extent to which cyber security is not just about ones and zeros, encryption and intrusion detection, but is also about human behaviours and societal cultures.

This should not really come as a surprise. In fact, the security of almost any technology concerns fundamentals and societal issues, just as much as it concerns the technology itself. Had we been writing a book about the security of cars in the late 20th century then the organization of the material in such a book might not have been structured so differently from this book. We might well have included:

- *Fundamentals*. This would cover the principles behind secure car design, including core security mechanisms such as anti-lock brakes, door locks, external lights, alarms, internal warning lights, seatbelts, etc.
- *Technology*. This would discuss how cars are designed and used to prevent security incidents. This might include ignition security controls, prevention of pressure build-up, fuel tank design, measures to control overheating, etc. It might look at security of road networks, including road infrastructure design and traffic control. It might also consider the security of additional features in cars such as entertainment and heating systems, and the risks they present to the likes of battery management.
- *Society*. This would look at car management, potentially including car manufacturer security, car maintenance and national roadworthiness licensing schemes. It might consider issues concerning car theft and road accidents. It might look at how car use can be tracked and the implications for drivers. It might also look at personalities and driving behaviour, how the apparent anonymity of being inside a car impacts

driving, and national driving cultures. It might include secure car design, including dashboard layouts and ergonomics. It might even close with a discussion on national driving safety campaigns and driver re-education programmes.

Does that all sound a bit familiar? (Maybe it sounds like a more interesting book!)

Pervasive digital environments

Of course, had we been writing a book about the security of cars *today* then it would not just be structured similarly to this book, it would cover much of the same content. Modern cars rely on cryptography to open their doors and start their engines. They have CPUs, OSs and maintain network connections back to their manufacturer. They drive on roads whose traffic light systems are digitally controlled. Today, cars are most commonly stolen by criminals using digital hacking technology. Modern cars are already computer systems. The 'cyber-cars' of the future may well be electronically powered, digitally automated and partially controlled by digitally networked road systems. Cyber security is just as much about cars as it is about traditional computers.

And this is true of an increasing amount of consumer technology, such as refrigerators and heating systems. It's also true of other forms of transport, such as trains and ships. It's true of manufacturing plants and power stations. It's true of satellites and missile launch systems. Cyber security is not a niche discipline concerning the security of specialist equipment. Regarding much of what life depends upon in the 21st century, cyber security is a significant aspect of security itself, in many cases the primary one.

Holistic cyber security

This book has hopefully illustrated not just how all-encompassing cyber security is, but also how interdependent all the various facets of cyber security are. Everything depends on everything else, and if one component of cyber security has a weakness then security might fail. Consider, for example, the many ways that a database on a corporate computer system might be compromised: poor cryptographic protection, unauthorized access, insecure data transfer, exploitation of a bug in the interface software, management failure to invest in sufficient protection mechanisms, a ransomware attack, deductions about protected content from metadata analysis, leakage of data by a disgruntled senior system administrator and so on. It only takes one point of failure. Every chapter in this book matters, as do the connections between them.

There's always more to learn

This book is an introduction to cyber security, but there's so much more to learn. There are many important cyber security topics we could not cover within the confines of this overview. We could dig deeper into every single topic covered in this book. We would love to have discussed additional topics such as digital forensics, ethical hacking techniques and cyber physical security. An entirely different book could be written on the roles of, and threats to, cyber security presented by artificial intelligence. In the end, we hope we have at least helped you start your cyber security journey, and we urge you to continue it!

GLOSSARY

Access control: The general process of managing the relationship between users and the resources of the computer system.

Access control list: The list of access rights that a principal holds to an object in a computer system.

Access control matrix: A simple representation of an access control policy by means of a table identifying the access rights of each principal (row) to each object (column).

Access control model: An abstract model that captures different aspects of how to implement an effective and consistent access control policy.

Access control policy: The specification of what access rights principals (users) have to resources of a computer system.

Access right: A way that a computer system's resources can be used (for example, read, write or execute).

Accountability: The ability to establish responsibility for an action.

Active adversary: An attacker who conducts actions that result in system changes such as data modification.

Address (memory): A specification of precisely where data can be accessed within the memory of a computer system.

Advanced Encryption Standard (AES): The most widely deployed block cipher, with a block size of 128 bits and variable key lengths of 128, 192 and 256 bits.

Adversary: Another word for an attacker.

Anonymity: A notion that relates to different degrees to which identification of an entity involved in a digital interaction can be hidden.

Anti-virus software: A host-based threat detection tool, primarily focused on identifying and removing known malware.

Application firewall: A firewall that is informed about aspects of the application logic of the system it aims to protect.

Asset: A resource within a digital environment that we wish to protect.

Asymmetric cryptography: Cryptography where the creator and consumer of cryptography depend on two different keys, one of which is secret and one of which can be made public.

Attack tree: A threat model that represents potential attack paths that an adversary might take to compromise a system.

Attribute: A label that is associated with an entity (of a computer system).

Audit: The provision of independent assurance to stakeholders that an audit subject matter is free from significant misstatement.

Authenticated encryption: A symmetric encryption technique which provides both confidentiality and data origin authentication.

Authorization: The ability to determine which digital resources an entity is permitted to access and what they can do with them.

Availability: The ability to access a digital resource whenever needed.

Backdoor: A secret weakness, most commonly used to describe a deliberate weakness in a cryptographic algorithm known only to the designer.

Bell-LaPadula (BLP) model: An access control model capturing consistent confidentiality requirements for a type of mandatory access control policy.

BGP hijacking: An attack on network routing.

BGPsec: A security extension to the border gateway protocol (BGP) that facilitates internet routing.

Biba model: An access control model capturing consistent integrity requirements for a type of mandatory access control policy.

Biometric: A measurable human characteristic used to authenticate to a computer system.

Biometric template: A data point generated during biometric initialization and subsequently referenced against during verification.

Binary hardening: The process of strengthening compiled binary executables, making them less vulnerable and more resistant to exploitation by attackers.

Black box testing: Evaluating the functionality of a system without having knowledge of its internal workings, source code or architecture.

Block cipher: A symmetric encryption algorithm that encrypts plaintext in blocks of bits at a time, where a typical block size is 128 bits.

Blockchain: A large open, distributed and immutable data structure constructed using hash functions and designed to provide data integrity of its contents.

Botnet: A network of malware-infected devices under the control of an attacker.

Buffer overflow: A vulnerability that occurs when a program puts more data into a region of temporary memory than it can handle, thus causing the computer system to overwrite to nearby memory.

Bug: A flaw in the design or implementation of a computer system and its software that leads to undefined or incorrect behaviour.

Business continuity: The development of specific plans and processes to enable organizational priorities to be maintained in times of disruption.

Capability: The list of access rights that a principal has to objects on a computer system.

Catfishing: The creation of fake social media accounts by using another person's personal information with the intention to engage in fraudulent activities such as romance scams.

Central Processing Unit (CPU): The core computer component responsible for executing instructions to run software applications.

Certificate authority: An issuer of public-key certificates.

Certificate revocation list: A list of public-key certificates that appear valid, but have in fact been withdrawn.

Challenge-response: An entity authentication technique based on sending a prover a nonce upon which they conduct a cryptographic computation in order to provide fresh evidence that they know the associated cryptographic key.

Checksum: A lightweight data integrity mechanism that can detect accidental but not deliberate modification of data.

CIA triad: A popular tendency to frame cyber security in terms of confidentiality, integrity and availability.

Cipher block chaining (CBC) mode: A mode of operation of a block cipher where each plaintext block is first combined with the previous ciphertext block before encryption.

Ciphertext: Data that is protected by encryption.

Code injection: An attack in which malicious code is inserted into a vulnerable application, causing it to execute unintended commands.

Common vulnerabilities and exposures (CVE): A standard for cataloguing publicly disclosed security vulnerabilities and exposures in software and hardware.

Common vulnerability scoring system (CVSS): A standard that assigns a numerical score to vulnerabilities that helps security practitioners to assess vulnerabilities based on their potential impact and exploitability.

Common weakness enumeration (CWE): A standard for cataloguing software and hardware security flaws, design errors or issues in software architecture that could lead to vulnerabilities.

Computer system: A group of interacting, interrelated and interdependent digital components (hardware and software) that form a connected whole.

Computer system security policy: A security policy that specifies how security controls are applied to the computer system in order to manage the relationship between users and the computer system resources.

Confidentiality: The ability to restrict access to data to only authorized entities.

Control: A measure put in place to address a risk.

Controlled invocation: The process of enabling a restricted and temporary elevation of privilege levels on a computer system.

Corporate regulation: A regulation produced by a regulatory body but not articulated in law.

Counter (CTR) mode: A mode of operation of a block cipher where a counter is encrypted and then added to a block of plaintext.

Counter with CBC MAC (CCM) mode: A widely deployed mode of operation of a block cipher that provides authenticated encryption.

Cross-site request forgery (CSRF): A vulnerability that allows an attacker to fool a user into executing unwanted actions on a web application.

Cross-site scripting (XSS): A vulnerability that enables an attacker to add harmful code to a website.

Cryptocurrency: A means of digital payment that is not governed directly by the traditional financial industry and normally offers a degree of anonymity.

Cryptographic algorithm: An instantiation of a cryptographic tool that is specified in sufficient detail that it could be implemented.

Cryptographic key: A relatively short piece of data that is input to a cryptographic algorithm and on which the resulting security depends.

Cryptographic protocol: A specification of exactly how cryptographic algorithms are used during an interaction between different system entities.

Cryptography: A toolkit of mechanisms enabling the provision of core digital security services.

Cryptojacker: Malware that hijacks a victim's computing resources in order to mine cryptocurrency.

Cyber Essentials: A simple UK cyber security management standard designed to help organizations engage in best practice.

Cyber resilience: A holistic concept relating to how an organization might assess its ability to cope with cyber security incidents.

Cyber threat intelligence: Information about possible attacks gathered by monitoring network activity.

Cyber-dependent crime: A crime that can be committed only through the use of digital technology.

Cyber-enabled crime: A traditional crime that is conducted using digital technology.

Cyberbullying: Offensive, intimidating, malicious or insulting behaviour intended to undermine, humiliate, denigrate or injure a recipient.

Cybercrime: An act punishable by law, which utilizes digital technology either to target data, systems, networks, technology or humans, or to facilitate the commission of further offences.

Cybercrime as a Service (CaaS): The provision of technological cybercrime tools for purchase or rent, or for collaborative usage.

Cyber security governance: Activities relating to what an organization sets out to do concerning cyber security (rather than how it does it).

Cyber security management: The process of systematically addressing the cyber security challenges that an organization faces.

Cyber security management system: Accumulation of all the processes and controls that an organization deploys to address cyber security management.

Cyberstalking: Repeated acts of threatening to harm, harassing, intimidating via messages or any other online activities with the purpose of annoying, alarming, threatening or making an individual afraid for their safety.

CyBOK: Cyber Security Body of Knowledge project.

Dark triad: Three personality traits that are correlated with offensive and malicious activities such as cybercrime-related behaviours.

Data anonymization: The removal or alteration of any data that explicitly links to an individual.

Data integrity: The ability to detect modification of data since creation by an authorized entity.

Data minimization: The principle of only collecting, processing and storing the minimum amount of personal data necessary to achieve a specific purpose.

Data origin authentication: A strong data integrity service that enables a verifying entity to not only detect deliberate manipulation of data, but also gain assurance of which entity was the authorized data creator.

Data sanitization: The process of permanently and securely removing or altering data to prevent later unauthorized access or recovery.

Decryption: The process of applying a decryption algorithm to remove data confidentiality.

Deep packet inspection: A packet filter firewall process that inspects packet contents belonging to the application layer.

Defence in depth: The principle that effective security is layered, with a secure system using many layers rather than relying on any single layer to provide adequate defence.

Demilitarized zone: A separate network that is isolated from internal services and on which public-facing services are placed.

Denial-of service (DoS) attack: An attack that aims to disrupt the availability of digital services by directing excessive traffic or requests to systems, networks or servers.

Dictionary attack: An attack, typically against password-based authentication, where an attacker exhaustively searches through all likely passwords until a valid password is found.

Differential privacy: A technique for adding controlled noise to data sets that enables statistical analysis to still be conducted while masking individual data points that could lead to breaches of privacy requirements.

Diffie-Hellman key exchange: A cryptographic protocol where two parties exchange public values and are then each able to compute a common secret from a private value and the other's public value.

Digital Signature Algorithm (DSA): A digital signature scheme based on the computational difficulty of computing discrete logarithms.

Digital signature scheme: An asymmetric cryptographic algorithm that provides non-repudiation (and hence both data origin authentication and data integrity).

Discretionary access control: An access control policy where access rights are assigned on an individual (principal) basis.

Disinformation: The deliberate distribution of false or misleading information.

Distributed denial-of-service (DDoS) attack: A denial-of-service attack where the disruption is coordinated through a network of malware-infected devices.

Domain name system security extensions (DNSSEC): A set of extensions designed to introduce security into the domain name system that supports internet addressing.

ECDH key exchange: An efficient form of Diffie-Hellman key exchange.

ECDSA: An efficient version of the DSA digital signature scheme.

Electronic codebook (ECB) mode: A mode of operation of a block cipher where each block is encrypted independently.

Elliptic-curve encryption: A public-key encryption algorithm based around the computational difficulty of computing discrete logarithms.

Encryption: The process of applying an encryption algorithm to provide data confidentiality.

End-to-end encryption: An encryption technique whereby data is encrypted on a sender's device and can only be decrypted on the receiver's device, but nowhere in between.

Entity: An abstraction that could represent, for example, a human being, an organization, a digital device or an application running on a digital device.

Entity authentication: The ability to confirm that a specific entity is engaged in a digital communication session.

Ethical hacking: Another term for penetration testing.

ETSI: The European Telecommunications Standards Institute.

Exception handling: Ensuring that a software application responds to unexpected conditions in a controlled, secure and predictable manner.

Exhaustive key search: A cryptographic attack which involves trying out every possible cryptographic key.

Exploit: A computer program that uses a vulnerability to cause incorrect or undefined behaviour in a computer system.

Exposure: An incident where an exploit is used.

Firewall: A technology that enables a network administrator to implement an access control policy on network communication.

Firmware: Software that controls hardware on a computer system.

Freshness mechanism: A technique for providing evidence that a communication is new (not a replay).

Fuzz testing: Providing unexpected, random or malformed inputs to a computer program to expose vulnerabilities and bugs that may lead to security issues.

Galois counter (GCM) mode: A widely deployed mode of operation of a block cipher that provides authenticated encryption.

General Data Protection Regulation (GDPR): One of the most influential privacy regulations that governs data protection.

Hacking: Unauthorized access or use of digital technology, typically by exploiting vulnerabilities or bypassing security controls.

Handshake: An exchange of messages at the start of a protocol that is normally used to establish initial parameters and sometimes establish cryptographic keys.

Hardware security module (HSM): A secure device which deploys a range of physical protection controls to protect against intrusion.

Hash function: A cryptographic algorithm that inputs some data and outputs an integrity digest value called a hash.

HMAC: A widely deployed message authentication code constructed from a hash function.

Homomorphic encryption: A form of encryption that enables computations to be performed on ciphertexts that have an equivalent impact on the underlying plaintext.

Honeypot: A dummy service that mimics a real service but does not provide any business-related functionality.

Hypervisor: Firmware that provides and manages computer system resources to create virtual machines.

Identity: The set of properties that make an individual (human) distinct.

Identification: The presentation of a claimed identity to a computer system.

Identity theft: The (unauthorized) collection of a victim's personal information with the intention of defrauding them.

IETF: The Internet Engineering Task Force.

Incident: Something significant and undesirable that impacts the cyber security of an organization.

Incident response team: Those responsible for handling the response to an incident.

Incomplete mediation: A type of vulnerability arising from an application failing to properly check all inputs or operations before acting upon them.

Indicators of compromise: Items of evidence that strongly indicate a network intrusion.

Input sanitization: The cleaning or modifying of input data to make it safe for a software system to process.

Input validation: The practice of ensuring that the data input by users or external sources to a program is both correct and expected.

Internal control: A process put in place by an organization's leadership to ensure that organizational objectives are met in terms of operational effectiveness and efficiency, reliability of reporting, and compliance with applicable laws and regulations.

Internet protocol security (IPsec): A set of extensions to IPv4 and IPv6 that build on cryptographic mechanisms to protect data.

Interrupt: An instruction for a computer system to switch tasks.

Intrusion detection system: A network monitoring technology that automatically checks for known attack patterns or suspicious activity on a network.

Intrusion prevention system: An intrusion detection system that can also actively take measures to intervene in suspicious activities that they detect.

ISO: International Organization for Standardization.

ISO/IEC 27000 security framework: A series of standards that support different aspects of cyber security management.

Jamming: An attack on the physical layer of a wireless network that emits a strong radio signal (noise) that makes regular transmission impossible.

Kernel: The core components of an operating system responsible for security and resource management.

Key derivation function: A cryptographic algorithm used to generate cryptographic keys.

Key encapsulation: An encryption technique where data is encrypted symmetrically using a symmetric key, and this is encrypted asymmetrically using the recipient's public key.

Key establishment: The process of getting cryptographic keys to the places in a system where they are needed.

Key length: A measure which relates to the security of a cryptographic algorithm.

Key management: The management of the lifecycle of a cryptographic key.

Keylogger: Malware that captures the keystrokes of a user entering data onto a computer system.

Keystream: A stream of pseudorandom bits generated from a symmetric key and then used by a stream cipher to encrypt plaintext.

Lateral movement: An attack strategy where a compromised host is used as a launchpad to mount attacks inside a network that then appears to originate from the compromised host.

Least privilege: The principle that anything running or accessing a computer system is only given sufficient capabilities to perform a task and nothing more.

Load balancing: A defence against DDoS attacks that distributes incoming network traffic across multiple servers, preventing any single server from becoming overwhelmed.

Logic bomb: Malware that installs itself on a computer system and then remains dormant until triggered by a specific event or condition.

Machine-in-the-middle: An attacker who controls a device on a network that lies in between two communicating entities and can modify data that is passed between them.

Malware: Software that can spread between systems with the malicious intention to interfere with operations.

Mandatory access control: An access control policy where access rights are assigned by means of a general classification system rather than on an individual basis.

Media access control (MAC) address: A unique identifier of a network adapter that connects a device to a network.

Memory zeroing: Ensuring that memory storing data is overwritten (zeroed out) before it is freed.

Message authentication code (MAC): A symmetric cryptographic algorithm providing data origin authentication (and thus data integrity).

Metadata: Data related to (for example) a communication that is other than the content (such as date and time of correspondence).

Microsoft security development lifecycle (SDL): A security-focused development framework that integrates security best practices into each phase of software development.

Misinformation: The unintentional spreading of inaccurate information.

Mode of operation: A means of deploying a block cipher in order to obtain a specific set of properties.

Model checking: The use of mathematics to prove or disprove the correctness of a software system's design or implementation against specified requirements, ensuring that it behaves as intended in all possible circumstances.

Monitoring: Data gathering that is specific in its application and overt.

Moving targets: A dynamic defence strategy where the attack surface is constantly changed or reconfigured.

Multifactor authentication: An entity authentication process that involves several different processes and often authenticates a combination of entities (for example, to detect the presence of both a human and a specific device).

Multiparty computation: A cryptographic technique that enables multiple parties to jointly compute a function while keeping their inputs private.

Mutual entity authentication: Authentication of both of two communicating entities.

NCSC: UK National Cyber Security Centre.

Network segmentation: A network security technique that involves separating services into single networks and isolating these networks using restrictive packet filter policies.

NIST: US National Institute of Standards and Technology.

NIST security framework: A cyber security management framework that was designed for US critical infrastructure providers but has subsequently been adopted by many organizations worldwide.

Nonce: A random number, often deployed as a freshness mechanism.

Non-repudiation: A strong data integrity service that enables a verifying entity to prove to a third party which entity was the authorized data creator.

Non-volatile memory: Persistent computer memory that remains even when the computer is switched off.

Object (in access control): A computer system resource.

One-time password: A strong password generated freshly for a single entity authentication attempt.

One-way function: A function that is easy to compute, but for which the input is hard to determine from the output.

Onion routing: An anonymity technique that utilizes a network of special routers that act as intermediaries between the originator and the destination of an internet connection.

Operating system (OS): The core piece of software on any computer system that enables users of a computer to make effective use of hardware resources.

Organizational security policy: A security policy that sets out, at a high level, what cyber security means to an organization in terms of the security principles that will be applied and where overall priorities should lie.

Packet filter: A rule-based firewall that can block network messages based on header information of the protocols running in the network layers.

Passive adversary: An adversary who only observes a system but does not make modifications.

Password policy: Part of a computer system security policy that enforces restrictions on password selection and any requirements on frequency of password change.

Patch: A repair that mitigates (or removes) a vulnerability.

Patch management: The systematic obtaining, testing and implementation of patches to vulnerabilities.

Penetration testing: A special type of security audit that involves skilled experts attempting to breach a system's defences using techniques similar to those that might be deployed by a malicious attacker.

Permission: Another term for access right.

Personal data: Data that can be linked to a human identity.

Personally identifiable information: Any information (data) that can be used to identify a particular individual.

Phishing: The use of digital messages appearing to originate from reputable, legitimate or known sources, with the intention to trick victims into taking an action.

Plaintext: Unprotected data (normally used with reference to encryption).

Port authentication: The process of requiring every device to authenticate to a central authority within a network in order to participate.

Port security: A network switch with additional security functionality designed to defeat various attacks based on manipulating media access control addressing.

Power analysis attack: An attack on a cryptographic implementation that uses detailed measurements of how much power a device consumes during specific operations in order to deduce information.

Principal (in access control): An entity (including a user) who requires access to resources of a computer system.

Privacy: The right to prevent personal data from being disclosed without an individual's explicit and informed consent.

Privacy by design: The principle of integrating privacy and data protection into the design and operation of products, systems and services from the outset.

Privacy-enhancing technology: A technological mechanism that can be used to enable privacy.

Privacy engineering: The discipline of designing and implementing systems that incorporate privacy protections directly into products and services.

Privacy impact assessment: A formal process that enables an organization to identify, assess and mitigate privacy risks.

Privacy policy: A policy that outlines how an organization collects, uses and safeguards personal data.

Private information retrieval: A technique to facilitate database queries without the database learning what data was accessed.

Private set intersection: A technique for enabling two database holders to deduce items of common data without revealing any data that the other does not hold.

Privilege: Another term for access right.

Privilege levels: A hierarchical means of allocating different levels of access to the core resources of a computer system.

Process scheduling: The determining of which programs on a computer system should be next in line to use core (CPU) resources.

Pseudonymization: Transforming data into a non-identifiable form by replacing sensitive information with fictitious data.

Pseudorandom: Randomness generated from the output of a cryptographic algorithm.

Public-key certificate: A common technique for binding a public key to data relating to it, including the name of the owner.

Public-key cryptography: Another name for asymmetric cryptography.

Quantum key distribution: A key establishment technique which requires two parties to possess special hardware and be connected by means of a quantum channel.

Race condition: A vulnerability that can arise when the behaviour of a system depends on the timing of uncontrollable events, leading to potentially insecure outcomes.

Random access memory: Another term for volatile memory.

Ransomware: A type of malware that encrypts data in such a way that only an attacker can decrypt it.

Reference monitor: The component of a computer (operating) system that acts as the guard that mediates access requests to computer system resources.

Replay attack: An attack where an adversary observes and records data, then later replays it with the intention of deceiving a receiver.

Responsible disclosure: The principle of disclosing a vulnerability to relevant parties, allowing time to fix the vulnerability before publicizing the details.

Reverse engineering: The process of analysing a system to understand its design and functionality without access to the original source code or documentation.

Risk: A complex concept that emerges from a combined analysis of the likelihood of a particular threat arising and the impact the threat might have should it manifest.

Risk assessment: The identification, quantification and prioritization of risks.

Risk attitude: An individual's intention to act on a risky situation.

Risk management: The overall process an organization deploys to manage the cyber security risks it faces.

Risk perception: An individual's judgement and evaluation of a hazard.

Risk treatment: The response to the assessment of risks.

Role-based access control: An access control policy where access rights are defined by the function (such as an employment role) of a principal within an organization.

Root of trust: A focal point within a (computer) system from which trust in the wider system can be derived.

Rootkit: Malware that is designed to take control of all or part of a computer system.

Round: A sequence of scrambling operations on data that is repeated a fixed number of times as part of a cryptographic algorithm.

Router: A device connected to two or more networks that takes care of forwarding packets from one network to another.

RSA: A public-key encryption algorithm based around the computational difficulty of factoring the product of two large primes.

Salt: A random value associated with a computer system user account that is used to counter certain password-related attacks.

Secure by design: The principle that security should be embedded in systems from the outset, not as an afterthought.

Secure channel: A cryptographically protected network layer, typically at least providing confidentiality and data integrity.

Secure element: A tamper-resistant hardware storage unit for storing secrets such as cryptographic keys.

Secure programming: The practice of creating software with security in mind.

Secure Shell (SSH): A protocol that enables secure connection to remote devices.

Security audit: An audit that reviews the implementation and effectiveness of security controls.

Security awareness: The conscious understanding of the need for security processes and how to respond to them.

Security behaviour: An individual's acts, responses and conduct in relation to security.

Security behaviour change: The modification of human security behaviour through some type of planned action (or series of actions).

Security culture: The collective attitude and behaviour of humans towards security within an organization.

Security education: The general process of equipping users with foundational knowledge relating to security.

Security hygiene: Another term for security behaviour.

Security operations centre: A centralized unit responsible for monitoring, detecting, responding to and managing cyber security incidents.

Security policy: A set of rules or principles governing cyber security within a context.

Security service: Core security functionality that we might want to realize when using a digital technology or service.

Security standard: A document that specifies how a cyber security system, process or technology should work.

Security training: Practical interventions, such as campaigns, courses and other knowledge transfer activities, designed to equip users with specific skills.

Separation of privilege: The principle that critical tasks should be divided amongst multiple parties or processes to prevent a single point of failure.

Sequence number: A counter value, most commonly deployed as a freshness mechanism.

Session identifier: An identifier used in each data exchange to link messages within the same session.

Shoulder surfing: An attack where an attacker retrieves a password by observing a user entering it onto a computer system.

Side channel attack: An attack that exploits different aspects of a cryptographic implementation in order to extract information.

Social engineering: Any act which influences individuals to act in fashions that may not be in their best interest.

Software security: The practice of designing, developing and maintaining software that protects it (and related components of computer systems) from unauthorized access, misuse or other attacks.

Spear phishing: Phishing that is targeted at specific individuals or groups.

Spoofing: An attack where an adversary injects false data in order to deceive a recipient.

Spyware: Malware designed to secretly monitor user activities and steal sensitive information without the user's knowledge.

SQL injection: A code injection where an attacker manipulates database queries that are managed using the Structured Query Language (SQL).

Stack canary: A value placed on the memory stack to detect and prevent buffer-overflow attacks.

Stream cipher: A symmetric encryption algorithm that encrypts plaintext bitwise (one, or at most a few, bits at a time).

Subject (in access control): A process running on a computer system that requires access to resources of a computer system.

Surveillance: Data gathering that is broad in its application and covert.

Symmetric cryptography: Cryptography where the creator and consumer of cryptography both depend on a shared secret key.

System hardening: The process of securing a computer system or network by reducing its overall surface of vulnerability.

TCP SYN flooding: An attack where an adversary sends many internet connection requests to a victim.

Threat: Anything that could exploit a vulnerability to harm or disrupt an asset.

Threat modelling: A systematic process to identify, assess and address potential security threats, vulnerabilities and risks in software systems.

Timing attack: An attack on a cryptographic implementation that uses detailed measurements of how long a device takes to conduct specific operations in order to deduce information.

Tor : An anonymity technology based on onion routing, most famously manifesting in the Tor browser for anonymous web browsing.

Transport layer security (TLS): A secure channel that sits on top of the networking transport layer.

Trojan: Malware that is disguised as legitimate software, enabling attackers to gain access to a computer system.

Trolling: Malicious online communication, such as the use of abusive, explicit and hurtful comments on social media, typically targeting a specific individual.

Trusted computing base: The hardware and core operating system (kernel) components that deliver key security functions.

Trusted execution environment: An isolated execution area in the memory of a computer system that provides additional security features.

Trusted platform module: An international standard for a secure cryptography processor that is designed to secure the hardware and software of a computer system through trusted cryptographic key generation.

Unilateral entity authentication: Authentication of only one of two communicating entities.

Usable security: The design of security processes and technologies that accommodate human users' needs and behaviour.

User space: The part of an operating system where resources such as application, libraries and drivers that interact with the kernel reside.

Verification (as part of computer system authentication): The presentation of evidence to support an identification claim.

Virtual machine: Functionality on a computer system that behaves like a separate computer system by borrowing resources from the available hardware.

Virtual private network (VPN): A secure channel used to link trusted networks over an untrusted network such as the internet.

Virus: A computer program (malware) that infects files and then spreads to other computer systems when transferred and executed.

Volatile memory: Working computer memory available to running programs while a computer is switched on.

Vulnerability: A weakness in a digital environment that could threaten the security of an asset.

Vulnerability scanning: The process of using automated tools to identify potential security flaws in software, networks or systems by scanning for known vulnerabilities.

Weakness: A defect in the design, development or configuration of software or systems that could, in turn, lead to bugs or vulnerabilities arising.

Web application firewall: An application firewall tailored for HTTP-based communication.

Whaling: Spear phishing that is directed at high-profile targets.

Wiper malware: A type of malware that deletes or destroys data with no possibility of recovering it.

Worm: A self-replicating computer program (malware) that can spread between different computer systems without any direct user interaction.

Zero-day exploit: An exploit that is based on a vulnerability that has been discovered but not disclosed by an adversary.

Zero-knowledge proof: A cryptographic tool that enables one party to prove the truth of a statement (such as knowledge of a value) to another without revealing any unnecessary information relating to that statement.

Zero trust: A system design approach that assumes no part of a network is automatically trusted.

Zombie: A compromised device that forms a component of a botnet.

INDEX

The index is filed in alphabetical, word-by-word order. Acronyms are filed as presented. '+' and numbers are filed as spelt out, excepting ISO standards, Ring privilege levels, and transport security layer versions, which are filed chronologically. Locators in roman numerals denote information within the preface.